THE IMPACT OF THE FRENCH REVOLUTION

THE IMPACT OF THE FRENCH

REVOLUTION

ON EUROPEAN CONSCIOUSNESS

Edited by

H. T. MASON and W. DOYLE

ALAN SUTTON
1989

ALAN SUTTON PUBLISHING
BRUNSWICK ROAD · GLOUCESTER · UK

ALAN SUTTON PUBLISHING INC
WOLFEBORO · NEW HAMPSHIRE · USA

First published 1989

British Library Cataloguing in Publication Data

The impact of the French Revolution on European
consciousness.
1. French Revolution, 1789–1799
I. Mason, Haydn, *1929*– II. Doyle, W.
944.04

ISBN 0-86299-483-7

Library of Congress Cataloging Publication Data

Applied for

Cover design by Martin Latham

Typesetting and origination by
Alan Sutton Publishing Limited.
Printed in Great Britain.

Contents

List of Contributors

Professor W. Doyle, Department of History, University of Bristol, 13 Woodland Road, Bristol BS8.

Dr. R. Bolster, Department of French, University of Bristol, 17/19 Woodland Road, Bristol BS8 1TE.

Professor W. Howarth, 53 Westbury Road, Bristol BS9 3AU.

Dr. N. Wilson, Department of French, University of Bristol, 17/19 Woodland Road, Bristol BS8 1TE.

Professor R. Peace, Department of Russian, University of Bristol, 17 Woodland Road, Bristol BS8 1TE.

Dr. B. Hamnett, Department of History, University of Strathclyde, Glasgow G1.

Dr. M. Broers, Department of History, University of Leeds, Leeds LS2.

Dr. B. Rigby, Department of French, University of Warwick, Coventry CV4.

Dr. A. Sanders, Department of English, Birkbeck College, Malet Street, London WC1E.

Professor N. Glendinning, Department of Spanish, Queen Mary College, Mile End Road, London.

Dr. T. Blanning, Sidney Sussex College, Cambridge.

Professor H. Reiss, 198 Stoke Lane, Westbury-on-Trym, Bristol BS9.

Dr. A. Grenville, Department of German, University of Bristol, 21 Woodland Road, Bristol BS8.

Professor S. Körner, 10 Belgrave Road, Bristol BS8.

Professor N. Hampson, Department of History, University of York, York YO1.

Introduction

What changes did the French Revolution effect upon the European mind? Such was the question, particularly apposite in this year of the bicentenary, addressed by the Colston Symposium in the University of Bristol. The speakers, all of them invited to contribute, tackled the problem on a deliberately wide front: literature, history, art, philosophy; France, England, Germany, Italy, Russia, Spain. These Transactions present the many-sided, interdisciplinary responses.

What was the French Revolution, to start with, and what can be learned from it? Professor Hampson attempts an overview, based on a lifetime spent in studying the great event. Now that the straightforward Marxist explanation, which held sway for so long in France, has collapsed in the face of Revolutionary complexities, no simple agreement on the significance or indeed the nature of the Revolution is any longer possible. Professor Hampson traces, instead, the growing gap, in the end unbridgeable, between Left and Right, for all the hopes of a common accord when the Bastille was stormed. He concludes with a wryly ironical lesson: revolutions are, on the whole, best avoided; yet they generate hope, that staple of human energy and endeavour.

Such detachment was unlikely to be experienced in the Revolutionary period or its wake. Chateaubriand, forced into exile because of the event, tried in later years, as Dr. Bolster shows, to make sense of it – with dismaying conclusions about human nature. While there were many specific causes, Chateaubriand could not exclude an unease endemic to the race whose presence constitutes a profound critique of European civilisation. Reactions from England and Germany revealed none of this painful complicity or guilt. Even the *Analytical Review*, most radical of English journals in the 1790's and therefore most sympathetic, took a cool, patronising line, as Dr. Rigby shows. By 1815 English writers were still more unequivocal. Dr. Sanders traces their distaste and fear at what Revolutionary ideology had wrought. Our own steady progressiveness through history was so much preferable to the topsy-turvy antics across the Channel. And yet . . . how brilliant the civilisation that had emerged in Paris by mid-century! German reports from Paris during the Revolution rivalled the English reactions in xenophobia. Germany, as Dr. Blanning brings out, was thought to have had its revolution already, bloodless and civilised in the shape of Kant. In this respect Goethe's hostility was characteristic; Professor Reiss

notes the horror felt by the great German writer at this betrayal of
Enlightenment principles and descent into anarchy. Grillparzer
was a little later to voice the same antipathy. As Dr. Grenville
makes clear, Grillparzer's Austrian background equipped him to
fear that the whirlwind would dissolve the Habsburg Empire itself
and lead to anarchic local nationalisms. Such responses serve to
confirm the weakness which Professor Körner discerns in Rousseau's concept of the General Will as in Kant's notion of the
categorical imperative: a moral dogmatism arises from this exaggerated assumption of the consensus involved.

Not all reactions, however, were so unambiguously hostile. The
Spanish artist Goya has long been seen as revolutionary; Professor
Glendinning argues, with considerable illustration, that while this
view is itself too sweeping, Goya's reformist attacks on inequality
relate to the spirit of the Revolution. Dr. Hamnett delineates the
way the Spanish constitutionalists in the same period, seeking an
answer to the collapse of absolute monarchy, found inspiration
from the Revolution for their goals of popular sovereignty and
unicameral legislature. Later on in Italy, argues Dr. Broers, the
Risorgimento saw it as central to their crusade for the overthrow of
Austrian rule and the establishment of a unitary State. Much
earlier in France, the Jewish community had called upon the new
order to press for and temporarily gain full citizenship; as Dr.
Wilson shows, the victory was brief, for Napoleon was soon to
terminate it.

As heir to the Revolution, Napoleon left his mark everywhere in
Europe. Professor Peace investigates his impact upon Pushkin,
Lermontov, Dostoevski, Tolstoy: an impressive cultural heritage
indeed, when one recognises the part Napoleon plays in the
creation of Raskolnikov (*Crime and Punishment*) or the making of *War
and Peace*. A similar inheritance has grown up in the theatre around
the two great figures of the Revolutionary era itself, Danton and
Robespierre, their conflicting temperaments and philosophies,
which Professor Howarth traces down as far as our contemporary
Anouilh, though the most incisive account still belongs to German
literature and Büchner's *Dantons Tod*.

The echoes, then, continue to reverberate. Professor Hampson is
surely right to consider the issues raised by the French Revolution as
still alive. This opinion receives independent confirmation from
Professor Doyle's "principles". Many of those principles grew up, he
shows, as the Revolution went along, in empirical reaction to events;
the Revolution invented itself as an ideology. Yet within these
ambiguities revolution made crystal clear the possibility of change,
by violence if need be. That hope, for many that fearful thought,
meant that the European world could never be the same again.

The Principles of the French Revolution

W. Doyle

Even the most bitter and determined opponents of the French Revolution were prepared to admit that it had principles; even if all these amounted to, in the words of Tolstoy's Vicomte de Mortemart, were 'robbery, murder and regicide'. But most of us, I suspect, when we think of the principles of the Revolution, would tend to adopt the response of the vicomte's opponent in that exchange at the start of *War and Peace*, Pierre Bezukhov. 'Those were extremes, no doubt, but they are not what is most important. What is important are the rights of man, emancipation from prejudices, and equality of citizenship'. But I wonder whether it was any of these things that, in July 1789, turned Kant into a news fanatic, or gave Caroline Böhmer hot flushes, or made Wordsworth feel that it was bliss to be alive? These were feelings stirred by news of the fall of the Bastille: but nobody knew, or could foresee, in the last fortnight of July 1789, what that event was to lead to, or how the next few years were likely to develop.

Even the Rights of Man had not been proclaimed on 14 July. It was to be another six weeks before the declaration embodying them was promulgated, and even then its precise content was far from a foregone conclusion. Nor did the French Revolutionaries remain content with it. It survived as the preamble to the Constitution of 1791, but in 1793 it was absorbed into a much longer and more far-reaching document adopted to begin the constitution of that year; and in 1795 it was swamped again in an even more long-winded statement of rights and duties. Which Rights of Man, then, might Pierre Bezukhov have had in mind? He had a number of different versions to choose from, even emanating from France; without considering those proposed by France's fellow travellers elsewhere, such as Tom Paine. Or take the slogan every schoolboy knows to be that of the French Revolution: *Liberty, Equality, Fraternity*. That, too, had not emerged as a revolutionary battle-cry when the Bastille was stormed. There had been much talk of liberty and liberties during the 'pre-revolutionary' struggles between 1787 and 1789; and of course the struggle to unite the three orders in the Estates-General, and ensure that deputies voted by head, was about

1

a sort of equality. But *Liberty:Equality*, as shorthand for what the Revolution was all about, did not begin to be used until very late in 1789; and *Fraternity* was only added much later, in 1793, when arguably fraternity was one of the last things the Revolution seemed to be all about. Or take symbols. Of course the Phrygian cap of liberty, the headgear of the freed slave, had always been associated with the idea of liberty, and was much used in 18th century iconography – particularly in countries like Great Britain, where the rhetoric of freedom was well entrenched and its emblems instantly recognisable. But French Revolutionaries only began to *wear* red caps in the winter of 1791–2. Anacharsis Clootz, the self-styled orator of the human race, first tried to launch the fashion in the autumn, to general derision; and although it eventually caught on in the Jacobin club in March 1792, amid the patriotic euphoria which carried the nation into war a month later, the fashion was always condemned as cheap and demeaning by serious-minded revolutionaries such as Robespierre. Even that most emotive and terrifying of all revolutionary symbols, the guillotine, was not perfected until three years after the Bastille fell. The deputies to the Constituent Assembly, who took themselves extremely seriously on the whole, were thrown into a rare fit of mirth when, late in 1789, Dr. Guillotin expounded his idea of a machine of execution that would make heads fly off in the twinkling of an eye. It was another two and a half years before such a device was accepted, and came into use. It would be easy to think of other examples. What they would all suggest is that the principles, ideas, style and habits of the French Revolution did not emerge all of a piece right from the start. Much that came to be indelibly associated with it was not present at the beginning, or often for some years after the beginning. What it meant, and what it was to mean to subsequent generations looking back on what seemed like a complete, integrated occurrence, largely developed as the Revolution went along, and usually in ways quite unforeseen. So far from being part of some rational, thought-out, or premeditated purpose, in fact, some of the most momentous things the Revolution came to stand for look very much like the product of accident, mischance, or miscalculation.

For instance, the Revolution represented probably the greatest attack on, and challenge to, the Catholic Church since the Reformation. It stripped the French Church of its wealth, reorganised its hierarchy, dissolved its monasteries. It stopped Peter's Pence, and annexed Papal territories unilaterally. Eventually it prohibited Catholic practice and deported or executed priests and religious in their thousands, and by the late 1790s the Pope was at the mercy of its armies. Yet none of this was intended, or dreamed of, at the outset. Everyone in 1789, even the clergy, thought the Church needed reform, and expected changes that would make it less wasteful, better organised, and more responsible to the spiritual and pastoral needs of French citizens. And there was certainly a good deal of less well-intentioned anti-clericalism in the air, as any reading of the *cahiers* of 1789 makes clear. But there was no desire to destroy the role that Catholicism played in national life: if anything, most people dreamed of strengthening it. Things began to go wrong not so much when tithe was abolished or Peter's Pence renounced, on 4 August 1789; or when Church lands were confiscated two months later; or even when regular orders were dissolved the following spring. The turning point was the attempt, with the Civil Constitution of the Clergy in the Summer of 1790, to bring the organisation and government of the Church into line with the organisation and government of the country at large, now being envisaged in the Constitution being prepared. At one level, of course, such an aspiration seemed rational enough. But again, even these constitutional principles had not been foreseen, except in the most general terms, in the summer of 1789. They were hammered out after that, and only then was it decided to bring the Church into conformity with them. Who, in 1789, would have thought of trying to exclude the Pope as completely from the affairs of the Catholic Church in France as the Civil Constitution of 1790 tried to do? Who would have dreamed of clergy being elected by the laity? The attempt to make beneficed clergy accept these and other principles as a prerequisite for exercising cure of souls, through the imposition of an oath, was the first great divide of the French Revolution; and although even then almost half the French clergy were still prepared to accept the new order, the Pope certainly was not, and nor were Catholic clergy anywhere else. From then on Rome and Revolution were deadly enemies; and however much that quarrel was later patched up, the suspicions it aroused were never again fully allayed, and the position and pretensions of the Catholic Church in France never went unchallenged again. The example, moreover, meant that that challenge would be echoed, more or less vehemently, in almost every country where Catholicism held sway.

An equally unpredictable chapter of accidents and miscalculations led to the second great trauma of the Revolution, the destruction of monarchy. Few things moved European onlookers more than the fate of Louis XVI and his family – whether in the ignominious failure of the Flight to Varennes, the mutinous and degrading scenes at the Tuileries on 20 June 1792, or, above all, the king's trial and execution. Even Tom Paine, who had denounced monarchy root and branch in the *Rights of Man* and fully believed the king to be guilty, pleaded with the Convention not to execute him;

and Wolfe Tone, founder of Irish republicanism, confided to his diary that he was sorry the execution was necessary. Only Frenchmen (and then of course by no means all of them) seemed to welcome regicide. And yet no such thought was in any Frenchman's mind, so far as we can tell, in 1789. There seems to have been hardly any overt republicanism, but rather the opposite: an almost boundless credulity about the extent of the king's good intentions. Men were still willing to believe that despotism was ministerial, that a monarch not misled by wicked or self-serving advisers would always wish for and work to bring about his subjects' wellbeing, that Louis XVI was happy to be redesignated King of the French, and accepted his loss of sovereignty. The Constitution the Assembly put together in those first two years was a monarchical one, even if that monarchy was now to be limited; and even after widespread republicanism took hold, after Varennes, a majority still seem to have believed that there was no alternative to a king at the head of the state, and that the king they had would accept the Revolution provided its popular excesses could be controlled. Here again, events, accidents and miscalculations eroded faith in monarchy, and paved the way to the first French Republic; but only slowly, and at a very uneven pace. And the other monarchs of Europe did not really feel threatened on their thrones by the French example until French armies began to win victories in the autumn of 1792, and the French declared that they intended to export the principles of their Revolution to whatever peoples asked for their fraternity and help. Not, then, until (in Danton's phrase) France threw down its gauntlet to Europe, and that gauntlet was the head of a king, did republicanism become an unequivocal identifying principle of the French Revolution – a good four years after it had begun.

Not, in fact, until the revolutionaries had become armed missionaries: but this, too, was an inconceivable idea in 1789. Of course, from a very early stage the French Revolutionaries considered themselves an example to the world – and there were from the start, too, enough admirers abroad to confirm to them that they were. Even in self-satisfied Great Britain, soaked in the rhetoric of Liberty, Richard Price and the Revolution Society were proclaiming before the end of 1789 that the French had caught up with and overtaken the English in the science of freedom in the space of a few months. But equally, the men of 1789 never dreamed of exporting the Rights of Man beyond French borders by force. They thought it self-evident that many abroad would wish to follow their glorious example, and assumed that others in revolt around the same time, such as the Belgians or the Poles, were engaged in doing so. But they themselves, they proclaimed, threatened nobody's sovereignty. They wished to live at peace with all who were content to live at peace with them; and in the famous Nootka Sound debates in May 1790 they brushed aside obligations assumed under the old dynastic diplomacy and declared that they would henceforth only make war in self-defence. Only 18 months later did they begin to rattle the sabre, and even then they could just about plausibly claim a defensive motive in that those against whom they were exercised were Rhenish princes sheltering the belligerent *émigrés* who threatened French security. Not until after the end of 1791 was all pretence of defensive war cast aside with the series of ultimatums issued to the Austrians; and even then it was another six months before the French became the armed missionaries who in the later 1790s would sweep across central Europe and Italy, destroying the established regimes there and setting up their own puppet states. Most people who experienced the French Revolution directly did so in the form of French soldiers conquering, marauding, extorting and requisitioning – yet these invaders were doing so in the name of a movement whose first thoughts about foreign affairs had been to offer peace to all and respect for the rights and integrity of other peoples.

A final, though somewhat different, example of how the Revolution's principles evolved, rather than burst all of a piece on Europe, is the case of popular power. Here at least was something that the Revolution began with. The fall of the Bastille witnessed the people in action, and the Parisian insurrection of which it was the culmination saved the National Assembly from dissolution by armed force. The people of Paris had saved the Revolution, and they knew they had. From then on they regarded it as their privileged role to be the Revolution's watchdogs – a role they first re-enacted in the October Days of 1789, and which attained its classic peak in the great sansculotte *journées* of 1792 and 1793. These were the scenes which so appalled most of the educated classes of Europe – the heads on pikes, the stringings-up on the street-lanterns, the September massacres and the jubilation of the crowds around the guillotine. And yet, these scenes were equally deplored by the vast majority of the educated classes of France, too; and by none more so than the deputies of the National Assembly whom popular action saved in July 1789. They deeply deplored the fact that they had had to be rescued from despotism on the streets. That was why they rushed to endorse the setting up of the National Guard by people just like themselves; why immediately after the October Days they passed the martial law decree to prevent future tumults; why most of them applauded the way this decree was invoked at the Champ de Mars in July 1791; and why they gave France a constitution in which only those with certain property qualifications were admitted as active citizens. In other words the men of 1789, the men who produced the original principles of the French Revolution, had no desire to see popular power established as one of those principles. They believed in equality: before the law, before the tax-collector, and of opportunity; but they never believed that power and authority should be allowed to fall into the hands of the uneducated or the unpropertied. And nor did the vast majority of their successors in the Legislative, the Convention, or the Directorial Councils. The popular role in the Revolution, at whatever stage, was at best a regrettable, and always transient, necessity. Establishing popular power was not what the Revolution was about, or intended to be about; and as soon as the Convention's deputies had the means at their disposal to break the grip of the sansculottes on their proceedings, they seized it. Their legacy to France, the Constitution of the Year III, for all its manhood suffrage, fixed qualifications for public office at a level far beyond what had been thought adequate by the men of 1789. Experience since that time had taught that those early safeguards had been nothing like enough. And when further experience, over the next four years, showed that even these new safeguards were not enough either (as repeated Jacobin scares in 1796, 1797 and 1798 proved) the political class threw in their lot with a dictator who made no secret of his determination to rule with the co-operation of solid men of property. To the vast majority of those who governed, or attempted to govern, France in the revolutionary decade, in other words, popular power was not one of the Revolution's principles: it had been a totally regrettable by-product which in the end it became the Revolution's first priority to eliminate.

The principles of the French Revolution, then, were not static, cut in stone, and invariable. They emerged uncertainly, reflected and were moulded by the play of events, and changed as the Revolution went on. And not only that: before the decade was out many of them, and by the time the Napoleonic episode was over, practically all of them, had been stood on their heads by the French and yet were still being vaunted as the authentic principles of the Revolution. It began as a revolt against despotism and centralisation; yet by as early as 1794 France had a more uniform, centralised government than she had ever had before – although it proclaimed itself a temporary, emergency regime designed to last no longer than the war. By the time another five years had elapsed the man who wrote the most cogent manifesto of 1789, Sieyès, had engineered the accession to power of a ruler beside whose power the so-called despotism of the Ancien Regime seemed effetely patriarchal, and whose rigid pattern of centralised authority made the rule of the intendants look like benign neglect. In 1789 the revolutionaries proclaimed the natural and imprescriptible rights of man as liberty, property, security, and resistance to oppression, all of which were to be guaranteed by the rule of law. And yet within weeks one tenth of the property in France, the lands of the Church, had been confiscated and then sold off (to underwrite a National Debt, incidentally, which was proclaimed sacred and yet was completely written off by 1797). Security likewise was thrown to the winds in 1789 owing to the revolutionaries' deep mistrust of all existing public forces: a decade of spectacular lawlessness ensued, whose extraordinary realities Richard Cobb has spent a scholarly lifetime introducing us to, and which was only brought to an end by the military efficiency of Napoleon. As to resistance to oppression and the supremacy of the rule of law, the Terror of 1793–4 had gone down as one of history's classic regimes of oppression; and the justice by which many of its victims were condemned as a mockery. In defence of it Saint-Just defined humanity as the extermination of one's enemies; and Robespierre, who in the early days of the Revolution had denounced capital punishment, ended up seemingly threatening a large proportion of the Convention with the guillotine. Proclaiming equal opportunities and an end to privileges based on birth, in the end the Revolution produced, and its leaders consciously sought from the earliest stage, a society dominated by, and governed in the interests of, rich landowners. The only talents post-revolutionary careers were open to were those honed by the sort of education that inherited wealth alone could buy.

Or consider freedom of thought and expression, the key to Pierre Bezukhov's 'emancipation from prejudices'. Initially, it is true, the press flourished as never before. But intimidation of those with unpopular opinions was a feature of the Revolution right from the start, as the woman publicly spanked in the Palais Royal on 9 July 1789 after she had spat on a portrait of Necker found out. Once the religious schism emerged the atmosphere grew far worse; popular pressure has now been clearly identified as a major factor in whether the clergy took the oath to the constitution or not. By the summer of 1791 special laws were being passed to curb the press, and within a year most right-wing journals had been harried out of business. Another year brought all the excesses of dechristianisation; and even after the dismantling of the Terror governments never gave up the power, or the practice, of regulating both the press and religious observance. With the advent of Napoleon, both became a central feature of government activity. Take, finally, revolutionary France's relationship with other peoples. Even as the Constituent Assembly was proclaiming that it threatened nobody it was happily cancelling the rights of imperial princes in Alsace and lending a sympathetic ear to those papal subjects in Avignon and

the Comtat Venaissin who were asking to be incorporated into
France. Almost the last public act of this Assembly, even though it
plainly realised by then that its religious policy had been mistaken,
was to annex these papal territories. The decree offering fraternity
and help to all peoples seeking to recover their liberty, it is often
forgotten, was revoked within five months for the quite impractical
promise it was. But before that was done something far more
ominous had been proclaimed: the doctrine of natural frontiers,
which warned all Belgians, some Dutch and many Germans that
they would be turned into French citizens whether they liked it or
not. Sooner or later, they were; and it is quite obvious that very few
of them did like it: witness the persistent passive resistance of the
left-bank Germans to their new French masters throughout the
1790s; or the great (though often overlooked) Belgian peasant
uprising of 1798. These peoples certainly wished to recover their
freedom: but what that meant in practice was freedom from French
oppression. Similar things could be said of territories not annexed
but occupied, looted and subject to puppet regimes that were
brusquely changed whenever they resisted whatever Paris wanted.
On the other hand the beleaguered Poles, appealing for French
help in 1794 against predatory neighbours preparing to partition
their country out of existence, received fine words but almost no
practical help from the self-styled liberators of Europe.

One could go on with such examples: but I hope the point is
sufficiently made. There was scarcely a principle with which the
French Revolution was identified, at the time or in later perceptions, that the French did not violate, flout, reverse or brush aside
during the Revolution's course. In other words, the Revolution
appears to have stood for nothing constant at all.

But perhaps that is precisely the point. As I began by observing,
people got excited about the French Revolution before they knew
what it was going to stand for. Frenchmen or foreigners, all they
knew before August 1789 was that France was to be regenerated by
the movement gripping it. Clearly what really appealed to that
generation was the idea of regeneration itself, and only very
secondarily what that process was meant to achieve. The world
could be *changed*; fresh starts *could* be made. That was the real
message of the French Revolution, whether it thrilled or appalled
hearers and onlookers. What by 1790 everybody was calling the
Ancien Regime had been a time when things changed slowly, if at
all. There seemed no prospect of making fundamental alterations to
government, to society, or to any human institutions or habits. It
was not that ideas were lacking. The Enlightenment had produced
an outburst of criticism, theorising and system-building
unprecedented in human history; and thanks to the equally

unprecedented enrichment of West European society since the sixteenth century more educated readers than ever before were in a position to share in the intellectual feast. But at the same time everyday experience taught them that to expect comprehensive or radical change was utopian. Yet only if the existing order of things were changed utterly could human beings be improved: that was the message of Rousseau, which appealed so powerfully to the educated men of the later eighteenth century. Society, existing institutions, had corrupted men's natural goodness. This analysis did not incite men to revolution; but it certainly made them welcome it when it happened. It offered them an unexpected, hitherto inconceivable opportunity to change whatever they wanted to change; even, for those so-inclined, to change everything, rebuild everything, from the ground up. Utopia, or at least the chance of utopia, had arrived; and everybody was able, or seemed able, to participate in making the very best of the opportunity.

> Not in Utopia, subterranean fields,
> Or some secreted island, Heaven knows where!
> But in the very world, which is the world
> Of all of us . . .

That in the end the opportunity was squandered was beside the point. Most of those who thrilled to the news in 1789 sooner or later became disillusioned with what it had led to. It is as well to remember that even Burke was moderately excited in early 1789, and Gentz, his German equivalent, was quite as euphoric as Georg Forster or all those other Germans proclaiming that a new age was dawning. But they all recognised, whether they continued to support the Revolution, or increasingly regretted the direction it was taking, or finally held it in abomination, that it represented a *principle of change*; and change on a scale never before deemed conceivable. It was this that unlocked men's minds and opened up European consciousness, in a permanent and quite irrevocable way. Of course the Revolution stood for nothing constant. After it had taken place, nothing was. And nothing would be, ever again. If, from now on, you did not like the world, you no longer sat around deploring its inadequacy, or wondering how by cultivating your garden you could at least marginally improve your bit of it. You turned to Revolution to change it. The French Revolution, therefore, not only introduced the possibility of comprehensive change; it also offered a different way of achieving that change, by violent revolt and tumult; reasoned, planned rebellion; and it offered a pattern over which future revolutionaries would brood and debate down the generations.

But it was not only those who wished to make changes whose outlook the Revolution changed forever. It also transformed the perceptions of those established authorities against whom they were ranged. Under the Ancien Regime the established authorities had not feared change. They had, indeed, in most countries, been its most persistent promoters for their own purposes, thereby attracting the charges of despotism that the men of 1789 and their foreign admirers hurled so readily against governments. But the French Revolution changed all that, too. It showed, in the very way it developed, which I was analysing earlier on, that one change could lead all too readily to another, and before you knew where you were to the overthrow of everything. Such a gospel, which soon enough came to be known in all ruling circles as Jacobinism, had to be resisted, both intellectually and practically. And so Conservatism was born, as much a product of the Revolution as the Rights of Man and the challenge to nobility and privilege. Ultimately it triumphed, in the sense that a generation after the Revolution began France and her upstart Emperor were at last defeated, the Bourbons were restored and calm returned to the continent. But the Ancien Regime was not restored, and never could be; and the triumphant allies of 1815 owed more of their success to what they had copied and borrowed from the French than to a refusal to learn from them. Thus, nobody, not even those who rejected it most vehemently, escaped the influence of the French Revolution, whether at the time or afterwards. That is why the theme of this Symposium is so important.

Chateaubriand and the French Revolution

R. Bolster

In the momentous summer of 1789, Chateaubriand was twenty years of age, had read the works of Rousseau and Voltaire, and was a fascinated observer of the great historical drama which was gathering momentum. A few years later, he was to look back with bitter disappointment on his earlier hope for great political progress in France, and describe himself as a member of a lost generation which had the misfortune to be born into one of those terrible periods when the world knows violent change. In 1797, even before the great military events of the Napoleonic era, he already compared the time he lived in to the fifth century of our era, with its great migrations and invasions. He did not yet know that he would experience the collapse of the Empire, followed by the revolutions of 1830 and 1848. Fortune had apparently smiled on the young Chateaubriand, born in Saint-Malo into a family of Breton nobility, and who, despite a severe upbringing, could look forward to a life of ease and privilege. He was the younger son, and could not expect a substantial inheritance, but his family succeeded in having him presented at Court. This distinction was essential for anyone who hoped to attain high rank in the military career which he had chosen, and Chateaubriand was aware of the injustice of a system in which the younger sons of provincial nobility had little chance of rising above the rank of captain, except by influence at Court. He recorded details of his presentation at Court in his Memoirs,[1] the accuracy of which is not always complete, but which are probably trustworthy in this case. The year was 1787, and the impressive pomp of Versailles gave him the feeling that Louis XIV was still present, seventy years after his death. Louis XVI, the actual occupant of the throne, could find no words to say to the young Chateaubriand, but made only a vague, regal gesture. Marie-Antoinette seemed enchanted with life. The memorialist remembers noting her beautiful hands, and recalls that they were soon to be tied by the executioner. Chateaubriand's dramatic vision of life, his emotive imagery, cannot be attributed to fashion. They are the natural expression of a sensibility formed by close encounter with tragedy. His sense of the fragility of life is the consequence of this experience. He saw a nation, considered the most civilised in the world, go out of control, become engaged in self-destruction. It was this disturbing spectacle which gave him a life-long obsession, almost pathological in its intensity, of the transience of things.

It was partly to counteract this sense of transience that the young Chateaubriand looked for historical truth, and undertook his first major literary work, his *Essai historique, politique et moral sur les Révolutions anciennes et modernes considérées dans leurs rapports avec la Révolution française*. Written in French and published in London in 1797, this work was composed during the author's exile in England which began in 1793. The preface of a later edition, part of the *Oeuvres complètes* of 1826, shows Chateaubriand looking back on the circumstances in which he composed the book. He had participated in the 1792 campaign against the French Republic, and had been wounded at the siege of Thionville. He had retreated, mostly on foot despite his leg wound, from Longwy to Ostend, and had been ill with both small-pox and dysentery. After a partial recovery, he had joined some Breton comrades who hired a boat with the intention of sailing to Jersey and later joining the royalists still active in Brittany. Unfavourable winds had forced the boat to land in Guernsey, where the weakness of Chateaubriand was such that he was placed on the ground, facing the sun, with every expectation that he would soon draw his last breath. Saved by the kindness of a fisherman's wife, who took him into her home, Chateaubriand reached England in the spring of 1793, still with the hope of returning to fight in France. But his health again declined, and at the age of twenty-five he was told by doctors that he could expect to live for one or two years at most. It was because he was no longer able to hold the sword in defence of the royalist cause that he took up the pen. His defence of this cause was not blind and unconditional, as he makes clear in the 1826 preface:

je ne me faisais aucune illusion, comme on le remarquera dans l'*Essai*, sur les fautes du parti auquel je m'étais dévoué.[2]

Chateaubriand's *Essai sur les Révolutions*, which he later described as bearing traces of bitterness and misanthrophy, was conceived as his first and last literary work. It can be said to have exerted a certain influence, as there is evidence that it was much read in the milieu of French exiles living in England and Germany, In France too it aroused some interest, and Maurice Regard has indicated[3] a very favourable review, published in *Le Républicain français* on June 26 1797, which speaks of the author's 'grande érudition' and predicts:

Cet ouvrage aura sans doute en France le même succès qu'il a obtenu dans les pays étrangers. Il reçoit déjà les honneurs de la traduction en Allemagne et en Angleterre.

Chateaubriand's literary career had begun successfully.

Started in 1794, the *Essai sur les Révolutions* is the result of years of study of ancient history, combined with much reflection on recent French events. The subject is impossibly vast, and indicates the inexperience of the writer, as it does his youthful confidence and vigour. It combines formal fragmentation with revealing insights, and is of evident historical interest. It is the work of a man who had lost his social position, his family, and all his possessions, but who had the intellectual courage to want to place in perspective a series of events still close in time, and which had been a bitter personal experience. The young historian formulates the following questions: Has the French Revolution any comparable precedents? What were its causes? Could such catastrophes be avoided? The first answer given is the confident assertion that History does repeat itself, and provide important lessons: knowledge of past revolutions is like a torch which enables humanity boldly to enter the night of future revolutions. Varying the metaphor, Chateaubriand also describes human history as a ladder of misfortune in which the revolutions form the rungs. The republican revolution in ancient Athens, he claims, had consequences very relevant to modern France. Firstly, the Athenian revolution did not bring happiness, but anarchy. The Athenians, similar in character to the French, changed their political system too frequently, and moved into a state of perpetual disorder. As in modern France, he asserts, there was great antipathy between the rich and the poor. And the severity of the draconian laws, comparable to those of Robespierre, produced insurrections, bloodshed, and cruel repression: France was not the first republic to have had savage laws and barbaric citizens, he stresses. After the draconian terror, the population of Athens, like that of modern France, was tired of atrocity. It wearily sought peace by giving power to one man, and, fortunately for the state, that man was Solon. In the history of Sparta too, Chateaubriand sees the same sequence: revolution, anarchy, then autocratic rule. He was, of course, aware of the more recent parallel afforded by the Revolution in England in the time of Charles I, but has little to say about it. The events of ancient Greece seemed to provide some reassurance, because they seemed to have a pattern. It is true that the apparent cyclical model did not point strongly to progress, but at least it was not chaos. Events in modern France seemed out of control, but it would be some consolation if a pattern could be discerned beneath the confusion. It would not be accurate to describe the theoretical models proposed by Chateaubriand as optimistic. He also uses the metaphor of a chain in which link follows link, in a manner apparently allowing no break in the sequence:

Chaque révolution est à la fois la conséquence et le principe d'une autre; en
sorte qu'il serait vrai à la rigueur de dire que la première révolution du globe a
produit de nos jours celle de France.[4]

His use of the expression 'cette fatalité qui règle tout' confirms the
pessimistic element in his thought at this time of ideological
seeking and uncertainty. It is a pessimism from which he was never
to distance himself completely.

Chateaubriand's vast claim about the interlinking of all political
upheavals, in a long chain stretching back towards the beginning of
time, does not prevent him from looking for other, more specific,
causes of the French Revolution. Among these causes he lists, not
surprisingly, the activity of the *philosophes*, and one notes that he is
less severe in his comments on Rousseau and Montesquieu than in
his remarks on Diderot, Voltaire and Helvétius. Their common
fault, he claims, was to destroy, and not replace that which they had
demolished. Another major cause of the events in France was, in
Chateaubriand's opinion, the American Revolution. By helping the
colonial insurgents, France had violated the sacred right of nations,
and without provocation.

> Grand exemple des malheurs qui suivent tôt ou tard une action immorale en
> elle-même, quels que soient d'ailleurs les brillants prétextes dont nous
> cherchions à nous fasciner les yeux, et la politique fallacieuse qui nous
> éblouit! La France, séduite par le jargon philosophique, par l'intérêt qu'elle
> crut en tirer, par l'étroite passion d'humilier son ancienne rivale, sans
> provocation de l'Angleterre, viola, au nom du genre humain, le droit sacré des
> nations. Elle fournit d'abord des armes aux Américains, contre leur souverain
> légitime, et bientôt se déclara ouvertement en leur faveur. Je sais qu'en subtile
> logique on peut argumenter de l'intérêt général des hommes dans la cause de
> la liberté; mais je sais que, toutes les fois qu'on appliquera la loi du Tout à la
> Partie, il n'y a point de vice qu'on ne parvienne à justifier. La révolution
> américaine est la cause immédiate de la révolution française.[5]

He adds that the sight of France covered in blood and ruins, its king
executed, its ministers in exile or killed, proves that there is some
justice in the world. He was not alone in seeing the events of
1789–1795 as a punishment of the nation, an opinion which was to
become orthodox in conservative circles after the return of the
monarchy in 1815.

In addition to the influence of the *philosophes* and that of the
American Revolution, Chateaubriand sees specific causes of the
French Revolution in the social forces in interplay in France. He
speaks of great antipathy between rich and poor, and sees it as a
significant factor. Claiming to have sympathy for the poor, he states
his belief, nevertheless, that there has been too much criticism of

wealth. The poor are infinitely more dangerous than the rich, and a fashionable form of philanthrophy had encouraged and released their destructive force. His perception of the masses is apprehensive and unflattering:

> La victoire s'attachera au parti populaire, toutes les fois qu'il sera dirigé par un homme de génie : parce que cette faction possède au-dessus des autres, l'énergie brutale d'une multitude pour laquelle la vertu n'a point de charmes, ni le crime de remords.

In addition, Chateaubriand explains his belief that the French nation, more than any other, is capable of going rapidly from indolence and insouciance to ferocity and destruction.

His opinion of the French nobility is almost as severe as his comments on the commoners, and he does not fail to explain the Revolution in part by the actions of the aristocracy. He is particularly outspoken in his criticism of those who frequented the court, accusing them of disastrous incompetence and ignorance of the national character:

> J'ai vu des hommes me dire en 1789: La Révolution! on en parlera dans deux ou trois ans d'ici, comme du Mesmérisme et de l'affaire du Collier! Dès lors je prévis de grands malheurs.

It was not by incompetence alone that the aristocracy contributed to the Revolution, argues Chateaubriand, claiming that it is a fact of history that republican revolutions are more frequently started by those who are rich and prominent than by the common people. He believed that a major cause of the Revolution was the vice of a small number of men, not all patrician, who had held power for too long: ministers who achieved and lost their position by intrigue in a continual changing of individuals and of systems. This had led to chronically weak government, as one generation of political insects, sucking the blood of the nation, was followed by another. That was the state of France in 1789, says the *Essai*, which asks: 'Pouvions-nous espérer échapper à une destruction épouvantable?'

The specific causes of the Revolution, as seen by Chateaubriand, can therefore be summarised: the ideological undermining done by the *philosophes*; the example of the American Revolution; the discontent of the common people; and the incompetence of the court and of successive governments. In addition to these specific factors, he speaks also of a more general cause, an alleged unspecific source of the Revolution, and this is surely his most novel and interesting contribution to the subject. He stresses the role of a purely psychological factor, distinct from class interest and the competition of social groups:

Malgré mille efforts pour pénétrer dans les causes des troubles des états, on sent quelque chose qui échappe; un je ne sais quoi, caché je ne sais où, et ce je ne sais quoi paraît être la raison efficiente de toutes les révolutions.

This unknown cause of political upheaval is all the more worrying, says Chateaubriand, because it cannot be seen in social man, and must therefore be innate in natural man and still lurking beneath the surface, with ominous power to disrupt:

Ce principe inconnu, ne naît-il point de cette vague inquiétude, particulière à notre coeur, qui nous fait nous dégoûter également du bonheur et du malheur, et nous précipitera de révolution en révolution, jusqu'au dernier siècle? Et cette inquiétude, d'où vient-elle à son tour? Je n'en sais rien: peut-être de la conscience d'une autre vie; peut-être d'une aspiration secrète vers la divinité. Quelle que soit son origine, elle existe chez tous les peuples. On la rencontre chez le sauvage et dans nos sociétés. Elle s'augmente surtout par les mauvaises moeurs, et bouleverse les empires.[6]

Chateaubriand foresees loud objections to his thesis that the French nation was not happy before 1789: he concedes that some of his readers will certainly describe this opinion as absurd, and protest that France was flourishing and contented. Behind the noise, the wealth of the cities, in spite of the smiling faces, says the young author of the *Essai*, was a hidden psychological reality:

Ceux qui ne voient dans un Etat que des voitures, des grandes villes, des troupes, de l'éclat et du bruit, ont raison de penser que la France était heureuse. Mais ceux qui croient que la grande question du bonheur est le plus près possible de la nature, que plus on s'en écarte, plus on tombe dans l'infortune; qu'alors on a beau avoir le sourire sur les lèvres devant les hommes, le coeur, en dépit des plaisirs factices, est agité, triste, consumé dans le secret de la vie; dans ce cas, on ne peut disconvenir que ce mécontentement général de soi-même, qui augmente l'inquiétude secrète dont j'ai parlé; que ce sentiment de malaise que chaque individu porte avec soi, ne soient dans un peuple, l'état le plus propre à une révolution.

In one of the most striking pages he would ever write, Chateaubriand abandons the objectivity of the historian and adopts a directly confessional mode:

Je l'ai aussi sentie, cette soif vague de quelque chose. Elle m'a traîné dans les solitudes muettes de l'Amérique, et dans les villes bruyantes de l'Europe; je me suis enfoncé pour la satisfaire dans l'épaisseur des forêts du Canada, et dans la foule qui inonde nos jardins et nos temples. Que de fois elle m'a contraint de sortir des spectacles de nos cités, pour aller voir le soleil se coucher au loin sur quelque site sauvage! que de fois, échappé à la société des hommes, je me suis tenu immobile sur une grève solitaire, à contempler

durant des heures, avec cette même inquiétude, le tableau philosophique de
la mer! Elle m'a fait suivre, autour de leurs palais, dans leurs chasses
pompeuses, ces rois qui laissent après eux une longue renommée; et j'ai aimé,
avec elle encore, m'asseoir en silence à la porte de la hutte hospitalière, près
du sauvage qui passe inconnu dans la vie, comme les fleuves sans nom de ses
déserts. Homme, si c'est ta destinée de porter partout un coeur miné d'une
désir inconnu; si c'est ta maladie, une ressource te reste. Que les sciences, les
filles du ciel, viennent remplir le vide fatal qui te conduira tôt ou tard à ta
perte.

In a metaphor which was often to be repeated, Chateaubriand sees
the human psyche bearing within itself this *maladie* which can
threaten civilisation. It must be stressed that he sees this psychological virus not as a consequence of the Revolution, as is sometimes thought, but as a cause.

In these passionately written pages, Chateaubriand's response to
the Revolution is an expression of weariness with the world, of a
melancholy which was to be echoed by more than one writer of the
next generation. Behind it lies the feeling that events are out of
control, that no hand of providence can be seen, that it is the nature
of humanity to have phases of perversity, crime and self-
destruction. His critique is radical, and aims at European civilisation in general. The *Essai* ends with an evocation of the author's
sense of liberation when he discovered the Canadian wilderness. He
recalls how, in a sort of delirium of happiness, he had gone from
tree to tree, rejoicing in the feeling that here were no roads, no
cities, no republics, no kings, and especially no laws. The only
people were harmless Indians, leading a simple, natural life. It was
already an old theme, but Chateaubriand was to give it new life,
and celebrate it unforgettably in his novel *Atala*.

The sincerity of this pessimistic analysis of European civilisation
seems clear. Yet it did also have a theoretical element in it, and
Chateaubriand never did return to America to attempt a new life
there. No doubt he felt that one had to be born to the Indian way of
life, and that of the European settlers did not appeal to him at all.
The author of the *Essai* simply seeks to convince his readers that
political liberty is an illusion, except for nomadic, primitive
peoples; that no European nation is ready for democracy; that the
best political solution for France would be enlightened monarchy.
This conclusion leads Chateaubriand to repeat one of his more
negative statements:

cette importante vérité, que l'homme, faible dans ses moyens et dans son
génie, ne fait que se répéter sans cesse; qu'il circule dans un cercle, dont it
tâche en vain de sortir.

If people could be convinced that there is nothing new in the world, they would lose that desire for change which is one of the greatest scourges of Europe.

But in spite of this vision of historical events moving in an endless circle, the *Essai* is not literature of despair, and it has rightly been asked whether there is such a literature. Destined to be read mostly by exiled French aristocrats and priests, it had the courage to make a statement which might not be welcome: that they had contributed to their misfortune. In years to come, Chateaubriand was to reassess the Revolution, and his first response to it, and modify his earlier vision of humanity moving in a circle. Looking back from the constitutional monarchy set up in 1815, he saw some progress, though he rightly believed it to be threatened by the policies of Charles X. The misanthropic and negative tendency in his earlier reaction to the Revolution he later described as the symptom of a troubled mind, similar to that of almost all those who had lived through the great crisis. It is important to note that his Memoirs, composed some decades later, are more severe than the *Essai* in their assessment of the leaders of the revolution. Time had not brought forgiveness. There are two main reasons for the greater severity of Chateaubriand's later opinion of the Revolution: firstly, his ideological movement away from the *philosophes* and secondly, the slowly matured conviction that it achieved nothing which could not have been obtained by peaceful means. In his Memoirs, he stated the belief that even before 1789 the aristocracy no longer dominated three sectors of power: the judicial system, the Church, and finance. He also believed that a constitutional monarchy could have been conceded about 1790, with Philippe d'Orléans as regent. The Memoirs[7] contain a remarkable hommage to the first achievements of the *Assemblée constituante*:

L'Assemblée constituante, malgré ce qui peut lui être reproché, n'en reste pas moins la plus illustre congrégation populaire qui jamais ait paru chez les nations, tant par la grandeur de ses transactions, que par l'immensité de leurs résultats. Il n'y a si haute question politique qu'elle n'ait touchée et convenablement résolue. Que serait-ce, si elle s'en fût tenue aux cahiers des Etats Généraux et n'eût pas essayé d'aller au-delà! (. . .) Les abus divers de l'ancienne monarchie y sont indiqués et les remèdes proposés; tous les genres de liberté sont réclamés, même la liberté de la presse; toutes les améliorations demandées, pour l'industrie, les manufactures, le commerce, les chemins, l'armée, l'impôt, les finances, les écoles, l'éducation publique, etc. Nous avons traversé sans profit des abîmes de crimes et des tas de gloire; la République et l'Empire n'ont servi à rien: l'Empire a seulement réglé la force brutale des bras que la République avait mis en mouvement; il nous a laissée la centralisation, administration vigoureuse que je crois un mal, mais qui peut-être pouvait seule remplacer les administrations locales alors qu'elles étaient détruites et que l'anarchie avec l'ignorance étaient dans toutes les têtes.

Made in 1821, the claim that the events of 1790–1815 had served no purpose can be seen as a plea for the use of peaceful and moderate methods in politics.

Chateaubriand's Memoirs, more descriptive and less theoretical than his *Essai*, are a significant contribution to our knowledge of the generation which lived through the Revolution. They differ from Michelet's romantic evocation, written after 1840, and by a man not born until 1798: it is not always the case that the historian can see more clearly from a distance. In contrast to a popular image of colourful and essentially lovable *sans-culottes*, Chateaubriand portrays the taking of the Bastille as an expression of brutal anger, an orgy of murder committed by a drunken rabble. Similarly, his account of the bringing of the captive king and queen from Versailles to Paris contrasts with that given by Michelet. The latter describes a holiday atmosphere, with the good-natured women of Paris in cheerful mood:

Les femmes portaient aux piques de grosses miches de pain, d'autres des branches de peuplier, déjà jaunies par octobre. Elles étaient fort joyeuses, aimables à leur façon, sauf quelques quolibets à l'adresse de la Reine.[8]

Chateaubriand, who was present at the scene, gives a very different impression:

Je courus aux Champs-Elysées : d'abord parurent des canons, sur lesquels des harpies, des larronnesses, des filles de joie montée à califourchon, tenaient les propos les plus obscènes et faisaient les gestes les plus immondes. Puis, au milieu d'une horde de tout âge et de tout sexe, marchaient à pied les gardes-du-corps, ayant changé de chapeaux, d'épées et de baudriers avec les gardes nationaux: chacun de leurs chevaux portait deux ou trois poissardes, sales bacchantes ivres et débraillées. Ensuite venait la députation de l'Assemblée nationale; les voitures du Roi suivaient: elles roulaient dans l'obscurité poudreuse d'une forêt de piques et de baïonnettes. Des chiffonniers en lambeaux, des bouchers, tablier sanglant aux cuisses, couteaux nus à la ceinture, manches de chemise retroussées, cheminaient aux portières; d'autres égipans noirs étaient grimpés sur l'impériale; d'autres, accrochés au marchepied des laquais, au siège des cochers. On tirait des coups de fusil et de pistolet; on criait : Voici le boulanger, la boulangère et le petit mitron! Pour oriflamme, devant le fils de saint Louis, des hallebardes suisses élevaient en l'air deux têtes de gardes-du-corps, frisées et poudrées par un perruquier de Sèvres.[9]

For Chateaubriand, this was no ludic festival, this was not a heroic people striding into the future. He records the fact that the Mayor Bailly, in his address to the captive king, described the people as humane, respectful and faithful. Louis XVI replied that he was very touched, and very pleased, and had come to Paris of his own free will. These statements, says Chateaubriand, were examples of the vile falsehoods, bred by violence and fear, which dishonoured all parties and all men at the time. In its sobriety, this account of revolutionary events is a valuable corrective for the sentimental image created by Michelet. Yet it is the latter, precisely because of its naive and patriotic sentimentality, which has stamped itself on popular imagination in France. Chateaubriand's account, stressing the role of illusion, of cynicism, of greed and crime, is the necessary antidote to that of Michelet. Chateaubriand, though a victim of the Revolution, had tried to be objective in his judgment, and the young author of the *Essai* had not hesitated to proclaim:

> il y a toujours quelque chose de bon dans une révolution, et ce quelque chose survit à la révolution même.[10]

The *Essai* had revealed him as an idealist who was not totally disenchanted about the possibility of political progress in the France of 1797. Chateaubriand would continue to feel the tensions, the hesitations, the confusions, the hopes and despairs of the time with an intensity known only by progressive aristocrats. Above all, his *Essai sur les Révolutions* has left us a dramatic and challenging statement about the eternally restless and self-destructive nature of humanity.

NOTES

1. *Mémoires d'outre-tombe*, Gallimard, Paris 1957, I, p. 130.
2. *Essai sur les Révolutions*, edited by M. Regard, Gallimard, Paris, 1978, p. 7.
3. Ibid., p. 1424 (notes).
4. Ibid., p. 253.
5. Ibid., p. 149.
6. Ibid., p. 263–5.
7. I, p. 174–5.
8. Michelet, *Histoire de la Révolution*, 1847–1853, I, book 2, ch. 9.
9. *Mémoires d'outre-tombe*, I, p. 174–5.
10. *Essai*, p. 338.

The Danton/Robespierre Theme in European Drama

W. D. Howarth

The nineteenth century was the heyday of historical drama. Alongside the poetic, idealising drama of Schiller, Manzoni and Victor Hugo, there existed a more prosaic evocation of the past, based on genuine historical scholarship, in the 'scènes historiques' of the 1820s in France – while, running through the century, the vigorous, popular historical melodrama continued to reflect a trivialising, anecdotal approach to historical events. In short, a broad spectrum, from superficial, if spectacular, entertainment to serious documentary narrative; on the one hand acknowledging the influence of Shakespeare, on the other anticipating the manner of Cecil B. de Mille. The outstanding illustration of the popularity of historical drama in this period was without a doubt the theme of Napoleon;[1] but while the real popularity of this subject only really dates from the 1830s, when we turn to the events of 1789–94 we find that from the beginning, polemical plays were written as a contribution to the unfolding of the events themselves. For instance, Laya's courageous anti-Jacobin play of 1793, *L'Ami des lois*, and the reply *l'Ami du peuple*, written by the citoyen Camaille-Saint-Aubin later in the same year, were both in effect political pamphlets in dramatic form. Of Laya, who attacked Robespierre under the name Nomophage ('devourer of laws'), Jacques Truchet writes: 'Il jouait le rôle d'un écrivain engagé prenant parti dans un conflit idéologique'.[2]

If Coleridge's pronouncement: 'In order that a drama may be properly historical, it is necessary that it should be the history of the people to whom it is addressed',[3] has any validity at all, it follows that a subject from recent history which had had such a profound impact on the life of every Frenchman of the time, should inevitably have continued to exercise a fascination for playwrights who had lived through the events, or who were the immediate descendants of those who had; and it is not difficult to understand the appeal of the Revolution throughout the century for playwrights and their audiences, who had lived through two further revolutions and were to suffer the traumatic failure of the Paris Commune in

21

1871. I shall leave on one side the purely anecdotal treatment of episodes, even those from the pen of major dramatists such as Alexandre Dumas *père*, whose *Chevalier de Maison-Rouge* (1847, written as a vehicle for Mélingue, the Errol Flynn of his day) is an early example of the romanesque, sentimental approach to the history of the Revolution that seems always to have been looked on with particular favour in this country: in his case, one might describe it as something like the plot of *A Tale of Two Cities* enacted in the manner of *The Scarlet Pimpernel*. Others besides Dumas chose to represent the political and personal conflicts of the Revolutionary period by means of a fictional narrative, leaving the major historical figures in the background – Sardou in *Thermidor* (1891), Edmond de Goncourt in *La Patrie en danger* (1889) – as Bernanos was to do much later in *Les Dialogues des Carmélites*, which was to be the basis for Poulenc's most moving opera of the same name in 1957. But for the most part, dramatists have chosen to offer the interpretation of an episode, or a sequence of episodes, involving the major figures themselves. The assassination of Marat has attracted a few authors, as has the execution of Louis XVI; but the overwhelming majority of plays deal with the rise and fall of Robespierre, the rivalry with Danton, the events of 9th Germinal and those of 9th Thermidor.

Most attempts to define historical drama have been so imprecise that it is open to doubt whether it can be regarded as a self-standing genre at all. My own criterion for a successful historical drama would be the playwright's ability to convince us of the specific nature of the events we are witnessing, as the unique product of historical forces operating at a given time and in a given place. We should all, I imagine, agree with Herbert Lindenberger in his excellent book *Historical Drama*, that the best examples of the genre have more to offer than a plain chronicle of fact: what we look for, like Lindenberger, is 'philosophical' rather than 'chronical' history.[4] And there could hardly be a richer subject for the playwright seeking to provide a philosophical commentary on the historical process than the events of 1793 and 1794: the contrast between purity of principle and the bloodthirsty barbarity of the end result; the destructive rivalry between leaders all equally devoted to the welfare of their fellow-Frenchmen; and indeed, what can only be seen as a mania for *self*-destruction. To quote Saint-Georges de Bouhélier, writing of his play *Le Sang de Danton*, performed at the Comédie-Française in 1931: 'Ce n'est pas un drame historique, au sens ordinaire du mot. C'est une tragédie du type de l'*Orestie*, ou de l'*Oedipe*'. Robespierre, he says, was destroyed by the pursuing Furies of a fatalistic process: 'le 9 thermidor fait écho au 9 germinal';[5] and at the end of Bouhélier's play, as Robespierre accepts his imminent death, he is made to cry: 'Germinal! germinal! C'est par toi que je meurs! O Danton, Danton! Comme tu m'as hanté, traqué, poursuivi! La vengeance des morts, voilà tout le drame!'

The best-known playwright to have treated the Danton-Robespierre relationship – or at any rate, the author of the play which is far and away the most highly regarded – was also motivated by a keen interest in the philosophy of history. Georg Büchner wrote to his fiancée in 1834, the year before the writing of *Dantons Tod*:

> I studied the history of the Revolution. I felt annihilated by the dreadful fatalism of history ... The individual is only foam on the wave; greatness is simply chance; the rule of genius is a puppet play, a ridiculous struggle against a pitiless law: to recognize it is the ultimate; to control it is impossible ... I accustomed myself to the sight of blood. But I am not the blade of a guillotine.[6]

There is nothing surprising in the fact that a young German should have been inspired to treat this subject, if one thinks of the tremendous impact of the Revolutionary events on the imagination of young radicals throughout Europe from Wordsworth and Coleridge onwards. The factual basis of Büchner's play calls for no particular comment; and the brief interview between Danton and Robespierre at the end of Act I, like the subsequent proceedings in the Assembly and the Revolutionary Tribunal, presents what one might call the standard view of the contrast between the two leaders. It is Büchner's manner, rather than the factual matter of his play, which lifts *Dantons Tod* out of the common run; and perhaps this can be characterised by saying that it reflects – and must more particularly have been seen by contemporaries as reflecting – the influence of Shakespeare's Histories. Not only is it an example of what Lindenberger calls 'philosophical' history (in that Danton emerges as a tragic hero, destroyed at least in part by his own temperament): it also borrows the characteristic Shakespearean structure, gradually piecing together its subject from the cumulative evidence of a series of disparate scenes until a whole finally emerges – a technique still quite strikingly novel in a period in which the *a priori* approach of the French tradition (typical of Hugo just as much as of Corneille) continued to dominate European historical drama.[7]

Like other plays on the Danton-Robespierre theme, *Dantons Tod* relies for its dramatic impact on the mutual interdependence of these two roles. The playwright who wishes to accentuate the sympathetic features of Robespierre's character must perforce cast doubt on the attractive qualities of Danton's sensual, hedonist nature; while the dramatist who chooses Danton as a sympathetic central protagonist will by the same token tend to create a Robespierre not only ascetic, but fanatical and intransigent to the point of inhumanity. Thus Büchner's hero, who would 'rather be guillotined than guillotine',[8] requires as dramatic contrast a Robespierre and Saint-Just for whom the Terror has become a very way of life.

By the time Büchner wrote *Dantons Tod*, however, a revisionist, pro-Robespierre tendency had already begun to manifest itself. Thus, an indifferent play of 1831, *Le 9 Thermidor, ou la Mort de Robespierre, drame historique non représenté* by one Bonnias – typical of the *scènes historiques* of the time in its mixture of public and private subject-matter – is accompanied by a lengthy pro-Robespierre preface:

> Ceci est une oeuvre composée sous l'inspiration d'une conviction profonde; c'est une réponse, sinon complète, du moins consciencieuse, aux calomnies et aux injures que depuis quarante années l'on n'a cessé de déverser sur la mémoire des illustres défenseurs de la cause populaire, de ces grands citoyens qui ont succombé sous les coups de l'intrigue dans la crise du 9 thermidor . . .
>
> Robespierre a été un homme extraordinaire; il eût été un grand homme s'il eût mieux connu son siècle. Il n'a apporté dans sa carrière législative que l'étude de l'histoire; il lui manquait celle du monde . . . Saint-Just était supérieur à Robespierre par l'étendue de son instruction et par son génie, mais il portait plus loin encore l'ignorance des hommes et du pays qu'ils voulaient instituer: tous deux étaient des premiers Romains vivant dans la corruption de l'Empire.

Such a formula – 'early Romans surrounded by the corruption of Imperial Rome' (the Girondins, Danton, and other opponents of Robespierre being identified by implication with moral and political corruption) – expresses in a striking form the 'alternative' view of Robespierre which, deriving from Charlotte Robespierre's biographical portrait of her brother and other similar sources, was not only to fuel the polemics of the professional historians, but also to underlie many of the historical dramas on the subject throughout the nineteenth century. For instance, it was Hamel's highly favourable biography of Robespierre (1865–7), together with later articles from the same pen, that were partly responsible for Sardou's corrective to what he saw as an over-partisan approach. Drawing attention to an early meeting with the veuve Lebas (daughter of Maurice Duplay, Robespierre's landlord), Sardou asks what value the first-hand testimony of someone like this, who had known Robespierre in a purely domestic situation, might possess:

> Quel Robespierre avait-elle connu? Celui de la maison paternelle, heureux de s'y voir cajolé, adulé, presque tendre pour Eléonore et ses soeurs, sobre, austère, chaste, ne parlant que par belles sentences et maximes! Celui qui,

aux veillées d'hiver, récitait des scènes de Racine et fredonnait la romance jouée par Buonarotti sur le clavecin; qui, les soirs d'été, jetait des sous aux petits Savoyards ou menait son chien Brount se baigner dans la Seine – et dans les excursions à Saint-Ouen, à Montmorency, cueillait pour ses jeunes amies des cerises dans les vergers, des bluets dans les champs!

Avec le temps, l'image du grand homme s'était idéalisée au point qu'elle le voyait beau! Sa tête de chat, aux pommettes saillantes, couturées de petite vérole; son teint bilieux, ses yeux verts bordés de rouge sous ses lunettes bleues, sa voix aigre, son verbe sec, pédant, hargneux, cassant; son port de tête hautain, ses gestes convulsifs; tout cela s'était effacé, fondu, transformé en une douce figure d'apôtre, martyr de sa foi pour le salut des hommes![9]

If personal memoirs are inevitably so misleading, it might seem better to stick to the more objective evidence of historical fact – as Sardou himself chose to do in *Thermidor*, at least as regards the major figures, by leaving the political events leading up to 9 Thermidor in the background, and devoting his foreground plot to the episode (historically authentic, despite its romanesque quality) of the ex-actor Labussière, who took a clerical job in the public prosecutor's office in order to save as many victims of the Terror as he could by destroying their dossiers before the cases came before the Tribunal. Despite this precaution, Sardou's condemnation of revolutionary judicial procedures – and his implicit condemnation of the politicians who had introduced them – was clear enough for this to become a *cause célèbre*, Clemenceau denouncing the play in the Assemblée Nationale with the phrase 'la Révolution est un bloc' – that is to say, it was impossible to attack the excesses of the Terror without undermining the fundamental principles of the Revolution and its importance as a unique historical example. Performances of Sardou's play were halted after the second night; and only five years later was *Thermidor* again allowed to be performed. The version given in 1896 contained two new final tableaux, showing the downfall of Robespierre on 9 Thermidor coinciding with the liberation of the young hero and heroine, en route for the guillotine, by a popular uprising. One of these tableaux, set in the Convention Nationale, was also adopted by Sardou as the closing scene of his later play *Robespierre* (premiered in London in 1899 with Henry Irving in the title role) – a much more conventional melodrama reposing on the romanesque fiction that the young hero Olivier, implicated in an anti-Jacobin plot in the days leading up to 9 Thermidor, turns out to be Robespierre's own illegitimate son by the daughter of the *notaire* to whom the young law student from Arras had been articled. Good historical melodrama, possibly; but hardly a serious contribution to the philosophy of history.

Other plays, however, were positively inspired by the revisionist historiography in favour of Robespierre. Louis Combet, author of *Robespierre, ou les Drames de la Révolution*, published at Lyon in 1888 and played in the Paris *banlieue* in the same year, claims in a foreword that his play had been refused by the principal Paris theatres because of its tendentious views. It is dedicated to Ernest Hamel, and the author writes:

> Ce drame n'est point une oeuvre de parti, c'est un essai de réparation et de justice. C'est un appel à l'impartiale histoire, pour la révision d'un jugement hâtivement rendu contre l'homme le plus pur de la Révolution française, et que la calomnie et la haine n'ont cessé de poursuivre jusqu'au delà de la tombe. [Il a été publié] dans le but de faire connaître au peuple qui ne lit pas, au moyen du Théâtre, qui doit être le complément de l'Ecole, la vérité sur Maximilien Robespierre, et rendre publiquement justice à une des plus nobles victimes de la haine, de la calomnie et des lâchetés humaines.

Combet's manner could not be more spectacular, though it depends more on zealous fervour than on historical demonstration: his play ends with a scene, no doubt inspired by Ingres's 'Apothéose d'Homère', in which Robespierre joins Christ, Confucius, Dante, Rousseau, Voltaire and 'tous les hommes illustres du passé' in front of allegorical figures representing Justice, Truth and History. By contrast, *Le 9 thermidor* of 1892, by a trio of authors: La Rode, Rolle and Crémieux, is more sober in its approach, though it denotes its anti-Thermidorian inspiration by making Thérèse Cabarrus the villain of the piece, motivated by a desire for vengeance on a mild, peace-loving Robespierre for having rebuffed her advances. This exercise in hagiography seems to have had a good reception, though the following press review was surely not written without a touch of irony:

> *Le Neuf thermidor*, c'est l'histoire de la Révolution découpée en tranches, dont la plus savoureuse est l'émouvant épisode de la chute de Robespierre. Le grand conventionnel est représenté dans une sorte de réalisme historique, où l'on retrouve aisément les points de vue et les opinions de Louis Blanc, d'Ernest Hamel et du savant professeur Aulard.[10]

A playwright of quite different calibre whose obsession with the Danton-Robespierre relationship, and with the whole corpus of French Revolution historiography, spanned a large part of his long career as a creative writer, was Romain Rolland; and it is his example that I should like to consider in some detail, in order to see how his attitude developed in response both to the views of the professional historians and to the changing political climate, national and international. Nobel prizewinner for literature, political publicist, associate of Gandhi and other leaders on the international stage, sensitive interpreter of the nature of creative genius in his biographies of Beethoven and Tolstoy, Romain Rolland is the most interesting French playwright to have been tempted by our historical theme; and the success of his long involvement with the subject is to be measured both by the epic breadth of the resultant *oeuvre*, and by the imaginative quality of some of the constituent episodes. His *Théâtre de la Révolution* owes its original inspiration to the same decade which saw the production of Sardou's two plays; but *Les Loups* (performed and published in 1898) was merely the first play in a projected sequence which the author himself called 'un vaste poème dramatique . . . l'Iliade du peuple de France'.[11] Elsewhere, he writes of his vision of a 'polyptique à douze panneaux';[12] in fact, the final version of *Le Théâtre de la Révolution* (completed on the eve of the Second World War, but not published as a whole until 1972) contains eight titles, as follows: *Pâques-Fleuries* (not performed; published 1926); *Le 14 juillet* (performed and published 1902); *Les Loups* (performed and published 1898); *Le Triomphe de la raison* (performed and published 1899); *Le Jeu de l'amour et de la mort* (published 1925; performed 1928); *Danton* (published 1899; performed 1900); *Robespierre* (not performed; published 1939); *Les Léonides* (not performed; published 1928).

The prologue and epilogue, both written in the late 1920s, when the scope of the whole project seems to have taken its final shape, are set across the border in Switzerland, and present episodes from the fortunes of the same two families, one aristocratic and the other bourgeois, in 1774 and again in 1797: this enables the playwright to suggest the paternity of Rousseau (who appears in person in *Pâques-Fleuries*) for the ideological principles underlying the Revolution, and to portray the impact on ordinary people, remote from Paris, of the new way of life these ideas had brought into being. In between, we have an interesting diversity of subject-matter and of manner: in the early *Danton* and the final *Robespierre*, the rivalries and conflicts of the major historical figures occupy the centre of the stage, while the other four plays are to a greater or lesser degree distanced from such direct focus on the Danton-Robespierre relationship by the choice of minor protagonists (whether historical or fictional) in a private or domestic setting. At the turn of the century, when he first worked on this material, Rolland tells us that he was haunted by 'le fantôme de Danton';[13] and the nature of this inspiration is clear from the earliest plays in the cycle. The factual account of Danton's downfall is conventional enough, as is the nature of the latter's opposition to Robespierre:

Pourvu qu'un homme ait l'estomac mauvais et les sens atrophiés, pourvu qu'il vive d'un peu de fromage et couche dans un lit étroit, vous le nommez

Incorruptible, et ce mot le dispense de courage et d'esprit. Je méprise ces vertus anémiques . . .

But what distinguishes Romain Rolland's Danton above all is his larger-than-life quality: ('gargantua shakespearien', he is called in the notes on the dramatis personae, while the text of *Le Jeu de l'amour* hints at a sort of mythic dimension when he is referred to as 'le mannekinpis shakespearien, Danton'). Unlike Büchner's hero, whose tragic flaw is the indecision and apathy by which he plays into Robespierre's hands, here the key to Danton's character is his preternatural love of life: a kind of self-love which, however different from Robespierre's 'orgueil', nevertheless leads him to underestimate the pygmies he sees himself as being surrounded by:

> Danton n'est point bâti sur la mesure des autres hommes. Des passions volcaniques incendient cette poitrine; mais elles ne font de moi que ce que je veux qu'elles fassent. Mon coeur a de vastes appétits, mes sens rugissent comme des lions; mais le dompteur est là. (*Il montre sa tête.*)

Together with this, he shows a degree of lucidity about the responsibility for the slaughter of innocent victims which is not at first shared by the morally irresponsible Camille Desmoulins and his child-wife Lucile; and we see how Danton has been conceived by Romain Rolland as a man forced by the pressures of history to assume a leader's role for which he was temperamentally not fitted. 'Colosse pourri' he may be in the eyes of his enemies, but Rolland endows him with a nobility, and a heroic stature, that are not recognisable in any other of the revolutionaries.

One other theme runs through *Danton*, and particularly through *Les Loups*: the relevance of the events of 1793–4 to the political climate of the late 1890s in France. In *Les Loups*, a *ci-devant* officer, D'Oyron – whom we are invited to consider as the same sort of outsider in the revolutionary armies as was a Jewish officer in the French army a hundred years later – is accused of complicity with the Prussian enemy, and convicted by the false testimony of a brother officer who has destroyed the documentary evidence. 'Que mon nom soit flétri', exclaims the commanding officer in the curtain-line of the play (for he suspects the truth) 'mais que la patrie soit sauvée'; while the following exchange between the same officer and his colleague with the disturbing conscience who wants to reopen the case:

> – Malheureux, tu vas jeter ici la haine, le soupçon, la guerre civile!
> – Que la justice se fasse, et que le ciel croule!

must have struck spectators in 1898 as going right to the heart of the issues raised by the Dreyfus affair.

Le 14 juillet carried the dedication, on its publication in 1902, 'Au peuple de Paris'; and in its foreword Rolland expressed his desire to 'rallumer l'héroïsme et la foi de la nation aux flammes de l'épopée républicaine, afin que l'oeuvre interrompue en 1794 soit reprise et achevée par un peuple plus mûr et plus conscient de ses destinées'. This is an early statement of the didactic purpose animating Rolland's revolutionary cycle – a purpose which had become more explicit, and more sharply focused, by the time *Robespierre* was written in 1939. The whole cycle is in fact a practical illustration of the views expressed in *Le Théâtre du peuple* of 1903. Here, Rolland had set out a programme for what he, Maurice Pottecher (to whom the volume is dedicated) and others had conceived as a new kind of popular theatre, 'qui opposât aux raffinements énervés des amuseurs parisiens un art mâle et robuste, exprimant la vie collective, et préparant, provoquant la résurrection d'une race'. *Le Théâtre du peuple* concludes with this challenging appeal to the rulers and educators of France: 'Vous voulez un art du peuple? Commencez par avoir un peuple'. As a means of consolidating the national consciousness, 'l'épopée nationale' is of particular value – for 'L'Histoire héroïque telle que je l'imagine n'est pas une lanterne à l'arrière d'un train, dont la lueur tremblotante éclaire confusément la route parcourue. C'est un phare dans la nuit, qui montre, d'un seul jet de flamme, la place du navire au milieu de l'océan'.

It goes without saying that this new concept of historical drama demands a new dramatic form: 'il faut à de telles oeuvres la flamme de toute une nation; sans elle, on ne peut écrire que des poèmes alexandrins, faits pour la distraction érudite de quelques académies'.[14] Hence the epic sweep of Rolland's whole cycle which, finding room for 'la satire bouffonne' and 'la pastorale' alongside 'le drame', 'voudrait être le tableau symphonique d'un cyclone de peuple'.[15] Hence the role given to ordinary people in certain of the episodes; hence, above all, the distinct emergence of a philosophy of history which sought to justify the Revolution, with all its cruelty, its self-defeating rivalries, its lack of a clear direction, as a necessary step in the evolution of a popular consciousness on a national level. This idealised view of the historical process is nowhere clearer than at the end of *Robespierre*, when the Thermidorians are threatened by the crowd, whereupon with Regnault's curtain-line: 'Peuples du monde, siècles à venir, à nous, à nous!', Hoche breaks into the 'Marseillaise'; and the dramatist comments, in what is more of a personal *profession de foi* than a stage-direction:

Et je voudrais qu'un Darius Milhaud ou un Honegger en fît sortir, en libre et fougueux contrepoint passionné, une puissante *Internationale* qui, enfantée d'elle, la recouvrît et l'absorbât.

Between the *Danton* of 1899 and the *Robespierre* of forty years later, Romain Rolland's view of the historical events, and particularly of the relationship between the eponymous protagonists, had undergone a considerable modification; and he now writes:

J'ose espérer que le vrai visage de l'histoire se reflète dans ce *Robespierre* – plus facilement que je n'ai pu le faire dans mon *Danton*, venu trop tôt, avant les fécondes investigations qui ont renouvelé l'histoire Révolutionnaire.

Drawing attention to contemporary tributes, paid to Robespierre even by his enemies, he asks:

Comment, après de tels témoignages rendus par ceux qui l'ont assassiné, a-t-il fallu attendre plus d'un siècle pour réviser enfin la cause de Robespierre? L'est-elle? Elle ne l'est point, en dépit de la généreuse divination de Lamartine, de la foi idolâtre d'un Hamel, des travaux d'archives passionnés de Mathiez et de son école. Le plus grand homme de la Révolution n'a pas encore en France sa statue.[16]

The Robespierre presented in Rolland's final play is far from being the product of hagiographical piety. Much is made of his relationship with ordinary people, and of the friendship of Saint-Just and Lebas for each other and for Robespierre; but the most significant modification is the suggestion, through the prominence given to the role of Fouché, that Robespierre in his turn, like Danton before him, was the victim of the intriguers and the manipulators. The play opens at the point at which *Danton* had closed; Robespierre and the Duplay family are watching the tumbril pass taking Danton, Desmoulins and their colleagues to the guillotine, and above the crowd noises Danton's offstage voice can be heard: 'Robespierre! j'ouvre la fosse. Tu m'y suivras ... A bientôt!' The presence of the dead Danton broods over this final play, but although Rolland may claim in his Preface that 'il y a là une fatalité aussi inextricable que celle où se débattait Oedipe', the predominant impression left with the reader is one of characters controlled by motivation that is all too human: by the failings of selfishness, cowardice, jealousy and the crude lust for power. However, Rolland's feeling for his subject is such that we remain aware, behind the cruelty, the treachery and the spite, of Robespierre's genuine love for his fellow-men and his belief in a future of justice and universal brotherhood. Anatole France makes his gentle cynic Jérôme Coignard say at one point:

La folie de la Révolution fut de vouloir instituer la vertu sur la terre. Quand on veut rendre les hommes bons et sages, libres, modérés, généreux, on est amené fatalement à vouloir les tuer tous. Robespierre croyait à la vertu: il fit la Terreur. Marat croyait à la justice: il demandait deux cent mille têtes.[17]

The paradox is one that underlies *Le Théâtre de la Révolution*, but without France's irony: for Romain Rolland was himself an idealist who believed in the perfectibility of human nature. As regards his talents as a playwright, it must be admitted that his *Théâtre de la Révolution* probably reads much better than it would perform. A reviewer of the 1939 production of *Le Jeu de l'amour et de la mort* suggests that this is due to the playwright's over-didactic manner:

[Il] prend des porte-parole et leur fait pesamment développer le pour et le contre, comme à quelque exercice contradictoire de Sorbonne . . . On sort de là plein d'estime pour la clairvoyance et la probité de M. Rolland, mais plein de rancune contre l'auteur dramatique. On devrait s'interdire la scène quand on est à ce point dépourvu du don d'insuffler la vie.[18]

The two celebrated spectacles presented by the Théâtre du Soleil – *1789* in 1970, and *1793* in 1972 – are in one sense the ultimate development, 150 years on, of the *scènes historiques* of the 1820s: there is the same deliberate rejection of any conventional dramatic shape, the same refusal to read the history of the past as a pattern of preparation, crisis and dénouement, or as a chronicle of the success and failure of a few individuals standing out from the crowd. But the notion of the spontaneous reconstruction of history in the making was surely also an indirect tribute to Romain Rolland and his 'Théâtre du peuple': the creation of a new, vital relationship between the audience and what is taking place on stage; the fulfilment of Rolland's vision of the democratisation of the theatre and its place in the community. However, there is no trace here of our Danton-Robespierre theme: this sort of sharply-defined dramatic conflict is not what the Théâtre du Soleil was about, nor does it correspond to the way in which Mnouchkine and her associates chose to see the history of the Revolutionary years.

I propose to finish, therefore, by looking briefly at a play from our own post-war period which uses material from the French Revolution in a more conventional dramatic form, but which focuses more squarely on the Danton-Robespierre relationship than most of the texts I have been considering. Like Peter Weiss in his *Marat/Sade* (1964), Jean Anouilh adopted in *Pauvre Bitos* (1956) an oblique approach to the Revolutionary material: in his case because the choice of subject was motivated by the playwright's wish to make a serious comment on the political situation in post-war France. The play is set in the 1950s, in the French provinces where a group of wealthy and successful characters, the social elite of their community, have been invited to a 'dîner de têtes', each of them being asked not only to come made up as one of the figures of the Revolutionary period – Danton, Camille Desmoulins, Tallien and so forth – but to rehearse the career and personality of the historical figure concerned, for the purposes of a spontaneous 'happening'. It emerges that the intention of the *animateur* of the evening's entertainment is to expose and humiliate one of the guests who is not one of their social circle: Bitos, an ambitious young lawyer from a very humble background, who has recently been posted back to this locality as public prosecutor, and is making a name for himself by his merciless vendettas against wartime collaborators. When Bitos arrives, he is identified with Robespierre not merely by wig and make-up, but because he is dressed in the latter's celebrated sky-blue costume. Antagonism between Bitos, the outsider, and his hosts develops with increasing dramatic tension, until the arrival of the young man briefed to play the gendarme Merda, whose pistol-shot brings to an end the first act. Act II takes place in the fevered imagination of Bitos, who has fainted at the pistol shot: in a dream-sequence he becomes Robespierre, while the other characters assume the roles they have been acting out. A third act returns us to the present, and the end of the play brings some sort of truce in the hostilities between Bitos and his tormentors.

Considered as historical drama, *Pauvre Bitos* would be unremarkable; and the play supports the view of Anouilh's critics, that history was never for him more than a pretext for a fancy-dress charade. But unlike his other 'history' plays, *Pauvre Bitos* exploits the theatricality of the charade, and uses the analogy between the political situation in post-war France and the events of the Revolution not only for striking technical effect, but in order to suggest telling parallels between past and present. The picture of the historical Robespierre, and his relationship with Danton and other contemporaries, may offer little that is original; but Bitos as a latter-day Robespierre is wholly convincing, as is the character who plays Danton, though he hardly emerges as the most humane of Robespierre's opponents. Artistically, the play does suffer from the lack of an attractive protagonist – neither the intransigent puritan Bitos nor the right-wing bullies who persecute him qualify for our sympathy – and contemporary criticism tended to accuse the playwright of misanthropy and cynicism. Pierre Fresnay, however, made a more perceptive comment when he said: 'On a écrit que c'est une pièce politique: c'est une pièce contre la politique, quelle qu'elle soit. On a dit que c'est une pièce de haine: c'est une pièce contre la haine';[19] and it still reads today as the most powerfully committed play of a dramatist who was often accused of being a dilettante entertainer: a humanist's protest against the witch-hunts of the post-war *épuration*, and against all forms of doctrinaire extremism, whether of the right or of the left.

In contrast to *Pauvre Bitos*, the recent *Danton Affair* by Pam Gems (Royal Shakespeare Company, 1986) is a crude historical melodrama. Büchner, Romain Rolland and Bouhélier had recognised in the antagonism between Danton and Robespierre the noble theme of human aspirations defeated by greater human failings; while even Anouilh's pessimistic view of the historical process had the benefit of being expressed in a theatrically most challenging form. Gems's play was based on the Polish original from the 1930s by Stanislawa Przybszewska, whose admiration for Robespierre led her to rewrite Büchner's play in an anti-Danton light. Gems has now used the same material again – but her determination to remain independent of both the German and the Polish interpretations has resulted in a play with no point of view at all. None of the main protagonists shows any nobility of spirt; the episodic construction merely adds to the arbitrary characterisation, in an atmosphere of strident vulgarity; and the Robespierre-Danton theme deserves much better than this painfully reductive treatment.

If Rolland's *Théâtre de la Révolution* stands out as the masterpiece, both in terms of its epic scope and of its philosophical insight, among the dramas devoted to our Revolutionary theme, it is equally true that playwrights of succeeding generations have continued to recognise the dramatic possibilities of the Danton-Robespierre confrontation, and have been ready to reinterpret the events of 1793–4 both in response to the changing perspectives of the professional historians, and as a vehicle for an imaginative artistic or philosophical commentary on the political prejudices of their own day. While there may perhaps be little to compare with *Dantons Tod* in terms of artistic achievement, we cannot fail to recognise the challenging potential of this theme which has made such a strong appeal to the imagination of playwrights over nearly two hundred years.

NOTES

1. See L.-H. Lecomte, *Napoléon et l'Empire racontés par le théâtre*, Paris, 1900; and my article 'Bonaparte on Stage', *Historical Drama* (*Themes in Drama*, *8*), Cambridge, 1986, pp. 139–161.
2. *Théâtre du xviiie siècle*, ed. J. Truchet, Paris, 2 vols., 1972–4, II, p. 1546.

3. Quoted by H. Lindenberger, *Historical Drama*, Chicago, 1975, p. 6.

4. Lindenberger, op. cit., p. 131 ff.

5. Preface.

6. Quoted by D.G. Richards, *Georg Büchner and the Birth of Modern Drama*, New York, 1977, p. 12.

7. See my article, 'History in the Theatre: the French and English Traditions', *Trivium*, I (1966), pp. 151–68.

8. *Dantons Tod*, II, i.

9. *La Maison de Robespierre, réponse à M. E. Hamel, sénateur*, Paris, 1895, pp. 74 ff.

10. Published in *Le Magasin théâtral*, 1892.

11. Written in 1900, at the time when *Danton* was performed. Quoted in the Preface to *Le Jeu de l'amour et de la mort*.

12. Preface to *Le Jeu de l'amour et de la mort*.

13. Preface to *Les Léonides*.

14. *Le Théâtre du peuple*, Paris, 1926, pp. 144, 140.

15. Preface to *Le Jeu de l'amour et de la mort*.

16. Preface to *Robespierre*.

17. *Les Opinions de Jérôme Coignard*, Paris, n.d. (Calmann-Lévy), pp. 25–6.

18. F. Ambrière, *Mercure de France*, 15. viii. 1939, Vol. CCXCIV, p. 117.

19. *Paris-Presse – L'Intransigeant*, 19. x. 1956.

The Poetry and Politics of Emancipation: The French-Jewish Response to the Revolution

Nelly Wilson

On 27 September 1791 the Constituent Assembly declared null and void all restrictions and privileges pertaining to members of the Jewish persuasion, hitherto known as the Portuguese nation[1] and the German nation,[2] and accorded them full citizenship.[3]

Nowadays the ambiguities surrounding the emancipation act, as it has come to be known, attract more attention than its significance. Why, for example, given the Constitution and the Declaration of the Rights of Man, did it take over two years (August 1789 to September 1791) of often acrimonious debate for the act to be passed? On the other hand, the Bordeaux community, arguing its case on *privileges* hitherto enjoyed, was granted citizenship eighteen months (January 1790) before all the others. Instead of abolishing privileges and inequalities, the Assembly seemed to perpetuate them and, along with them, the anomalies which might arise. Thus a Bordelais living in Paris[4] was recognised as a citizen, while his neighbour, who similarly prayed in Hebrew but who did not have the good fortune to have been born in Bordeaux, was not so considered; and this in spite of the fact that many Parisian Jews were by then already serving in the National Guard. It was ultimately the appeal to logic and to the Constitution that carried the day. Or so it would seem, for some historians have suggested that accident may have played its part in the final passing of the act, a number of opposition deputies having already gone home by the time it came to the vote. However that may be, whatever one's interpretations about how it came about and what was ultimately achieved, most people will agree that, first, the emancipation decree marks a turning point in the history and consciousness of modern Jewry, until then the most oppressed ethnic minority in Christian Europe; secondly that it had a profound influence on the French Jewish community throughout the nineteenth century and beyond. After Napoleon's tampering with it in 1808, the act was fully restored in 1818 and respected thereafter by successive regimes until Vichy.

Explaining the significance of Day One of the new era to his community, the Lorraine leader at the time, Berr-Isaac-Berr, exclaimed: yesterday we were still wretched slaves; today, 'a memorable day which we shall celebrate for evermore, we are not only men and citizens but Frenchmen!'. Being a deeply religious man, he thanked the Almighty for having inspired the 'immortal legislators of France' who had brought the purest joy to 40,000 unhappy serfs and transformed them with one stroke of the pen into 'des enfants de la patrie'. And he ends this lyrical section of his *Lettre d'un Citoyen*, signed 'Juif, Citoyen Actif', by expressing the inexpressible to the Nation and the King: 'the extent of our gratitude and our unwavering submission'.[5]

The main components of what was to develop into a common French-Jewish discourse on the Revolution are already present in these few lines. And I would like to begin by considering some of them.

We have, first of all, the dramatic 'before and after' view of things, with the implicit rejection or repression of what went before. In an ironic depiction of how, in the early decades of the Third Republic, primary school children were taught the impact of the French Revolution, Péguy recalled that the *instituteur* would tell them that until 1789 France was plunged into an abyss of darkness. After 1789 light shone everywhere. In the Thursday catechism classes, *monsieur le curé* would say the exact opposite. Jewish Republicans were even more prone to thinking in terms of the great divide – which their clergy confirmed – with the result that French history was shortened and Jewish history discontinued. As early as 1790, Berr-Isaac-Berr expressed the hope that with the passing of the emancipation act both persecutors and persecuted would throw 'un voile sur tous les temps passés'.[6] Eleven years later (1801) his son, Michel Berr, wrote: 'Having become more French than Jewish, I hardly dare to discover the abyss of horrors (i.e. persecutions) since I cannot recall them without feeling shame for my country from whose midst came some of our persecutors'.[7]

The feeling of shame was increasingly extended to the persecuted ancestors who in the struggle for survival, it was said, acquired the vices (ruse, dishonesty, usury, fanaticism, etc.) of which the outside world accused them. In its efforts to prove its 'regeneration' since 1789, assimilated Jewry often tended to see its past, the ghetto 'juiverie' of old, with the eyes of its opponents. As a consequence, much of the cultural life that went on in the 'dark' ghettos was not rediscovered until much later, under the influence of German Jewish scholarship. Even so, as Julien Benda remarked à propos his father, the ardent patriotism of French Jews was not attached to the soil or the distant past, nor to any specific city or village. *La patrie* was the French Revolution.[8]

The emancipated were similarly anxious to prove to themselves and to the outside world that 1789 had put an end to Jewish history, henceforth absorbed into French history. This 'end' view found its most widespread form of expression in the rejection of the term *Juif* not merely on account of its pejorative associations but because, according to Berr-Isaac-Berr, writing in 1806,[9] its etymological derivation from and historical association with Judea was no longer meaningful, an idea forcefully expressed in the *Archives Israélites* in 1842: 'The adjective Jewish no longer makes any sense because the Jew whose soul is in Jerusalem and whose body is in France no longer exists'. Both lay and spiritual leaders insisted that, in the words of Théodore Reinach, 'after 1791 it is inappropriate to speak of French Jews. They are French citizens professing *la religion israelite*'.[10] With the substitution of the term Israelite for Jew, first proposed by Berr-Isaac-Berr, went the rejection of any notion of a Jewish people with a continuing history of its own, any manifestation of national feeling. Thus Reinach was not only hostile to modern Zionism, as one might expect, but he dismissed it on the grounds that it was 'incompatible with the principles of 1789'.[11]

Rejection of or unfamiliarity with the past, particularly the martyrological past, made it difficult to identify, to express solidarity with persecuted brethren. An extreme example is provided by Bernard-Lazare (1865–1903), a young intellectual angered by the entry into France in the 1880s of Russian immigrants fleeing from pogroms. 'What do I . . . an Israelite of France, have in common with these descendants of the Huns',[12] he asked. He later bitterly regretted his disassociation but only after having himself experienced persecution during the Dreyfus Affair. Actually, deep down, the community did feel solidarity but it did not dare express it publicly. The poetry of *civis gallicus sum* dictated a political strategy of silence, of waiting for non-Jewish personalities or organisations to take up the fight, of behind-the-scene interventions. There are several such instances of the politics of emancipation, none more eloquent than the silence observed by the community at large during the Dreyfus Affair.

To return to Berr-Isaac-Berr's letter of 1791. His pride of belonging to *la patrie* combined with an overwhelming sense of gratitude towards it were to be echoed throughout the century. The expression 'enfants de la patrie' has a literal meaning in our context, for the Jews at the time saw themselves as minors who had come of age, as hitherto abandoned and therefore wayward children now anxious to mend their ways, learning to be citizens, to exercise *useful* trades, to speak French. To speak French as the mother-tongue became an over-riding concern, to the point where schoolchildren in Metz were punished if overheard speaking Yiddish among themselves. The Metz leader, I.B. Bing, even characterised Yiddish, widely spoken in the North-East before the Revolution, as an 'unintelligible jargon'[13] invented by way of protection against a hostile outside world. Berr-Isaac-Berr, for his part, was forever deploring his own inexperience in the 'national tongue', 'the language of freedom'. If the image of minors learning to be French-speaking adult citizens soon disappeared, that of France as *la patrie-mère*, not adopting but welcoming back to the fold children once cast out, remained. It is in this sense that James Darmesteter spoke of France as 'la patrie retrouvée'.

The Lorraine leader's promise of unwavering obedience to the 'Nation and the King' was similarly kept by the community in subsequent years. With the possible exception of the traumatic experience of the Terror, it welcomed all post-1789 regimes, composed odes to Louis XVIII, Louis-Philippe, Napoleon III. The ruler most celebrated, not infrequently in Hebrew and in adaptations of the Psalms, was Napoleon, at least until the 'infamous' decree of 1808. This official apolitical stance does not necessarily betoken insincerity; it is more an expression of fidelity to the law and the charter represented by the government in power, mingled with a fear of being seen as 'bad', rebellious citizens. But it does mean that individual dissidents (Adolphe Crémieux, Bernard-Lazare, Léon Blum and others) were a political embarrassment. In general, the Third Republic came as a great relief; it allowed French Jewry, Republican at heart, to reconcile public and private allegiance.

We even have in Berr-Isaac-Berr's letter of 1791 a hint of something that was to develop greatly with the years. He looked upon the emancipation decree as God-inspired and upon France as the Chosen Nation of modern times. Another contemporary expressed his feelings thus: 'France is our Palestine; its mountains are our Mount Zion; its rivers are our Jordan: let us drink the living waters of its springs, the waters of freedom'.[14] From poetic analogies of this kind there emerged in due course a phenomenon unique to French Jewry, that of Franco-Judaism which transfers to France values and aspirations traditionally associated with Judaism. Republican France assumes the role of Israel. As one rabbi put it, on the occasion of the centenary of the Revolution in 1889: France has been 'chosen by the Almighty who directs the destinies of humanity to bring about the emancipation of all the oppressed, to spread throughout the world the lofty and beautiful ideas of justice, equality and fraternity which formed once upon a time the patrimony of Israel'.[15] It is difficult to think of any section of French society which celebrated the centenary with greater enthusiasm and solemnity than the Jewish community: commemorative services were held in synagogues throughout the country; rabbinical sermons, a collection of which was published (1890) under the characteristic title of 'The French Revolution and the French Rabbinate', celebrated 1789 as the second exodus from Egypt, the modern Passover, the second Sinai Law, the coming of the Messianic age. What is implicit in these analogies is a transformation of the concept of exile and the spirit of messianism. The idea that the golden age has arrived, that progress is an historical law, a matter of natural evolution, owes more to the Enlightenment than to the prophetic, pessimistic and ultimately more revolutionary concept of a cataclysm announcing the messianic age which may or may not follow the apocalypse; the ideal city, in this context, lies ahead, is awaited and prepared for without certainty of attainment.

For all its worship of the French Revolution, late nineteenth-century French Jewry was not on the whole revolutionary. In common with the politically and socially conservative liberal bourgeoisie to which it largely belonged, the well assimilated Jewish middle class believed itself to be living in the best of all possible countries and Republics. It counted its blessings and honoured the French Revolution as the eleventh commandment. In this kind of central Franco-Judaism, as distinct from the more rebellious variants active on the periphery, much of the questioning and fiery spirit of both the Revolution and of Judaism tended to be lost.

It is in this respect perhaps that the early Jewish response to the Revolution, that on the part of men who actually fought for emancipation and who had initiated the debate during the last decade of the ancien régime, is significantly different. For all their bourgeois respectability, flowery rhetoric and constant assurances that the Jewish nation was resigned and not of rebellious spirit, the 'syndics' (i.e. community representatives) of Alsace, Lorraine and Metz did in fact not resign themselves either to the chaotic ancien régime system of arbitrary privileges and no rights,[16] or later, to the Constituent Assembly's apparent inability or unwillingness to apply the declaration of Rights to the most oppressed section of French as well as Jewish society.

The battle began in the late 1770s with Cerf Berr's account of the plight of Alsatian Jewry, the first such effort designed to attract public attention. On the advice of Moses Mendelssohn, it seems, the *mémoire* was published as part of *De la Reforme Politique des Juifs* (1782), a French translation of the seminal work by the German Christian historian Dohm. On a more immediately successful level the Alsatian leader used his court connections to campaign for the abolition of the degrading headtax (abolished in 1784) and, armed with a royal decree and a great deal of tenacity, he fought his way into Strasbourg, closed to Jewish settlement since 1349. Thus, in spite of the opposition of the city fathers, the Cerf Berr family demonstrated, albeit on a small scale, that in Alsatian cities, as well as in Bordeaux, Jews could live side by side with their Christian neighbours without provoking catastrophes or riots. The real problem, however, was how to transform the privileges of the few into rights for all. In a personal letter to the King (1788), Cerf Berr had the boldness to suggest full citizenship as the solution to the question of Jewish settlement.[17]

Neither Cerf Berr nor his colleagues from Metz (Isaie Beer Bing) and Nancy (Berr-Isaac-Berr) participated directly in the famous essay competition set by the Metz Royal Society in 1785 on a subject dear to their hearts: 'How can the Jews in France be rendered happier and more useful?' The syndics were busy however, briefing friendly contestants, notably the abbé Grégoire and Adolphe Thiéry. Less inhibited or diplomatic, the Polish-born son of a rabbi recently settled in Paris, decided to enter the competition and represent the Jewish nation; not to have done so, observed Zalkind Hourwitz in the preface to his essay, significantly entitled *Apologie des Juifs*, would have been to miss the opportunity of enlightening the outside world whose total ignorance of things Jewish he found astonishing.[18] I.B. Bing was evidently beginning to feel this too for even before the Royal Society made public its decision, he published his own apology (*Lettre à l'auteur anonyme*, 1787). The Metz prize, incidentally, was finally shared, in 1788, between a Catholic priest (the abbé Grégoire), a Protestant lawyer (Thiéry) and a Polish Jew (Hourwitz). All argued that oppression was the main cause of the unhappy Jewish situation. The competition and the debate it provoked on the eve of the Revolution represent a crucial stage: they were instrumental in the King's decision (1788) to set up a commission headed by Malesherbes to look into the Jewish problem; subsequently, they provided a reference point in the Constituent Assembly's discussions, with the abbé Grégoire continuing to act as chief spokesman for emancipation. The Metz competition also marks a turning point in the awareness of the Jewish leaders that they must fight their own battles, rather than rely on or simply brief friendly spokesmen, if they were to achieve the kind of 'regeneration' they had in mind. I.B. Bing's above mentioned *letter* is in this respect highly instructive. It set the tone, themes and tensions of Jewish emancipationist writing for the next decade or so.

The immediate provocation was an unsigned pamphlet, *Le cri du Citoyen contre les Juifs de Metz* (1786), emanating from an Army officer, Latour-Foissac (generally thought to be a pseudonym for Aubert-Dubayet). What alarmed Bing most were the obvious Voltairian sources of the author's arguments. Here was a new kind of atheist anti-Judaism, product of the Enlightenment, which not only struck at what Jews most cherished about their religion, namely its ethics, but whose predictable effect would be to revive and even justify the old Christian anti-Judaism which had seemed to be on the wane. Voltaire was a problem to 'enlightened' Jews. On the one hand they admired 'ce grand génie [qui] a infiniment contribué à la tolérance'. On the other hand, as observant Jews they regarded Voltaire's attacks on religion in general as destructive of social and moral values and were devastated in particular by his anti-Jewish diatribes (how generous of the enlightened philosopher, remarked Bing, that he did not wish to burn the Jews in spite of all the vices he attributed to them!).[19] It was time to explain Judaism, to refute common charges, to give chapter and verse, to present the Jewish view of Judaism.

Thus a bold defence of Judaism became a prominent feature of Jewish emancipationist writing. It is invariably accompanied by an equally outspoken critique of the present deplorable state of mind of the faithful, the result not of Jewish teaching, it is argued, but of outside oppression which causes that teaching to be debased in the struggle for survival. 'A persecuted nation cannot be a prodigy of civilisation', Bing observes. Grant the Jews freedom of movement, access to all professions, admission to public schools and institutions and they will prove to be good citizens and good Jews. As it is, without community care, things could be far worse. In 1789, looking back on the Metz competition, Bing is almost angry that the *usefulness* of the Jewish people to French society should have been a matter for debate. How the community has managed to preserve its humanity in the midst of so much inhumanity might have been a more pertinent subject to examine, he suggests.[20]

Bing's pre-revolutionary apology comprises two further elements of interest, both taken up and developed by Berr-Isaac-Berr after 1789: a profession of fidelity to the faith and the vision of a pluralist society in which different faiths co-exist. Convinced that their religious beliefs were not incompatible with their duties as men and citizens, the syndics made no attempt to rationalise, christianise, gallicise or modernise them. Let us fight for our freedom, urged Bing, but '. . . demeurons inaltérables dans le culte de nos pères, ne sacrifions pas à des avantages passagers.' And if, he added, this be considered superstitious, then 'je vous avouerai volontiers que nous le soyons toujours en dépit des progrès de la philosophie'.[21] The remark is evidently addressed to Voltaire's disciples in the first instance, but it may also have been intended for such conversionist friends as the abbé Grégoire, whom Berr-Isaac-Berr later chided for denigrating 3047 pages of Talmudic text as comprising only a few 'paillettes d'or égarées dans la fange'. Could it be that the abbé was not sufficiently familiar with Talmudic language? He similarly objected to Grégoire's characterisation of the rabbinical mentality as 'le fléau de la raison'.[22] With such friends, who needs enemies?

Most non-Jewish emancipationists, whether Christian or non-religious (Mirabeau, Clermont-Tonnerre) did indeed present something of a problem for friend no less than foe stipulated a necessary dejudaisation; the only difference being that the latter made emancipation *from* Judaism a prerequisite for political emancipation, while the friends hoped that one would naturally follow from the other, that, once a free and equal citizen, the Jew would cease to be Jewish, perhaps convert to Christianity or, in Mirabeau's words, prove himself to be 'more Man than Jew'. The dynamics of emancipation and acculturation did indeed tend towards a certain dejudaisation later in the century; but it was not something that Cerf Berr, Bing or Berr-Isaac-Berr ever contemplated. If anything the latter thought that Revolutionary France had moved closer to his position. It is worth recalling the remarkable opening of his address to the Constituent Assembly before which he appeared on 14 October 1789 to plead the case for his still unemancipated brethren. Awed by the solemnity of the historic occasion – the first time a Jewish delegation was admitted to Parliament – but not overawed, he did not altogether speak as a suppliant asking for favours but as someone who claims his rights which should never have been taken away. 'I come in the name of the Eternal, author of all justice and truth, in the name of God who has bestowed on all the same rights and prescribed to all the same duties'.[23] In other words, liberty, equality and fraternity may well have ancient roots.

An original idea in the early Jewish emancipationist dream concerned the retention of spiritual and cultural autonomy side by side with political equality. Bing first hinted at this in 1787 when he suggested that 'deux nations (i.e. French and Jews) ... entre lesquelles il règne une sorte d'égalité politique et dont la religion est fondée sur les mêmes principes moraux'[24] can live harmoniously side by side. His post-revolutionary version (1789), though less bold in its formulation, was bolder still in its pluralist concept since it stipulated *full* equality of citizenship without this entailing the community's 'incorporation absolue' into the State.[25] No doubt the desire for communal autonomy was dictated by a mixture of immediate practical needs (the collection of communal taxes in order to settle debts and maintain social services) and long-term religio-cultural aspirations. Whatever the motives, the notion itself of group autonomy was audacious. Nothing could have been more contrary to Jacobin ideology in this respect than the 'Pétition des Juifs établis en France' presented to the Assembly on 28 January 1790. It comprises a plea for what amounts to, in effect, the separation of Church (i.e. religion) and State and for the latter's recognition of spiritually diverse 'colonies de citoyens'. No wonder the Assembly found it difficult to reach a decision.

In order to retain a certain amount of autonomy, Berr-Isaac-Berr was prepared to go down a slippery path. He was prepared to strike a bargain with the bishop of Nancy who was most alarmed at the prospect of Jews, once accorded citizenship, being eligible to high public office. Berr-Isaac-Berr, who may well have respected this fear to a certain extent, proposed that in return for voluntarily renouncing the right to serve on the judiciary and on local councils, the Jews of the North-Eastern provinces should be allowed to remain an autonomous community with its own courts (in litigation between Jew and Jew) and the right to appoint its own rabbis and representatives.[26] Understandably, the would-be citizens in whose name the bargain was proposed were alarmed and hastily and publicly rejected it.

More than most leaders, the paternalist Berr-Isaac-Berr feared the effects of the community's sudden dissolution. He was remarkably lucid in his realisation that the 1791 decree marked the end of one battle and the beginning of another: in the eyes of the world emancipation or regeneration, to use the term in vogue at the time, was conditional on yesterday's slaves proving themselves to be paragons of virtue overnight, transforming themselves from pedlars into peasants, from hated moneylenders into skilled craftsmen; on living down the myths and legends of centuries. In other words, emancipated Jewry was on probation. Most of all he feared that if that miraculous progress did not come about as quickly as people expected, then the opponents of emancipation would seem to have scored a victory: the Jew would be regarded as incorrigibly degenerate, beyond regeneration, or, at best, as regenerable provided he ceased to be Jewish. Such were his sombre reflections when, on 30 May 1806, Napoleon convened an Assembly of Jewish Notables and, a little later, an international Grand Sanhedrin modelled on the rabbinic court of ancient times.

Why Napoleon went to the trouble of staging this elaborate charade and how half of European Jewry came to be duped by it is a long and far from clear story. The enthusiastic French response is understandable. Indeed, if we take the Lorraine leader's views to be reasonably representative, then it must be said that the 'immortal Emperor' began by heeding the wishes of his Jewish subjects, and he did so on a scale and with a pomp which profoundly moved them. A year prior to the setting up of the Assembly, Berr-Isaac-Berr had pleaded with the government to create some such body, with the dual purpose of restoring order to communal affairs, in disarray since the Revolution, and, once set up, of concluding a concordat as had been signed with the other Churches.[27] Such a covenant would not only serve as formal confirmation of the claims previously made in various apologia and petitions concerning the compatibility between religious principles and national law, but would also accord the Jewish religion official recognition and equality with the other faiths.

Had Napoleon's Jewish policy been limited to the creation of a centralised consistorial system and to the concordat between Synagogue and State embodied in the Sanhedrin's decisions – the one generating an unprecedented degree of order and unity and the other conferring on Judaism the dignity of being a State-protected religion – it is likely that he would have retained the profound gratitude of his French Jewish subjects. The emancipationist dream seemed complete: observant Jew and patriotic Frenchman could live fully in both worlds. The dream, as we know, was shattered by one of the decrees of 1808. For certain regions, notably Alsace-Lorraine, it amounted to a repeal, albeit for a temporary ten-year probationary period, of the rights of citizenship granted in 1791. The whole community was shocked into silence. One can only guess at the feelings of men such as Berr-Isaac-Berr. In a sense the repeal realised his worst fears but, by a sad irony, it was the work of the Emperor whom he had hailed as saviour.

The consistorial system, with its motto of 'Patrie et Religion', proved ideal for spreading and maintaining Franco-Judaism. The latter acquired an interesting variant conceived by rebellious individuals on the periphery of the Establishment, a deviation which takes us back to some extent to the spirit of the early emancipationists. Whereas Franco-Judaism gallicised Jewish ideals, certain thinkers (Bernard-Lazare, James Darmesteter, Alexandre Weill, Joseph Salvador) tended to judaise the Revolution, interpreting it in the light of Jewish revolutionary traditions, symbolised in the Jew as the born agitator, never satisfied, always aspiring to better things in the here and now. The idea the ancient Hebrews had of God, observed Bernard-Lazare, made earthly tyrants unacceptable; no *man* shall be called master. Similarly, their conception of life and death made them fight for justice and equality in this world. This was the essence of the prophetic spirit.[28] James Darmesteter, for his part, presented the Jew as the eternal dissident, the man who protests, who argues and reasons, even with God.[29] One of the most fascinating versions of this trend is to be found in Joseph Salvador's Utopia *Paris, Rome and Jerusalem* (1859), with Rome (pagan antiquity and Christianity) representing the past, Paris the present and Jerusalem the future. Humanity, regenerated by revolutionary France and the ideals of ancient Jerusalem which inspired it, will return one day to Palestine to build the New Jerusalem.

It is an original response on the part of a minority, but it is most unlikely that French revolutionary ideology was inspired in any conscious way by the ideals of prophetic justice or Mosaic law; as unlikely as the antisemitic idea current in the late 19th century that the Revolution was the result of a Jewish-Masonic plot.

NOTES

1. The Sephardi communities of the Bordeaux and Bayonne areas who originally came from Portugal and Spain and whose settlement in the South-West goes back to the 16th century.

2. The Ashkenazi communities of the North Eastern territories (Alsace, Lorraine, Metz and surrounding area) which came under French rule at different times.

3. This also came to include the communities of Avignon and the Comtat Venaissin (Carpentras, Cavaillon and L'Isle-sur-Sorgue) which had been under papal jurisdiction until 14 September 1791.
   Exact figures are difficult to establish for the pre-Napoleonic period; it is generally estimated that the total *number* of Jews did not exceed 40 to 50,000 (i.e. 0.16% of the country's total population). The distribution, however, was very uneven, with 78% concentrated in the North-East.

4. Paris, where Jews were not allowed to reside except with special permission, counted some 500 legal residents plus a certain number of temporary 'passport' holders and no doubt quite a few illegals.

5. Berr-Isaac-Berr: *Lettre d'un citoyen . . . à ses confrères, à l'occasion du droit de Citoyen actif . . .*, 1791, in *La Révolution française et l'émancipation des Juifs*, Editions d'Histoire Sociale, 1968, Vol. 8, No. 9, pp. 4–5.
   This last, eight-volume work (henceforth abbreviated to Edhis) comprises the essential primary source material, i.e. petitions, letters, addresses, etc. I have also consulted the British Library's excellent collection of revolutionary pamphlets relevant to the subject (notably those comprised in FR 170, 1–30; and 1363.d. 1. 1–14). For a brief selection of the most directly useful secondary literature see note 16.

6. Berr-Isaac-Berr: *Lettre à Monseigneur l'Evêque de Nancy*, 1790, Edhis, Vol. 8, No. 8, p. 15.

7. *Appel à la Justice des Nations et des Rois*, 1801, Edhis, Vol. 8, No. 11, p. 18.

8. J. Benda: *La Jeunesse d'un clerc*, 1936.

9. Berr-Isaac-Berr: *Réflexions sur la régénération complète des Juifs*, 1806, Edhis, Vol. 8, No. 12, p. 12.

10. Th. Reinach: *Histoire des Israelites depuis l'époque de leur dispersion à nos jours*, 1884, p. 340.

11. Ibid. (1901 edition), p. 311.

12. Bernard-Lazare: 'La solidarité juive', *Entretiens politiques et littéraires*, October 1890.

13. *Lettre du S^R I.B.B. . . . à l'auteur anonyme etc.*, 1787, Edhis, Vol. 8, No. 1, p. 41.

14. Quoted in S. Dubnov: *History of the Jews*, Vol. 4, p. 534.

15. *La Révolution française et le rabbinat français*, 1890, p. 94. See also M. Marrus: *Les Juifs de France à l'époque de l'Affaire Dreyfus*, 1972, pp. 112–13.

16. Jewish life under the ancien régime was governed by royal 'privileges' which in effect restricted the freedom of movement and activity of the majority. Jews were privileged, for example, to settle in certain parts of Alsace but not in others, to trade but only in old clothes, to live in Metz but only in one quarter. These privileges varied widely not only between the relatively wealthy and privileged South-West and the poverty-stricken North-East but also within a particular region. In Alsace they were not allowed to reside in the big cities, whereas a limited number were tolerated in neighbouring Nancy and Metz. In certain places they were subject to special local taxes (Metz) or no-go areas on certain days (Lunéville), etc. Generally speaking, in Alsace, Lorraine and Metz, they were prohibited from owning property, joining guilds, attending public schools, exercising the liberal and most other professions. There were individual exceptions.

    See:

Les Juifs et la Révolution Française, ed. B. Blumenkrantz and A. Soboul, 1976.

D. Feuerwerker: *L'émancipation des Juifs en France*, 1976.

L. Kahn: *Les Juifs de Paris pendant la Révolution*, 1898.

S. Posener: 'The immediate economic and social effects of the emancipation of the Jews in France', *Jewish Social Studies*, Vol. 1. 1939, pp. 271–326.

17. Quoted in P. Girard: *Les Juifs de France de 1789 à 1860*, 1976, p. 42.

18. Zalkind-Hourwitz: *Apologie des Juifs*, 1789, Edhis, Vol. 4, pp. 8–10.

19. I.B. Bing: *Lettre . . . à l'auteur anonyme d'un écrit intitulé: le cri du Citoyen contre les Juifs*, 1787, Edhis, Vol. 8, No. 1, p. 30, pp. 4–5. Hourwitz also admired Voltaire, and even tried to imitate his ironic style, but he was equally puzzled and disturbed by the master's anti-Judaism.

20. I.B. Bing: *Mémoire particulier pour la communauté des Juifs établis à Metz*, 1789, Edhis, Vol. 5, no. 10, p. 13.

21. *Lettre . . . à l'auteur anonyme etc.*, op. cit., pp. 30–32.

22. *Lettre du S^R Berr-Isaac-Berr à M. Grégoire*, 1806, pp. 5–8. (British Library Collection).

23. Berr-Isaac-Berr: *Discours prononcé à la Barre de l'Assemblée Nationale*, 1789, Edhis, Vol. 5, No. 6, p. 3.

24. I.B. Bing: *Lettre . . . à l'auteur anonyme etc.*, op. cit., p. 55.

25. I.B. Bing: *Mémoire particulier . . . etc.*, op. cit., p. 26.

26. *Lettre à Monseigneur l'Evêque de Nancy*, 1790, op. cit., pp. 18–19.

27. Berr-Isaac-Berr: *Réflexions sur la régénération . . .* op. cit. The work was written in July 1805 and published the following year.

28. Bernard-Lazare: 'L'esprit révolutionnaire dans le judaïsme', *Revue Bleue*, May 1893.

29. J. Darmesteter: *Coup d'oeil sur l'histoire du peuple juif*, 1880.
                    Les Prophètes d'Israel, 1892.

The Napoleonic Theme in Russian Literature

R.A. Peace

During the reign of Catherine II (also known as 'The Great') the political and social ideas of eighteenth-century France were championed by no less a person than the empress herself. She corresponded with Voltaire and Diderot and as an enlightened monarch sought political guidance in the ideas of Montesquieu. It seemed as though Catherine was about to produce a new and enlightened liberal constitution for Russia based on the very political, social and moral ideas which would later form the philosophical underpinning of the French Revolution. Yet, although there was much liberal talk and encouragement of Russia's home-grown philosophers, nothing of real political substance emerged. Russia itself was not as ready for such bold ideas as its empress appeared to be. For one thing there were the newly-established privileges of the gentry class, privileges confirmed by Catherine herself as the political basis of her own power, yet privileges radically at odds with the interests of the peasants, who formed the vast majority of the population.

The greatest shock to Catherine's professed liberalism came from the peasants – the Pugachev uprising of 1773–5 which very nearly swept her from power. Then some fourteen years later revolution broke out in France, and her flirtation with liberal ideas ended in bitter disillusionment and recrimination.

The accession to the throne of Catherine's son Paul I in 1796 coincided with Napoleon's first victories in Italy. Paul, who was probably the most autocratic of all Russia's rulers, hated the French Revolution and was persuaded to join the Second Coalition against France in 1799, sending the ageing but brilliant general Suvorov to fight against the French in Italy. Unfortunately Suvorov's successes did not please his allies, the British and the Austrians; their attitude towards Russia angered Paul, who now saw in the rise of Napoleon a new force for stability in Europe. The very next year, 1800, in a typical *volte face*, Paul allied himself with Napoleon in the Second Armed Neutrality against Britain.

The new alliance, however, was short-lived – Paul was murdered in a palace coup in 1801, and was succeeded by his son, Alexander

I. Alexander had been brought up on the liberal ideas of his grandmother, and educated by a Swiss tutor La Harpe. The excesses of his father made him admire the ideals of the French Revolution. He surrounded himself with a group of young liberal-minded men, one of whom, Stroganov, had actually been the librarian of the Jacobin Library in Paris and was a pupil of the French Jacobin, Romme. Just as Paul's policies had been determined by opposition to his own mother, so those of Alexander had inevitably to take a different turn from the policies of his father. He hastened to make his peace with Britain and found his tolerance of Napoleon greatly stretched by his self-proclamation as emperor in 1804 as well as by his murder of the duc D'Enghien, to whom Alexander was related by marriage. In 1805 Russia joined the Third Coalition against France, but Napoleon's brilliant series of victories against the continental powers and Alexander's growing disillusionment with his allies, particularly the lack of support from Britain, forced him into a *volte-face* equally as abrupt as that of his father. In the treaty signed between Alexander I and Napoleon at Tilsit (1807) Russia now became France's ally – a situation which was again reversed in 1812 by Napoleon's invasion of Russia.

The disastrous retreat of *La Grande Armée* from Moscow – ravaged by the Russian winter; harassed by Russian partisans; with Kutuzov's main army following all the time in the rear – finally exploded the myth of Napoleon's invincibility, but it did more than this, it brought Russia for the first time truly into Europe, not only as a military force to be reckoned with, but more importantly for the Russians themselves, it gave them a more real sense of actually belonging to Europe. A Soviet scholar writing recently on the war of 1812 and the evolution of Russian prose has compared the importance of 1812 to that of the French Revolution itself; for if the latter changed Europe, the former certainly changed Russia.[1]

On invading Russia Napoleon had sought to win popular support through a revolutionary and democratic gesture: he promised the Russian serf his freedom, and yet it was the unemancipated peasant soldier who defeated Napoleon. In a typical Russian irony, an army of bonded serfs brought freedom to Europe, but got no freedom itself in return, and by a further irony, their masters, the Russian officers stationed in Europe, fell prey to those very ideas against which, ostensibly, they had taken up arms – the heady ideology behind the French Revolution and the practical radicalism of Napoleon himself. It seemed as though direct contact with the West had grafted radical, social and political ideas on to the Russian soul more effectively than the foreign empress Catherine had been able to do in the previous century, and when these officers came back to Russia, they formed debating societies and secret revolutionary groups, starting a movement which led to the Decembrist uprising of 1825.

The suppression of the revolt by the new tsar, Nicholas I, seemed to bring the curtain down on the Napoleon-dominated reign of his predecessor Alexander I, but it was only the interval after the first act: the ideas of the French Revolution were to find a receptive stage for dramatic development in nineteenth-century Russia, where they would interact with other ideas from Germany and England, and provide a dénouement in the following century in Russia's own home-grown revolution.

I have begun with this brief sketch of the historical background, not because it is not sufficiently well-known, but in order to emphasise salient features in the history of the period, which are reflected in the literature we are about to examine. In the first place history shows us a striking ambivalence of response, not so much to the Revolution as to the figure of Napoleon himself, be it on the part of Paul or of his son Alexander I. Despite vacillations of attitude even the autocratic Paul is forced to concede Napoleon's importance; while his son, defeated at Pratzen Berg, is reputed to have sat on the ground and cried, saying 'We are all babies in the hands of a giant'.

The idea of the strong man of the will had its own peculiar appeal to the Russians. Behind their own sneaking admiration for Napoleon one often senses the presence of another figure – Peter the Great, who in the words of Pushkin 'pulled Russia up on to its haunches'.[2] The idea of the giant, of two giants – one Napoleon, the other Russia – is found in the poetry of Lermontov. Yet if Russia were a giant, it was a sleeping one, and it was that other giant Napoleon who challenged it to its intellectual awakening. It is therefore no accident that the Napoleonic theme in Russian literature is closely interwoven with ideas and ideals.

In its original conception Tolstoy's monumental novel, *War and Peace* was an attempt to deal with the origins of the Decembrist movement. It did not quite encompass this, either in its time scale or its ideological focus, but it ends with a philosophical epilogue, which develops a whole theory of history and historical causation round the figure of Napoleon.

Napoleon imposed on Russia an awakened national consciousness, a sense of her own historical mission. At the same time, he was associated with the ultimate stage of the French Revolution and the foremost ideas of Western Europe. His activities, his very personality, provoked moral questions on the nature of power, the right of might and whether ends could ever justify means. All these issues are reflected in the Napoleonic theme as it developed in Russian literature.

Pushkin, by common consent, is regarded as the founder of modern Russian literature, and his treatment of the Napoleonic theme is particularly instructive. As a young boy Pushkin had lived through the Napoleonic invasion and from the age of fourteen to the end of his life in 1837, Napoleon was for him a constant preoccupation. Apart from the published works in which Napoleon appears, Pushkin throughout his life left many unfinished drafts of verses devoted to Napoleon.

One of his earliest poems – the recollection of his school days at the Imperial Palace near St Petersburg: *Vospominaniya v Tsarskom sele* – was written in 1814. It deals with the French invasion, the occupation and subsequent conflagration of Moscow, and the rout of the French army. In an odd way this section of the poem almost seems to anticipate Tolstoy's later treatment of these events in *War and Peace*. Pushkin's emphasis is also on mass movements rather than leaders. Indeed the way Napoleon is depicted does not seem to make him entirely central to these events, and the portrait that does emerge is negative. Pushkin's reference to Napoleon as the instigator of bloody deeds seems curiously oblique:

> Blesnul krovavyy mech v neukrotimoy dlani
> Kovarstvom, derzost'yu venchannogo tsarya;
> Vosstal vselennoy bich – . . .

> There flashed the bloody sword in the unpacifiable hand
> Of a tsar crowned by insolence and deceit.
> There arose the scourge of the universe.

At the end in defeat, this figure again seems almost anonymous:

> Gde ty, lyubimyy syn i schast'ya i Bellony
> Prezrevshiy pravdy glas, i veru i zakon
> V gordyne vozmechtav mechom nizvergnut' trony?
> Izchez, kak utrom strashnyy son.

> Where are you, the favourite son of fortune and of war,
> Despising the voice of truth, faith and the law,
> Dreaming in your pride to tumble thrones by the sword?
> You have disappeared as does a terrible dream in the morning

In 1814 these events are still fresh in Pushkin's mind, and Napoleon, although on Elba, was still a threat.

The reference in the poem to the favourite son of Fortune and of War (Bellona) seems to echo the words uttered by Napoleon himself at 18th Brumière when he claimed to be accompanied by the God of Fortune and of War. Pushkin returns to the theme of fortune, or luck, in a poem of 1815, *Napoleon on Elba*, where

Napoleon is portrayed apostrophising luck as a malicious seducer, and yet as a former, faithful protector and guardian who had brought him to the throne and covered his brow in laurel wreathes.

There was a legend, apparently current in *La Grande Armée*, that Napoleon was accompanied by a little red man who gave him advice, but who deserted him at Waterloo. (The story is also recounted by Balzac.[3]) Shorn of its supernatural elements, the theme of luck is one that Tolstoy will develop in his treatment of Napoleon in *War and Peace*.

When Pushkin learned of Napoleon's death in 1821, he wrote a more positive tribute to him in his poem entitled *Napoleon*. He was, after all, a great man – as the opening couplet makes clear:

> Chudesnyy zhrebiy sovershilsya.
> Ugas velikiy chelovek.

> A marvellous destiny has been accomplished.
> A great man has been extinguished.

He is a 'giant' (*velikan*), but he is also a 'tyrant' – the word *tiran* conveniently rhyming with *velikan*. He may have quashed the new-born freedom of the French and offered them war and destruction in its place, but he had been repaid in the snows of Russia. The poem ends on a very positive note:

> 'May that cowardly man be covered in shame, who on this day will trouble his uncrowned shade with a stupid reproach. Praise to him. He has shown the Russian people a lofty destiny, and from the gloom of exile has bequeathed eternal freedom to the world.'

Thus we see that for Pushkin, Napoleon – far from being the one who suppressed 'new-born freedom' when alive, now on his death is hailed as a figure who has bequeathed eternal freedom to the world.

Freedom is a quality also associated with another romantic hero of the age – Byron and, when in 1824 Pushkin wrote a poem in response to the death of Byron, freedom was its central theme. It is symbolised in the title: *To the Sea (K moryu)*, as the opening line makes clear, apostrophising the sea as the very element of freedom – *svobodnaya stikhiya*, and it represents freedom for Pushkin himself. He had, he says, contemplated fleeing from Russia by sea, and had he done so, he believes that one object in the ocean waste would have impressed his soul – the cliff, the grave of fame, where Napoleon died:

> Tam on pochil sredi mucheniy
> I vsled za nim, kak buri shum

Drugoy ot nas umchalsya geniy
Drugoy vlastitel' nashikh dum.

There he found rest amid torment
and following him like the noise of a storm
Another genius sped from us
Another ruler of our thoughts

Yet it is Byron who is mourned by freedom itself (*ischez oplakannyy svobodoy*) – Byron who sang so much of the sea and, like the sea, was himself an untamed element. Thus the fate of Napoleon immediately evokes for Pushkin the new loss of Byron – the very symbol of freedom itself, and both Napoleon and Byron are described as 'rulers of our thoughts' (*vlastitel' nashikh dum*).

Pushkin obviously sees Napoleon and Byron as the two outstanding romantic heroes of his generation. In his novel in verse, *Eugene Onegin*, he gives a portrait of the typical 'superfluous man' of his time, and throughout Onegin is many times likened to Byron and the Byronic hero, Childe Harold. Indeed the thought actually occurs to the heroine, Tatiana, that Onegin may be little more than a 'Muscovite in a Harold cloak' (*Moskvich v garol'dovom plashche*), when, in his absence she visits his study, and sees there two very modish icons – a portrait of Byron and a statuette of Napoleon. As cult-figures the significance of these heroes is not just personal to Onegin, it is general: Napoleon is the ideal to be aimed at by every coldly egocentric man so typical of Pushkin's own generation: '*My vse glyadim v Napoleony/ Dvunogikh tvarey milliony dlya nas orudiye odno*' (We all aim at being Napoleons/ The millions of two-legged creatures are for us merely a tool).

This is an idea which Pushkin appears to develop more fully in his short prose work of 1833, *The Queen of Spades*. Its hero, Herman is a young Russian with a German name, who in profile bears a physical resemblance to Napoleon, but he also shows Napoleonic features in the very ruthlessness with which he sets about to win a fortune, using as his 'tools' an aged countess and her companion, and in the process becoming responsible for the countess' death.

The arena for his self-promotion is not the battle field but the gaming tables. Nevertheless, the modern Napoleonic man is pitting the force of his own egocentric will against that other, perhaps more essential, Napoleonic quality – luck, but fortune in the end does not smile on him, as ultimately it did not on Napoleon himself.[4]

Napoleon as a man of the will exerted a strong fascination for Pushkin, as he did for many Russians. The titanic hero shaping the destinies of thousands of his fellow-men is the subject of his long poem (also written in 1833) *The Bronze Horseman*, though the titanic figure in question is here Peter the Great. At the beginning of the poem he too, like Napoleon, is associated with the sea, and he, too, is thinking grandiose thoughts: 'On the shore of desolate waves/ He stood, full of lofty thoughts' (*Na beregu pustynnykh voln/ stoyal on dum velikikh poln.*), an obvious echo of his earlier poems on Napoleon: *Napoleon on Elba* of 1815, depicting his hero as 'full of rebellious thought' (*matezhnoy dumy poln*) and the poem of 1821, with its injunction to 'rest amidst the desolate waves' (*Pochiy sredi pustynnykh voln*).

According to the Soviet critic Reizov, in such works as *The Negro of Peter the Great*, *Poltava* and particularly *The Bronze Horseman*, the image of Peter I embraces ideas which occurred to Pushkin from, as he calls it, 'his many encounters with Napoleon', and he quotes Pushkin writing in French, comparing the revolution effected by Peter the Great with that of Robespierre and Napoleon:

'Les moyens avec lesquels on accomplit une révolution ne sont plus ceux qui la consolident. Pierre I est tout à la fois Robespierre et Napoléon (La Révolution incarnée) [PSS, 1949, XII, 205][5]

A central issue in *The Bronze Horseman* is the relationship between the sublime vision of the titan and the ordinary everyday lives which must be sacrificed to this greater truth. It is a related issue which Pushkin addresses in his poem of 1830, *The Hero*, in which he looks at the greater truth of Napoleon himself and the lesser truths that could stain his name. The poem was written in response to the publication in 1829–30 of memoirs supposedly from the pen of Napoleon's secretary, Louis Bourrienne, in which among other things, the heroism of Napoleon's visit to the plague victims in Jaffa was discounted. The memoirs later proved to be a forgery, but Pushkin, unaware of this, responded with this poem, bearing the questioning epigraph 'What is truth?' and written in the form of a dialogue between a poet and his friend. In reply to his friend's query, the poet confesses that his greatest hero is Napoleon, and that he considers the noblest moment in Napoleon's career to be his visit to the plague hospital in Jaffa. When the friend objects that Bourrienne in his memoirs has disproved the valour of this act, the poet replies:

T'my nizkikh istin mne dorozhe
Nas vozvyshayushchiy obman.

The deceit which uplifts us is dearer to me than a whole host of base truths

– a phrase which despite its syntactical complexity in the original Russian has very much entered into the language and has been taken up by authors such as Dostoyevsky, Chekhov and Gorky.[6]

Hero-worship of Napoleon is also seen in Pushkin's successor Lermontov, whose poetry is strongly influenced by Byron. In the novel, *A Hero of Our Time*, which bears as its epigraph a quotation from Pushkin's *Eugene Onegin*, Lermontov draws the portrait of the 'Byronic' young man, whom he sees as typical of his age. Yet despite the Byronic overtones, the moment of the hero's defeat is Napoleonic. He has just shot a friend in a ruthlessly conceived duel, lost the woman he really loves, and in an attempt to regain her has ridden his horse to death. In despair he sinks to the ground and weeps, and then, so we are told, he 'sleeps the sleep of Napoleon after Waterloo'.[7]

In his poetry Lermontov seems to return obsessively to the figure of Napoleon, but in his early poems, as was the case with Pushkin, the heroic pretensions of Napoleon have to contend with the poet's own patriotic sentiments. Thus in two early poems Lermontov projects both Napoleon and Russia as two giants, but soon we find him using associative imagery reminiscent of Pushkin's treatment of the Napoleonic theme. In a poem of 1829 entitled *Napoleon* the fallen hero is depicted on St Helena, 'Where the wave beats against the high shore' (*Gde b'yet volna o breg vysokiy*) – the sea is a potent symbolic presence. In another poem of 1831, *St Helena*, Napoleon is identified with the storm, as he had been, along with Byron, in Pushkin's poem *To the Sea*. Although Napoleon is defeated, he is a hero who flew past his generation like a storm (*On proletel kak burya mimo nas*).

In 1840, when Lermontov was temporarily under arrest, he responded to the news that the French government was contemplating bringing back the body of Napoleon for burial in France, by a poem written in imitation of J.C. Zedlitz's *Geisterschiff* – *Vozdushnyy korabl'* 'The Airborne Ship'). In this poem, Napoleon returns to France from his grave in a flying ship to find that all his marshals and even his son are dead. When, however, on 15 December 1840, the French government's project became fact, Lermontov gave vent to real anger in his poem 'The Last Resting Place' (*Posledneye novosel'ye* – literally 'The Last Housewarming'). His veneration for Napoleon is obvious from his own autograph copy, in which all words relating to Napoleon are written in capital letters, not merely all the pronouns, but such associative symbolic words as 'sea' and 'cliff'. St Helena is a more fitting place for his hero, he argues, as there he is guarded by his own element – the sea:

Gde storozhil ego, kak on nepobedimyy,
Kak on velikiy okean.

Where he is guarded by the ocean, which is like him unconquerable and great.

Later in the century a new Napoleon came to power in France, Napoleon III, and with him a new invasion of Russian soil, the Crimean War. Inevitably old memories were stirred in Russia. Tolstoy, who had fought in the Crimean War and written some notable sketches of his own impressions of it, started work in the 1860s on a long epic novel, *War and Peace*, in which he sought to recreate the earlier Napoleonic period. Dostoyevsky, too, who owed his return to literary life to the Crimean War (in as much as the more enlightened regime that succeeded the defeat and death of Nicholas I allowed him back from Siberian exile) – he too at this time also became fascinated with the Napoleonic theme, and used it as a central ideological strand in his novel *Crime and Punishment*.

In 1865 the Russian translation of Napoleon III's book, *L'Histoire de Jules César*, caused quite a stir in St Petersburg. The author, ostensibly discussing the life and deeds of Julius Caesar, was in fact uttering an apologia for his own uncle Napoleon I. He divided humanity into 'ordinary people' and heroes, and sought to justify the right to absolute power of figures such as Caesar, Napoleon I and of course, by extension, himself. Dostoyevsky's hero Raskolnikov also has Napoleonic aspirations. He, too, divides up humanity into those with a right to absolute power and the rest – the mass of people who are mere material to be used. Given this theory, he himself must make a choice; he must define himself: is he a Napoleon or a louse? Dostoyevsky's novel is in effect a complex and subtle examination of the thesis of Napoleon III. Raskolnikov tries to prove his Napoleonic potential by committing murder. He appears to bring the crime off undetected, yet there is something within him which subverts his ruthless ambition. He is tormented by an unexpected spiritual struggle and ultimately some inner drive causes him to confess his crime.

The deed by which he has chosen to prove himself is the murder of a defenceless old money-lender, and he himself comes to realise that the equation of this crime with the grander exploits of Napoleon is completely incongruous. Even the fact that he has felt the need to prove himself shows that he is not really a Napoleon. Yet Dostoyevsky seems to be arguing that Raskolnikov is by no means an exceptional case: he is merely a prey to ideas that are in the air. Thus he overhears a conversation outlining the theoretical justification for the very same crime which he himself intends to commit, and Dostoyevsky underscores the point that such ideas were a commonplace of the times. The detective Porfiry, who suspects Raskolnikov all along, principally because of the article he has written on exceptional people and the masses, links these fashionable ideas more specifically with Napoleon: 'Who then is there in Russia, who does not consider himself to be a Napoleon?'

(*Kto zh u nas na Rusi sebya Napoleonom ne shchitayet?*) – a pronouncement which seems to look back to Pushkin's assertion: 'We all aim at being Napoleons/ The millions of two-legged creatures are but a tool for us'.

Pushkin's own treatment of the Napoleonic theme in *The Queen of Spades* also seems to have conditioned elements of Dostoyevsky's plot. Pushkin's Herman, the hero with the Napoleonic profile, in the ruthless pursuit of his aims causes the death of a defenceless old woman, and at the same time makes blatant use of her young companion, Lizaveta Ivanovna. Raskolnikov's crime involves two comparable women. Indeed Lizaveta Ivanovna is also the name of the old money-lender's companion, her younger half-sister, who unwittingly becomes Raskolnikov's second victim. Both Pushkin and Dostoyevsky set their action against the background of St Petersburg, the city whose improbable existence was decreed by that Russian ruler of exceptional will – Peter the Great (in *Notes from Underground* Dostoyevsky calls St Petersburg the most concocted city in the whole world). Pushkin, too, in *The Bronze Horseman* had depicted the plight of ordinary mortals condemned to lead their lives in Peter's city, and the grim social realism which is such a feature of *Crime and Punishment* may also be related to this Pushkinian theme; for the novel abounds in the abject victims of Peter's original effort of will – the urban mass of wasted human material, above which Raskolnikov wishes to raise himself.

Dostoyevsky's treatment of the Napoleonic theme is, of course, far more complex and far richer than that of Pushkin. The ideological content of *Crime and Punishment* contains a strong religious element. Yet even here, in an oblique, but typically Dostoyevskian fashion, we come back to the theme of Napoleon. Dostoyevsky (and for that matter Tolstoy too) was fascinated by the Russian religious sects – the *raskol'niki*, and it is no mere chance that dictates the name of Dostoyevsky's Napoleonic hero – Raskolnikov. The official Orthodox church had anathematised Napoleon, pronouncing him antichrist, but many *raskol'niki* believed the official church itself to have been taken over by antichrist, and so an iron logic of reversal suggested that if an apostate church interpreted the invasion of Napoleon as the coming of antichrist, it must indeed be rather the second coming of Christ. A cult of Napoleon, therefore, grew up among some of the *raskol'niki* which led to the formation of a sect known as the *Napoleonovy*.[8] Dostoyevsky does not make this identification explicit, but it adds an ironic aura to the sectarian motif which is such an important strand in his novel.

The identification of Napoleon with antichrist is also made at the beginning of Tolstoy's novel, *War and Peace*. The action opens in St Petersburg high society, at the salon of Anna Scherer, where they are discussing the events of 1804: Napoleon crowning himself as emperor, the murder of the duc d'Enghien. It is Anna Scherer herself who calls Napoleon 'antichrist'. The young Pierre Bezukhov, however, is Napoleon's chief defender at this gathering, and there is a great deal of irony in this fact, since it will be he who later in the novel comes to believe literally in the identification of Napoleon with antichrist, and through a cabalistic interpretation of the letters of Napoleon's name and those of his own, identifies Napoleon as the 'beast of the Apocalypse' and himself (le Russe Bezukhov) as the person preordained to kill him.

It is in these higher echelons of Russian society that we see most clearly the crisis of identity forced upon the nation by the onset of the Napoleonic wars. High society was dominated by French culture. Russian aristocrats often spoke French more naturally than Russian, and there is a certain piquancy in the fact that Kutuzov, the national hero destined to triumph over Napoleon, reads French novels before he goes to sleep. Here is a society which has suddenly found France, its spiritual and cultural home, equated with the national enemy – a society forced back upon itself and vainly trying to find its own cultural roots. In Tolstoy's depiction of Moscow society in 1812 we see that fines are instituted for speaking French.

Nevertheless, before the events of 1812 condemnation of Napoleon is not universal. In the salon of Anna Scherer the older generation may deplore Napoleon's actions and what he stands for, but he finds strong champions among representatives of the younger generation. In fact at this stage of the novel he is the hero of Tolstoy's own heroes – Pierre Bezukhov and Prince Andrey.

Pierre stoutly defends Napoleon at Anna Scherer's and it is clear that he sees him as the upholder of democratic principles, the saviour of the French Revolution both from itself and from the Bourbons. Napoleon is great, Pierre argues, because he towered above the Revolution, suppressed its abuses and preserved all that was good in it: equality of citizenship, freedom of speech and press, and that this was the only reason that he possessed himself of power. Such views obviously embarrass his hostess, but Tolstoy himself attempts to put them in their true context, the context of youth:

'The Revolution was a grand fact', continued Monsieur Pierre, betraying by this desperate and challenging statement his extreme youth and desire to give full expression to whatever was on his mind.'⁹

Tolstoy's other hero, Prince Andrey, comes to his friend's aid:

'One must admit', continued Prince Andrey, 'that Napoleon on the bridge at

Arcola, or in the hospital at Jaffa shaking hands with the plague-stricken, is
great as a man . . . but there are other things it would be difficult to justify.'[10]

This reference to the plague victims and to less creditable things in
Napoleon's career seems almost like an echo of Pushkin's poem *The
Hero*, and there is more than a hint of the 'elevating deceit' in Prince
Andrey's attitude to Napoleon; for it later transpires that his own
veneration of Napoleon is as great, if not greater than that of Pierre,
but whereas Pierre sees in his hero the embodiment of the
democratic values of the Revolution, Prince Andrey, the professional soldier, venerates in him the military leader.

Pierre's attitude is moral, it is concerned with larger human
questions. Thus he is against the forthcoming war because it is not
a war for freedom, it is, as he puts it: 'To help England and Austria
against the greatest man in the world – that is not right.'[11] By
contrast, Prince Andrey's attitude to Napoleon seems more nar-
rowly self-centred, he admires the Napoleonic will and even seeks
to emulate the personal career of Napoleon – in this he seems closer
to Raskolnikov who says:

'A real *ruler of men*, a man to whom everything is permitted, takes Toulon by
storm, carries out a massacre in Paris, *forgets* an army in Egypt, *wastes* half a
million men in his Moscow campaign, and gets away with a *bon mot* in Vilna
. . .'[12]

Prince Andrey, for his part, is fascinated by the significance of
Toulon, the first bold step in Napoleon's career. It becomes for him
an obsessive personal image. He, too, like Raskolnikov feels that a
woman stands between him and his Napoleonic ambitions, but in
his case it is an unloved wife. He tells Pierre:

'You talk of Bonaparte, but Bonaparte while he was working his way step by
step towards his goal – he was free; there was nothing for him but his goal and
he reached it. But tie yourself up with a woman and like a convict in irons you
lose your freedom! And all your aspirations, all the ability you feel within you
is only a drag on you, torturing you with regret.'[13]

Pierre's concern for freedom in the abstract, centred on the figure of
Napoleon, has, in his friend Prince Andrey, become reduced to a
mere concern for personal freedom. Yet both in their different ways
seem to reflect the Pushkinian idea that 'We all aim at being
Napoleons'. In the case of Pierre it is comic; thus he is interrupted
in an embarrassing flight of fancy:

'But before Pierre – who at that moment was imagining himself to be his hero
Napoleon, in whose person he had already effected the dangerous crossing of

the Channel and captured London – could pronounce Pitt's sentence, he saw a well-built and handsome young officer entering his room.'[14]

Prince Andrey's Napoleonic reveries, by contrast, are more serious, as we see in his reaction to Bilibin's news that the French have crossed the Tabor bridge:

'The news grieved him and yet it gave him pleasure. As soon as he heard that the Russian army was in such a hopeless situation, the idea occurred to him that it was he who was destined to extricate it from that situation – that this was his Toulon that would lift him from the ranks of obscure officers and open to him the path to glory! As he listened to Bilibin, he was already picturing himself arriving at the camp and there at the council of war, giving an opinion that alone could save the army, and how he would be entrusted personally to execute the plan.'[15]

The full dilemma of Prince Andrey's position – his self-identification with a hero who is now his enemy – is revealed when he learns with a 'thrill of delight' of the defeat of the Austrian allies and looks forward to the Russians' encounter with the French, and we are told:

'But he feared that Bonaparte's genius might outweigh all the valour of the Russian troops, and at the same time he could not bear to entertain the idea of his hero suffering disgrace.'[16]

Before the battle of Austerlitz Prince Andrey repeatedly imagines how the forthcoming encounter will present him with his Toulon. Instead, of course, he is wounded, and lying on the battle field, he meets his hero face to face for the first time. A great change has taken place in Prince Andrey; he has now not only experienced the *reality* of warfare, but is faced with the imminence of death:

'He knew that it was Napoleon – his hero – but at that moment Napoleon seemed to him such a small, insignificant creature compared with what was passing now between his own soul and that lofty limitless firmament with the clouds flying over it.'[17]

The imminence of death, in true Tolstoyan fashion, has opened up a greater spirituality for Prince Andrey; gone are the narrow, self-centred interests of his career, focused, as they were, on the figure of Napoleon, and in its place another Tolstoyan virtue has come to the surface: the family – that extended ego, at odds with narrow Napoleonic egocentricity:

'The quiet home life and peaceful happiness of Bald Hills passed before his imagination. He was enjoying the happiness when that little Napoleon appeared, with his indifferent narrow look of satisfaction at the misery of others, and was followed by doubts and torments, and only the heavens promised peace.'[18]

For Pierre, too, the cult of Napoleon is also ousted by a form of mystical experience. He becomes a Freemason, and (as we have already seen) begins to identify Napoleon with the 'Beast of the Apocalypse'.

A similar shift in attitude is also discernible on the part of the author himself. It is not that Tolstoy shows any veneration for Napoleon comparable to that of his own heroes, but nevertheless, before Napoleon sets foot on Russian soil, Tolstoy does appear to allow him both dignity and military ability. At the battle of Austerlitz Napoleon is depicted as in control of events. He can see what is going on with the naked eye – how different from the way he is described at the battle of Borodino, where Napoleon can see nothing, not even through his telescope, and where his pretence to be in charge is thoroughly debunked: he is not in control of anything.

As the novel progresses Tolstoy's projection of Napoleon seems to get more and more negative. He is merely a vulgar little man, with an overweening view of his powers, the mobile facial features of an Italian and the sentimentality of a Frenchman – a sentimentality always conceived of in terms of 'ma chère mère'. He is almost cast as Pushkin's Napoleonic hero Herman – a gambler:

> 'Who after a long run of luck during which he recklessly flung his money about and won every time, suddenly finds, just when he has carefully calculated all the chances of the game, that the more he considers his play, the more surely he loses.'[19]

As the novel proceeds Tolstoy's tone becomes more moral, almost as if he is dotting the i's of what Dostoyevsky is suggesting less didactically in his treatment of the Napoleonic theme in *Crime and Punishment*. Thus Raskolnikov's words on 'the real *ruler of men* who gets away with a *bon mot* in Vilna' seems to find an echo in Tolstoy's novel:

> 'From the sublime' (he saw something sublime in himself) 'to the ridiculous there is only one step', said he. And for fifty years the whole world has gone on repeating 'Sublime! Grand. Napoléon le grand. Du sublime au ridicule il n'y a qu'un pas!'
> And it never enters anyone's head that to admit a greatness not commensurate with the standard of right and wrong is merely to admit one's own nothingness and immeasurable littleness.

For us who have the standard of good and evil given us by Christ nothing can claim to be outside the law – And there is no greatness where simplicity, goodness and truth are absent.'[20]

Tolstoy's historical argument, as it develops, is focused on the will of the superman, and in typical Russian fashion, this argument is not only about Napoleon, it is also about Peter the Great:

'To historians who believe that Russia was shaped by the will of one man – Peter the Great – and that France was transformed from a republic into an empire and French armies marched into Russia at the will of one man – Napoleon, the argument that Russia remained a power because Napoleon had a bad cold on the 26th August may seem logical and convincing.'[21]

Tolstoy's mockery is obvious: Napoleon was no more in control of events than a child 'holding on to the straps inside a carriage and imagining that he is driving it'.[22]

If the force which drove Napoleon back out of Moscow was not superior Russian military strength and cunning, but a series of fortuitous, negative events, then – argues Tolstoy – this was also true of Napoleon's career up to that point: it was a series of lucky events – it was *sluchaynosti, milliony sluchaynostey*: 'Chance, millions of chances, invest him with authority, and all men everywhere, as if by agreement together, cooperate to confirm that power.'[23]

Tolstoy, it seems, has taken Napoleon at face value, when the latter talked of the importance of luck in military affairs, and his use of what could well be the Pushkinian-inspired image of the Napoleonic gambler seems more than apt. Yet in unfolding the Napoleonic theme Tolstoy has developed a theory of history, in which mass movements determine the course of historical events, not the will of so-called leaders:

'In 1789 fermentation starts in Paris: it develops and spreads, and finds expression in a movement of people from west to east. Several times the movement is directed towards the east and comes into collision with a counter-movement from east to westwards. In the year 1812 it reaches its extreme limit – Moscow – and then with remarkable symmetry, the counter-movement reaches the departure point in the west of the first movement – Paris – and subsides.'[24]

Thus Tolstoy, who took the bold step of writing an historical figure into his fiction, takes the even bolder step of writing him out of history.

Throughout the nineteenth century Russian writers attempted to shed their own light on the long shadow cast by Napoleon on their culture, but as we have seen their attitudes were highly ambivalent:

was he a hero of the will and an ultimate force for good? or an overweening tyrant who caused mass suffering? It is a debate which also looks back to Russia's own homegrown colossus – Peter the Great, and yet it also looks forward: the implications of this debate have contemporary relevance; for Russia's own revolution over a century later also threw up a man of the will, a law-maker, the bringer of a new social order, with pretensions to flawless military leadership – Stalin. In the Soviet Union the debate over base truths and elevating deceit continues to this day.[25]

NOTES

1. A.V. Arkhivova, 'Voyna 1812 goda i evolyutsiya russkoy prozy', *Russkaya Literatura*, Vol. 28, No. 1, 1985, p. 39.
2. i.e. in part II of *The Bronze Horseman*.
3. i.e. in the section 'Le Napoléon du peuple' of the novel *Le Médicin de Campagne*, (cf. B. Reizov, 'Pushkin i Napoleon', *Russkaya literatura*, Vol. 9, No. 4, 1966, p. 50.
4. cf. Napoleon's own use of gambling imagery. When he was asked in 1897 why he stopped at Leoben instead of marching on to Vienna, he replied: 'Because I was playing at 21, and I held at 20'; and at Waterloo: 'This morning still had 90 chances out of 100 in our favour. Bulow's arrival cost us 30, but we still have 60 against 40.' (quoted in *The Mind of Napoleon: A Selection of His Written and Spoken Words*, edited and translated by J. Christopher Herold, New York, 1955, pp. 45–6).
   Napoleon's comment on the debacle of 1812 was that it was not his luck that had failed him, but he that had failed his luck. (Ibid., pp. 44–5.)
5. See: B. Reizov, op.cit. p. 58.
6. Cf. Dostoyevsky's 'Pushkin Speech', Chekhov's story *Gooseberries* and Gorky's *Conversation about the Trade*.
7. Later Hippolyte Taine would compare France herself to a horse ridden to death by Napoleon. See: Pieter Geyl, *Napoleon For and Against* (trans. from Dutch by Olive Renier) Revised edition, London, 1962, pp. 139–40.
8. See: K.K. Grass, *Die russischen Sekten*, Leipzig, 1907, Vol. 1, pp. 562–3; also P.I. Mel'nikov-Pechersky, 'Pis'ma o rasskole', *Sobraniye sochineniy v shesti tomakh*, Moscow 1963, Vol. 6, p. 238; and F.C. Conybeare, *Russian Dissenters*, Harvard Univ. Press, 1921, p. 370.
9. L.N. Tolstoy, *War and Peace* (trans. and with an introduction by Rosemary Edmonds) Harmondsworth, 1957, Vol. I, p. 21.
10. Ibid.
11. Ibid. p. 27.
12. F. Dostoyevsky, *Crime and Punishment* (trans. with an introduction by D. Magarshak) Harmondsworth, 1966, p. 291 (adapted).
13. *War and Peace*, Vol. I, p. 31.
14. Ibid., p. 60.
15. Ibid., p. 185.

16. Ibid., p. 141.
17. Ibid., p. 339.
18. Ibid., p. 341.
19. Ibid., Vol. II. p. 954.
20. Ibid., pp. 1267–8.
21. Ibid., p. 931.
22. Ibid., p. 1193.
23. Ibid., p. 1346.
24. Ibid., p. 1401.
25. It is perhaps politically significant that Reizov's article of the mid-1960s 'Pushkin i Napoleon', which makes much of the parallel between Peter I and Napoleon, and draws extensively on unpublished Pushkin fragments, nevertheless omits to mention the poem 'The Hero'.

Spanish Constitutionalism and the Impact of the French Revolution, 1808–1814

Brian R. Hamnett

Spanish constitutionalists sought legitimacy in the medieval past and in the philosophy of St. Thomas Aquinas. They repeatedly denied French Revolutionary influences. Liberal leaders such as Agustín Argüelles frequently distinguished the Spanish constitutional experiment from the experience of Revolutionary France. The profound traditionalist complexion of the Spanish risings against the French in 1808 made this distinction imperative. When looking back at the two constitutional experiments of 1810–14 and 1820–23, the Liberal poet and politician, Manuel Josef Quintana, said of his generation that, 'we were far from possessing the revolutionary maxims which have been charged against us. We had seen the military despotism which had resulted in France from so much social upheaval. The enthusiasm of the most revolutionary among us had been dampened and the eyes of the most deluded had been opened.'[1] Allegations of French Revolutionary influences understandably reached a climax in the aftermath of the royal coup of May 1814 and again following the collapse of the second constitutional régime in October 1823. One of Ferdinand VII's closest collaborators in the months after the dissolution of the Cortes, Blas Ostolaza, who had been a Peruvian substitute deputy, denounced the Cortes for having introduced French republican ideas into Spain, describing as 'national' everything that had previously been described as 'royal'. The Cortes had deceitfully usurped the king's sovereignty and forcibly baptised everyone as 'citizen'. The Spanish constitutionalists were nothing but 'monkeys imitating our enemies . . . everything in their programme was based on the Napoleonic measures for the regeneration of Spain.'[2] Although Blas Ostolaza's assertions were wild and extreme, such sentiments had gained currency during the last eighteen months of the first constitutional period. The question of French influences has been much debated. The Cortes followed the French National Assembly's adoption of separation of powers, and likewise sought to create a unitary state with a written constitution and a rational administration. Controversy focused particularly upon two central aspects: the attribution of sovereignty to the nation, and the unicameral nature of the reconstituted cortes. Precisely such developments had alarmed Spain's senior statesman, Gaspar Melchor Jovellanos, who in the 1780s and 1790s had been in the vanguard of the intellectual circle urging the crown to take the lead in reform. An exponent of Enlightened Absolutism, he had later fallen increasingly under the influence of British political forms by way of reaction to the events in France after 1792.[3] Writing in August and September 1811, at the height of the discussion concerning the nature of representative government in Spain, Jovellanos deplored the idea of sovereignty of the nation. He identified it with egalitarianism; he deplored the fact that the Supreme Central Junta's advocacy of an upper chamber had not been realised and that the Cortes convened in September 1810 in a unicameral form. Jovellanos and a later and growing conservative position identified sovereignty of the nation with 'the exclusion of representatives of the privileged estates and the meeting of all representatives in one chamber alone.' Such a system, he argued, would overthrow the entire balance of political life, since it stripped the crown of its effective power and gave too great an authority to the 'nation', a state of affairs that would ultimately lead to a 'democratic constitution', an idea he did not support.[4]

It was those two issues – sovereignty of the nation and a unicameral legislature – that sharply illustrated the break with the past. No amount of obscurantist medievalism could disguise the fact that those ideas reflected the French experience during the 1790s.[5] The constitutional experiment in Spain was an attempt to discover a viable and durable alternative to the absolute monarchy which had collapsed in 1808, and to the type of institutions and practices associated with the *ancien régime*. In this, France and Spain shared a common experience, even though their circumstances differed widely. The most striking divergence, to say the least, was the very fact that France and Spain were at war between 1808 and 1814 for the entire duration of the first Spanish constitutional experiment. The question of French influences and supposed imitations should be seen within that context, since allegations of Bonapartist or Jacobin sympathies could be politically perilous. That was especially so, since the first written constitution to be introduced in Spain was the Constitution of Bayonne, offered in 1808 by the French Emperor to Spanish notables assembled on French soil. This Constitution came out of the French revolutionary tradition, in the sense that it rejected, as the Constitution of 1791 had done, the *ancien régime* structure of society based upon estates and corporations, in favour of the principles of equality before the law and representation according to population. Nevertheless, it combined with this the type of brevity and practicality associated with the Constitution of the Year VIII (December 1799), which had, in contrast to 1791, not contained any definition of sovereignty.[6] Spanish Liberals found much to admire in Bonapartist legislation, since it attacked many of those problems of long duration which Bourbon ministers, using the plenitude of power claimed by the absolute monarchy, had singularly failed to resolve. Napoleon's Chamartín Decrees of 4 December 1808, for instance, proclaimed the outright abolition of seigneurial jurisdiction and extinguished the Inquisition, anticipating the actions of the Cortes by three to four years. Joaquín Lorenzo Villanueva, Liberal cleric and deputy in the Cortes for Valencia, stressed that the Bayonne Constitution provided Napoleon with one of his greatest advantages in Spain, because it offered Spanish reformers and constitutionalists an alternative to a discredited absolutism for the first time. In a similar vein, Argüelles blamed the puny achievements of the resistance regime between 1808 and 1810 on the Supreme Central Junta which he saw as the principal opponent of reform. Liberals in the Cádiz Cortes were conscious that the outcome of the war in the peninsula depended upon their ability to destroy the effectiveness of the propaganda of the Bonapartist regime in Madrid. They were anxious to gain an ideological victory over the Spanish supporters of King Joseph, whom they branded as '*afrancesados*' and collaborators. Nevertheless, they were aware at the same time of a prevailing traditionalist sentiment throughout the 'patriot' zone and that many of the social and economic structures of the *ancien régime* still survived in Spain.[7]

The neo-Gothic element in Spanish constitutionalism resulted from a concerted attempt by intellectuals, usually historians, to place the legitimate roots of the new political order into a solid historical past that antedated the absolute monarchy. The Habsburgs and Bourbons were increasingly portrayed as foreign dynasties that had altered Spain's 'fundamental laws', her 'ancient constitution'. In medieval roots both liberals and conservatives sought justification for their positions. The appeal to tradition, however, lacked the substance of British constitutionalism, for instance, since absolute monarchs and their ministers, both in Spain and in France, had made profound inroads into the type of corporate representative institutions that had survived from the Middle Ages into the seventeenth and eighteenth centuries. For this reason, the political ideas of Francisco Martínez Marina, the archetypal constitutionalist of this historical school, raised more problems than they resolved, since they exposed the radical divergence between the Cortes that actually met in September 1810 and the historical cortes in each of the component kingdoms of the peninsula. Any argument of direct continuity lacked conviction. Even so, Martínez Marina, and Liberals who adopted all or part of his views, argued that the Cádiz Cortes and the Constitution of 1812 restored and improved 'our ancient institutions'.[8]

Profound elements of scholasticism ran through Spanish constitutionalism. According to Villanueva, the doctrine of sovereignty of the nation itself derived from Aquinas' *Summa Theologica*, which, he argued, should be the guiding work for Spanish Liberals. The Cortes had re-established Spain's 'fundamental laws', in accordance with which the cortes together with the king formed and sanctioned the laws, a tradition practised in Spain before the lifetime of the Angelic Doctor. Villanueva attempted to found a theory of the 'general will' in Aquinas, rather than in Rousseau. He had examined, he said, the writings of St. Thomas in order to discover what could be said concerning the present state of Spain where there was no monarch in residence, and from these readings he had concluded that the faculty of modifying the institutions within a monarchy fell to the representatives of the kingdom, the *procuradores a cortes*. Accordingly, the measures adopted since September 1810 had been 'neither theory nor fiction, nor, worse still, a doctrine opposed to legitimate political practice, but, on the contrary, pure water from the Angelic source.' Hence, those who attacked the work of the Cortes after 1814 were also attacking its Thomist foundations.[9]

Villanueva rejected the allegations of royalist clerics, such as Fray Agustín de Castro, a monk of the Escorial, that the Cádiz Constitution of 1812 was nothing but a 'scandalous copy' of the French Constitution of 1791. Castro had published on 12 and 16 May 1814 an attack on the arrested Liberal deputies in the anti-constitutionalist *Atalaya de La Mancha*, in the pages of which he denounced them as traitors and rebels. In order to rebut these charges, which he regarded as calumnious, Villanueva listed ten basic differences between the two Constitutions. The 1791 Constitution had, for instance, established religious toleration, whereas the Cádiz Constitution upheld the Catholic establishment. Under the provisions of the Civil Constitution of the Clergy (1790) and the 1791 Constitution, members of the judiciary and ministers of religion were to be elected, a principle expressly rejected in 1812. The Cortes had preserved the king's right to declare war and make peace, and to dispose of the armed forces, and so on.[10]

The discussion concerning French influences raised the broader question of the imperfections of the 1812 Constitution, a subject which transcended the growing polarisation of the years 1813 and 1814 between Liberals and conservatives. In his reflections on the Constitution written in London in 1812, José María Blanco ('Blanco

White') argued that it was better to have some constitution, than none at all. Spanish Liberals, however, were anxious to transform the Cádiz Constitution into unassailable fundamental law as fast as they possibly could. They feared traditionalist opinion; they were wary of the military; they were haunted by the notion of an absolutist reaction. Accordingly, they were prepared to ride rough-shod over dissenting opinion, and violated many of their own precepts. Blanco sought to make a plea for a British type of balance, and pointed out that several excesses that appeared in the Consti-tution and that characterised subsequent Liberal practice derived from the French revolutionary experience. He listed six basic defects. The oath required from future deputies to observe the Constitution without alteration within an eight-year period created the potentially destabilising effect of making the Constitution permanent, even though the Cortes itself shared in the exercise of sovereignty. Precisely this sharing faculty, moreover, opened the way for ambiguities in the relationship between king and cortes. Articles 132–153 of the Constitution, in fact, contradicted this, by reserving legislative faculties exclusively for the cortes and allowing the king only a right to veto. Blanco argued that such a right, given those circumstances, could only serve to humiliate the king, just as Louis XVI had been humiliated during the French Revolution. Its exercise threatened to make the king odious in the eyes of his people, especially if demagogues were allowed full play. Instead, Spain should have adopted the British practice of allowing King, lords, and commons equal legislative power in Parliament. Blanco's list of defects was most impressive. The adoption of the 1791 Constitution's practice of a tier system of election destroyed the direct relationship between deputies and people, and removed all popular influence upon the final selection of these deputies. The prohibition of re-election in a forthcoming cortes prevented legisla-tors from gaining experience, especially serious in a country such as Spain without a tradition of representative government. Blanco argued in 1814 that the Liberals produced their own ruin. The framers of the Constitution, parts of which were impracticable, had regarded themselves as infallible. Liberal intolerance had reached a pitch of 'delirium' in 1813–14, when the committees of press censorship had acted like a secularised Inquisition. Worst of all, the attitude of the king had not been seriously taken into account: the Liberal régime had expected him to swear to observe the entire Constitution without allowing the possibility of any changes. For such reasons a totally different situation existed in Spain when Ferdinand VII returned from captivity in May 1814 to that which prevailed in France when Louis XVIII returned to the throne.[11]

II

The deputies in the Cortes in general and most Liberals in particular were not the possessors of national wealth. Of 70 deputies considered to be Liberals in 1814, 23 were merchants, a considerable minority among the total of some 170 deputies in the Ordinary Cortes of 1813–14. Merchant support tended to be evident at the base levels rather than in the political leadership, which fell, as might have been expected, chiefly to members trained in the legal profession who had often held some civil service office under the *ancien régime*. A major pressure group, for instance, was the Junta of Cádiz, which was formed after the collapse of the Supreme Central Junta in Seville late in January 1810. This Junta became the key influence in political life; it consisted of some twenty merchants and officers of the armed services. The Cádiz Junta was the mouth-piece of the mercantile community: this body opposed all commercial concessions to Spanish Americans and sought to maintain full colonial control in the Indies. Subsequently, Tomás Istúriz, a member of one of the chief Cádiz commercial houses, presided over the Junta. The Istúriz family, along with the Valencia merchant and banker family, the Bertrán de Lis, would become leading Liberal opponents of Ferdinand VII's absolutist régime of 1814–20.[12]

Behind the Cortes were many individuals who aspired to become holders of wealth. Most notable among these was the small group of financiers, who had received *vales reales* since the 1780s guaranteed against the sale of appropriated village commons or church properties. This group saw in the Liberal capture of power in September 1810 more than just a constitutional experiment, but a means of transferring landed property to themselves through the exercise of state power. *Vales reales* during the war years after 1795 resembled the French Revolutionary *assignats*, which had been guaranteed against the sale of nationalized church property. If the political changes in Spain after 1810 constituted in any sense at all a bourgeois revolution, then the bourgeoisie involved was not primarily industrial or commercial, but *rentier*. This *rentier* class had, of course, already played a major role under the *ancien régime*, and its pressures after 1808 signifed continuity rather than rupture. These creditors formed an inner group at court, in the civil service, or in the merchant-financier category, and were in no sense provincial outsiders. The same type of government bond-holders existed both under the *ancien régime* and in the Liberal era. Liberalism, then, did not represent exactly a bourgeois revolution in opposition to the structures of power before 1808, but an attempt to keep the same people in power in face of nobiliar reaction and popular opposition. Under the *ancien régime*, the principal groups financing the government had been merchants and civil servants. With the mismanagement of the war and the decline in value of government bonds, this group pressed the government to guarantee their bonds against further loss. Since the government was bankrupt, this could not be done by cash, and, in consequence, attention focused upon corporate property, which had already come under attack in the legal theories of the *ilustrados*. Liberal ideology and bondholder self-interest conveniently converged in the 1800s and 1810s. On both accounts, the hostility of the Church could be expected. However, the objectives of disamortization differed between the time of the *ilustrados* and that of the Liberals: the former argued for rational exploitation of the soil and the broader distribution of proprietorship; the latter in 1811 and 1813 concentrated upon sale of corporate property and abolition of mortmain and entail, in order to rescue the state from bankruptcy. The collapse in value of government bonds in the mid-1790s determined this difference of emphasis. The first disamortization legislation had been passed in 1798 by the government of Charles IV. The Cortes' measures in 1811 and 1813 extended this procedure further.[13]

Many of these *agiotistas* or government creditors, generally described at the time as 'capitalists', were noblemen. Those who benefited from Liberal measures tended to be creditors, aspiring rural middle sectors, and merchants anxious to improve their social status through landownership. By the second half of the nineteenth century, the Liberal state and the new landowners had realigned alongside the old in a common defence of the social order.

The deputies in the Cortes tended for the most part to be salary-earners – civil servants, clerics with livings, law graduates. As in the case of the French National Assembly of 1789–91 lawyers predominated in influence, if not in numbers. There were also, in fact, 66 members of the armed forces in the Cortes in 1810 (counting both proprietary and substitute deputies), 30 of whom were senior officers above the rank of lieutenant-colonel. Several leading Liberals came from families with distinguished positions in the universities and the bureaucracy. José Canga Argüelles (b.1770), Secretary of Finance from November 1810 until August 1811, was the son of a lawyer and university professor, who until 1787 had been fiscal of the Andiencia of Zaragoza. Both Canga and his fellow Asturian, Agustín Argüelles (b.1776) graduated from Oviedo University. Canga received his doctorate from Zaragoza University, and was admitted to the *Royal Aragonese Society* in 1794 and to honorary membership of the *Economic Societies of Friends of the Fatherland* in Madrid, Asturias and Sanlúcar de Barrameda between

1800 and 1803. He joined the Ministry of Finance in 1798 and served in the Accounts Office for the Amortization of Government Bonds. By that time his father had also moved to Madrid as fiscal of the Council of Castile. Canga himself transferred to the Secretariat of State in 1803 and became Intendant of Valencia from 1805–8. He was a member of the 'patriot' Supreme Junta of Valencia in 1808. Agustín Argüelles had been secretary to the Bishop of Barcelona in 1798, had subsequently worked under Leandro Fernández de Moratín, one of the *afrancesados* of 1808, in the Secretariat for the Translation of Foreign Languages, and after 1805 moved to the department of Amortization of Government Bonds. From mid-1809, he had acted as secretary of the Supreme Central Junta in Seville under the presidency of Jovellanos. Villanueva (b.1757) was a member of the Royal Academy of History and on the Council of the Inquisition had been a protégé of the Inquisitor General, Ramón José de Arce, who became a supporter of Joseph Buonaparte. Diego Muñoz Torrero (b.1761), author of the decree on sovereignty in September 1810, had been Rector of the University of Salamanca in 1787–89. Of those not in the Cortes but in the forefront of Spanish Liberalism, Quintana (b.1772) was the son of a Salamanca University professor of canon law, and himself became fiscal of the Junta of Commerce and Money from 1795 until 1808. Well-versed in classical and French literature, he published his main literary works between 1797 and 1805. Both he and Blanco White (b.1775), the son of a Seville merchant family, were at different times editors of *El Semanario Patriótico* between 1808 and 1811. The father of Álvaro Flórez Estrada (b.1766) was a friend of Campomanes and Jovellanos. Flórez Estrada himself became Principal Treasurer of Court Revenues in 1796. With the Conde de Toreno (b.1786), an Asturian nobleman, he was a member of the insurgent Asturias Junta from August 1808 to May 1809. In Cádiz he founded *El Tribuno del Pueblo Español* which published from November 1812 until July 1813. He was Intendant of Seville in 1813–14. The Liberals, whether inside or outside the Cortes, did not at the time constitute a political party with a recognizable organisation, although a number of newspapers did propagate their ideas. Rather, they were a group of men who agreed on certain basic issues such as the formation of a representative form of government and a number of reforms designed to alter the legal structure of society. A leadership cadre had emerged, mostly consisting of men in their 30s, who had been associated with one another since at least the time of the Supreme Central Junta. A complicated network of personal relationships existed both within and beyond this group.[14]

III

Napoleon's Chamartín Decrees had removed all internal customs
barriers, reduced the existing religious communities by two-thirds
and abolished seigneurial jurisdiction and feudal dues – sweeping
measures which strikingly contrasted with the ineffectual Bourbon
policies of the eighteenth century. This legislation, however,
applied only to territory effectively under French control. Valencia
and Galicia, for instance, where *señoríos* predominated, remained for
a long time under patriot control. The Constitution of Bayonne had
abolished entail, and thereby struck at the territorial basis of
nobiliar power. These attacks on jurisdiction, incomes, and lands
helped to account for the adherence of the greater part of the
Spanish nobility to the patriot cause, the implication of which was
the alliance with the numerically small reforming element within
the patriot zone. The *señoríos* formed one of the principal resources
of the titled nobility, whose properties amounted to states within
the state. Both the French and the Spanish Bourbon governments
had sought to dislocate the society of estates and were hostile to
centrifugal elements. In Spain, however, absolutist ministers had
experienced little real success in pushing back the frontiers of
seigneurial power, whether in terms of restricting jurisdictional
privileges or of altering the balance of power in the municipalities.
The nobility managed to delay the Cortes' abolition of entail in a
way they had not been able to do at Bayonne. The Cortes' decree of
8 June 1813 attempted to increase the amount of land in use, but
came to no decision with regard to entail as such. Finally, on 21
March 1814 the Council of State concluded that entail was detrimental to national prosperity, but any projected measures vanished
with the royal coup of May 1814.[15] When the Cortes came to deal
with the question of *señoríos*, it employed a phraseology which
recalled the French Constituent Assembly's claim to have abolished the 'feudal system' in France on 4 August 1789. In Spain, the
framers of the decree of 6 April 1811 were intending to establish a
clear legal distinction between the exercise of jurisdiction and
rights of proprietorship: the former were removed and the latter
reinforced. In this sense, the decree of 1811 could not be described
as revolutionary. As the Liberal deputy and later minister, Francisco Martínez de la Rosa, pointed out in 1822, the model for the
decree of 1811 had indeed been the French law of 4 August 1789,
but the objective had been the reinforcement of legitimate property
rights. Furthermore, Spain had its own precedents of restricting
seigneurial jurisdiction in the proposals of Campomanes and
Jovellanos, which antedated the French Revolution. Even so,

deputies in the Cortes during the debates on this subject over the period, 1810–13, frequently used language similar to that heard in the French Constituent Assembly. It was logical that they should, since they believed that Spain was engaged in a similar political process. Yet, at the same time, they rejected the imputation that they were embarking upon a social revolution, rather than simply clarifying the law. However, that in itself did little or nothing to respond to the urgent social grievances in the localities concerning seigneurial privileges, and it certainly did not assist the recruitment of peasant communities into the Liberal camp. On the contrary, Spanish Liberals strove, by and large successfully, to prevent social revolution in the countryside. The example of loss of control by the French state after 1787–89 was constantly before them. In France the peasant revolts of July and August 1789 had presented the National Assembly with an unexpected crisis of property in the countryside: the old régime was falling faster than the deputies, anxious to uphold property rights, had anticipated. The decree of 4 August had responded to what had already been occurring in the countryside. In effect, 'feudalism' and the fiscal practices of the old régime were abolished from below.[16] The nightmare of the Cádiz deputies, furthermore, was a prolongation of the Spanish chaos and violence of 1808 into a similar experience to that of the *Grande Peur* of 1789. This was especially the case since, despite their obvious traditionalist characteristics, the Spanish risings at their popular base had not presupposed any defence of the social status quo in the countryside, least of all with regard to seigneurial power. The priorities of the Cortes, however, were stabilization through the establishment of a unitary and centralized state and the clarification of private property rights. These two elements came together in the decree of 1811.[17]

The definition of private property rights, freedom of movement for capital, land, and labour, the stimulation of private enterprise in response to free market forces – these were essential aspects of the political theory of Spanish Liberalism from the 1810s onwards. Quite clearly, such a platform found no place for seigneurial jurisdiction, though Argüelles and Manuel García Herreros were quick to stress that abolition implied in no way at all that landlords' rights had been removed as well. The decree of 1811 conformed only imperfectly to the aspirations of those Valencian deputies who had first introduced discussion on the question at the end of March 1811. One of them, Antoni Lloret, a lawyer from the town of Alberic, which lay within the *señorío* of the Duque del Infantado, one of the richest noblemen in Spain, proposed with Villanueva's support the abolition of both jurisdiction and territorial rights. A fellow Valencian deputy, Pere Aparici, warned the Cortes of the crisis in the countryside, and questioned the validity of nobles' titles to land acquired after the expulsion of the Moriscos in 1609.[18]

The census of 1797 revealed 402,059 noblemen, most of them modest farmers living north of the Duero and little different in socio-economic terms from a middle peasantry. In Andalusia, in contrast, only 5% of the total peasant population owned land: the majority worked as day-labourers on private land, especially in the provinces of Jaén, Córdoba, Seville, Granada, and Murcia. The nobility owned half the land in Extremadura and two-thirds in La Mancha and Seville. In the two western Andalusian provinces of high population density, Seville and Córdoba, probably only one-sixth part of the land was actually cultivated.[19] It seems to have been the case that the material position of the landed nobility generally improved during the latter part of the eighteenth century, in response to the rise in prices and rents. The growth of population from an estimated 7 million in 1724 to a possible 12 million by 1808, a trend not reversed by repeated dearths, put pressure on available land, especially since Spain's perceptible economic recovery during the intervening period had taken place largely in the geographical peripheries of the peninsula. An inadequate infrastructure accounted for the existence of a dual economy, with the peripheries able to relieve dearth by importation of foodstuffs. By the second half of the century, the inability of agriculture to feed an increasing population had become apparent. In response to the Madrid food riots of 1766, Charles III had commissioned a report on land reform from the provincial Intendants, but nobiliar opposition had blocked publication until 1784. When Jovellanos published his Agrarian Reform Report in 1795, the time for reform had been superseded by the general European reaction to the French Revolution.[20] Valencia had a tradition of litigation and rural rebellions against the burden of tithes, government monopolies, and seigneurial dues, the highest in Spain. At frequent intervals the peasant communities of the *huerta* stood in opposition to the beneficiaries of the *ancien régime*. Rising prices from the 1760s and slack payment of wages worsened labourers' conditions. Banditry grew to serious proportions, and government orders from the early 1780s into the 1800s attempted in vain to deal with the problem, which was equally serious in Andalusia as well. The war after 1795 hit Valencia's silk and wine trades, and precipitated further price rises. These pressures combined with those of military recruitment to explain the outbreak of rural rebellion in 1801 particularly among the small farmers of the *huerta*. The repercussions of this rebellion had still not subsided when the region rose again in 1808 against the imposition of French rule and local government collaboration.[21] In Valencia and Catalonia, rural communities were struggling as much against their own landlords as against the French invaders. In certain areas of Catalonia, the rural milita, the *somatenes*, set up their own local committees.[22] In Valencia, virtually an agrarian revolt was in progress by 1811, a situation which undoubtedly influenced the position adopted by the Valencian deputies in the Cortes. The Cortes was attempting to deal with a situation that had got out of hand.[23] Valencia and Galicia, however, were the two most densely populated regions in Spain. Together they also possessed the largest number of lay and ecclesiastical *señoríos* in the peninsula. In Valencia, the Cortes heard on 12 April 1813, only one-eighth of approximately 500 towns did not have their magistrates appointed by seigneurs. In Galicia, 380 towns and villages fell within lay *señoríos*, 239 within ecclesiastical, and only 35 under direct government administration. In two regions of Andalusia, Seville and Córdoba, seigneurial jurisdiction predominated.[24]

The decree of 1811 left nobiliar territorial rights intact, but removed all exclusive privileges such as monopoly of fishing rights, water usage, pasture, hunting areas and open lands, wine and oil presses, furnaces and ovens. All existing tenants' contracts were upheld and rents were to be paid in the normal way. The Cortes transformed the traditional rural relationship of lord and vassal into that of landlord and tenant. The decree did, however, specify that all land titles had to be validated before proprietorship could be confirmed. Inevitably, this opened the way for widespread litigation on the subject, to which not even the restoration of Ferdinand VII in 1814 put an end.[25] Many communities believed that the Cortes had abolished all dues previously required by landlords and accordingly refused to pay. In some instances, landlords' properties were occupied, such direct action encouraged by sympathetic local lawyers. Given the collapse of the Bourbon administration at the local level, landlords could no longer count on the public authorities to uphold their position when confronted by an assault from below.[26] Faced with direct action at the local level in Valencia, Alicante, Murcia, and western Andalusia, the Cortes appointed a committee to draw up a supplementary law designed to clarify the decree of 1811. This committee encompassed a broad range of Liberal opinion, and included both Aparici and García Herreros. Again Aparici raised the question of land titles, while Lloret maintained that few benefits had been felt from the law of 1811 as a result of nobiliar obstruction. The clarifying law of 6 August 1813 reaffirmed the abolition of seigneurial jurisdiction and all dues and obligations, but upheld landlords' property rights.[27]

Redistribution of private land was not a Liberal policy objective. On the contrary, Liberals saw in the furtherance of private economic interests the principal means of stimulating the economy into growth. With that aim, they sought to reduce village corporate properties to private ownership and thereby fulfil the earlier goal of the *ilustrados*, who had pressed for the release of property on to the market. The axe fell, as it were, not on the territorial nobility, but on the peasant villages and the rural small towns, as it would later on ecclesiastical corporate property during the widespread disamortization procedures after 1835 and 1855. Throughout the period, 1810–1860, it appears that lay landlords reinforced their position, with the result that many features of the *ancien régime* in the countryside continued well into the Liberal era: they complemented it, rather than contradicted it. The rural population, accordingly, could expect little to their advantage from Liberalism, and the tendency towards recruitment into traditionalist movements became pronounced. The Cortes found itself not only geographically isolated in Cádiz, but also caught precariously in the middle between nobiliar intransigence and rising peasant militancy. Spanish Liberals, for such reasons, failed to create a popular base among the rural majority. As a result of this failure they unwittingly fixed the time limit of the first constitutional experiment by enabling a traditionalist recovery of nerve during the course of 1813 and the early months of 1814. That, in turn, created the conditions in which a royal coup d'etat, supported by the conservative section of the armed forces, could put an end to the Cortes, nullify the Constitution, and terminate Spain's first attempt to work out the basis for a liberal, representative system.[28]

By 1812–14, Liberalism gained ground in certain areas of Spain's geographical periphery. However, the recovery of territory in the traditional heartlands, with the gradual collapse of the French military position, obscured these developments. In political circles attention naturally focused on the Cortes, particularly when the Ordinary Legislature opened in Madrid early in 1814. In this Cortes deputies of a conservative complexion, hostile to the radical provisions of the 1812 Constitution, which they identified with the excesses of the French Revolution, probably commanded the majority. The Liberal ministry, alarmed at the prospect of seeing its work undone, remained determined to hold on to power. Accompanying this political polarisation at the centre, the outlines of a geographical division of opinion could also be discerned in the last months of the first constitutional period. The royal coup of May 1814, however, further obscured the development of a Liberal base in the cities of the periphery. With the growth of a clandestine opposition to Ferdinand VII's first absolutist regime (1814–20), Liberal support in Cádiz, La Coruña, Málaga, Cartagena, Murcia, Alicante, and Valencia became apparent, as did the existence of opposition masonic cells in Granada and Madrid. The industrial littoral of Catalonia, with Barcelona at its core, became for the first time strongholds of Liberalism. This region had played no direct part in the first constitutional experiment, since French forces remained in control there into the early months of 1814. On the Catalan littoral business and worker support for the Liberal cause were evident in the period, 1817–23, while in the Catalan interior traditionalist sentiment remained supreme.[29]

Spain, with its geographical proximity to France, its historical involvement in the mainstream of European affairs, and its common experience of absolutism, understandably could not escape the impact of either the French Revolution or the conservative reaction to it. Perhaps that explained the anxiousness of Spanish constitutionalists to disclaim direct revolutionary influences. The execution of the king and queen, the experience of the Terror, and then the dictatorship of Bonaparte, not only provoked a revulsion in Spanish reforming circles but also provided counter-revolutionaries with powerful weapons of propaganda. Spanish constitutionalists were aware, nevertheless, that they shared with their French counterparts a common desire to discover a viable alternative to an *ancien régime* in crisis. They sought, however, to place the roots of the new representative system in Spain's own medieval past, and, thereby, to circumvent the allegations of illegitimacy. Absolutism, though, had severely weakened the traditional cortes of the Spanish kingdoms, with the result that entirely new legal and political structures had to be introduced after 1808. Fiscal breakdown and mounting rural tensions made fresh solutions imperative. Neo-Gothicism and traditionalist hankerings could not disguise the extent of the changes proposed. Spanish constitutionalists did not regard the French Revolution as a model, and only viewed it as a guide to their own actions in the sense that it showed them what to avoid. They did not copy France, as extreme conservatives alleged; they were caught up in their own domestic problems and to a large extent were overcome by them. The ground had not been prepared for the reception of radical changes, and wartime conditions frustrated their application. In fundamental aspects, Spanish Liberals followed in the tradition of the *ilustrados*, who had sought to use the absolute monarchy as the instrument of reform: the monarchy had collapsed in 1808; a Bonaparte ruled in Madrid. Another instrument of reform had to be found by the 'patriots' of Cádiz – the sovereign, unicameral assembly. Yet, conservative hostility to the aims of the *ilustrados*, the reaction to the

French Revolution, the politicisation of the nobility, the popular risings, the growing importance of the military in political life – all these factors weakened the narrowly-based reformist circles in Spain, divided as they were between support for Bonapartism and the multifarious 'patriot' coalition. By 1812–13 the consensus within that coalition for reforms of one kind or another had collapsed, and a deepening polarisation took place that would last more than a century and a half.

NOTES

1. C.W. Crawley, 'English and French Influences in the Cortes of Cadiz, 1810–1814', *Cambridge Historical Journal* VI (1939), pp. 176–208. Diego Sevilla Andrés, 'La Constitución española de 1812 y la francesca de 1791', *Saitabi* VII, nos. 33–34 (1949), pp. 212–34, and 'La Constitución de 1812. Obra de Transición', *Revista de Estudios Políticos* 126 (Nov.–Dec. 1962), pp. 113–41. Federico Suárez Verdeguer, *Conservadores, inovadores y renovadores en las postrimerías del antiguo régimen* (Pamplona 1955) and *La crísis política del antiguo régimen en España, 1800–1840*, (Madrid 1958). María Esther Martínez Quinteiro, *Los grupos liberales antes de las Cortes de Cádiz* (Madrid 1977), pp. 170–186. W.D. Hargreaves-Mawdesley, *Spain Under the Bourbons, 1700–1833. A Collection of Documents* (London 1973), no. 132, pp. 261–275, see p. 262. According to Luis Sánchez Agesta, *Historia del constitucionalismo español*, (Madrid 1964), pp. 58–9, it was difficult to separate the sources of the Cortes' work, since the format and content were modern, but the principle usually referred back to legitimate Spanish traditions.
2. Joaquín Lorenzo Villanueva, *Apuntes sobre el arresto de vocales de Cortes* (Madrid 1820), pp. 34, 110–11.
3. Gaspar Melchor de Jovellanos, *Memoria que dirigió a sus compatriotas rebatiendo las calumnias divulgadas contra los individuos de la Junta Central* (1810), in *Obras* 8 tomes (Barcelona 1839–40), VII, pp. 189–90, 214–19. Richard Herr, *The Eighteenth Century Revolution in Spain* (Princeton 1958), p. 321, refers to Jovellanos' revulsion towards the Jacobin régime in France.
4. *Cartas de Jovellanos y Lord Vassall Holland sobre la guerra de la independencia (1808–1811)*, 2 vols. (Madrid 1911), II, pp. 76–7, 523–7.
5. Martínez Quinteiro, *Los grupos liberales*, pp. 155–65, 170–86.
6. A. Duguit and H. Monnier, *Les Constitutions et les principles lois politiques de la France depuis 1789*, (Paris 1852), pp. 118–29. For discussion of the Constitution of the Year VIII, see M.J. Sydenham, *The First French Republic, 1792–1804*, (London 1974), pp. 226–30. Irene Collins, *Napoleon and His Parliaments, 1800–1815*, pp. 10–14. Louis Bergeron, *France Under Napoleon* (Princeton 1981), pp. 5–13. For the Bayonne Constitution, see Carlos Sanz-Cid, *La Constitución de Bayona* (Madrid 1923).
7. See Brian R. Hamnett, *La política española en una época revolucionaria, 1790–1820*, (Mexico 1985), pp. 95–102. Miguel Artola, *Los afrancesados*, (Madrid 1953) and Hans Juretschke, *Los afrancesados en la guerra de la independencia* (Madrid 1962).

8. Francisco Martínez Marina, *Teoría de las Cortes o Grandes Juntas Nacionales de León y Castilla* (Madrid 1813), 3 vols., I, pp. xlix–1, 1–7, 37–46, 190–91; II, pp. 199–201. J.A. Maravall, 'El pensamiento político en España a comienzos del siglo XIX. Martínez Marina,' *Revista de Estudios Políticos* 81 (May–June 1955), pp. 29–82. Martínez Marina (b. Oviedo, 1754) became a member of the Real Academia de la Historia in 1786 under the presidency of Compomanes.

9. Joaquín Lorenzo Villanueva, *Las angélicas fuentes o el tomista en las Cortes*, (Cádiz 1811–13), 2 vols. edited by Rafael María Baralt and Nemesio Fernández (Madrid 1849), I, pp. 43–46, 55, 58, 61–62. Lucienne Domergue, 'Notes sur la première edition de langue espagnol du 'Contrat Social', 1799', *Mélanges de la Casa de Velázquez* III (1967), pp. 375–413. All Rousseau's works were translated into Spanish by José Marchena in France during the 1790s, finishing with *Du Contrat Social* (not necessarily by Marchena) in 1799. By the end of that year, some 200 copies were already in Spain.

10. Villanueva, *Apuntes*, pp. 11–18. For the French Constitution of 1791, see J.M. Roberts and R.C. Cobb (eds.), *French Revolution. Documents*, vol 1., (Oxford 1966), pp. 347–365. That Constitution, moreover, abolished nobility as such; this the 1812 Constitution did not do.

11. José María Blanco ('White'), *El Español*, 8 tomes (London 1810–1814), V (1812), *Breves reflexiones sobre algunos artículos de la Constitución española*, pp. 76–80; 81–95; 119–24; VIII (1814), pp. 295–308. See *Constitución política de la monarquía española* (Cádiz 1812) arts. pp. 35–103 (tier system); 141–56, 170–3 (royal power); 375–9 (reform of the Constitution).

12. Timothy Anna, *Spain and the Loss of America* (Nebraska 1983), 55. Michael P. Costeloe, *Response to Revolution. Imperial Spain and the Spanish American Revolutions 1810–1840* (Cambridge 1986), pp. 118–123.

13. Miguel Artola, *Estudio Preliminar* to vol 98, Biblioteca de Autores Españoles: *Memorias de Tiempos de Fernando VII*, II (Madrid 1957), pp. v–lvi. Juan Brines Blasco, 'Deuda y desamortización durante el Trienio Constitucional (1820–1823),' *Moneda y Crédito* 124 (March 1973), 51–67, pp. 52–3, 60–61.

14. Martínez Quinteiro, ibid., pp. 41–3, 47, 52, 63–8, 80–6, 241–4. Constantino Suárez, *Escritores y artistas asturianos*, (Madrid 1936), I, pp. 405–20; II, pp. 279–95. Luis Alfonso Martínez Cachero, *Alvaro Flórez Estrada. Su Vida, su obra política y sus ideas económicas*, (Oviedo 1961), pp. 19–29, 38–56.

15. Bartolomé Clavero, *Mayorazgo. Propiedad feudal en Castilla, 1369–1836* (Madrid 1974), pp. 325–6, 331–5, 354–6. Salvador de Moxó, *La disolución del régimen señorial en España*, (Madrid 1965), pp. 20–58.

16. Theda Skocpol, *States and Social Revolutions: A Comparative Analysis of France, Russia and China*, (Cambridge 1980), pp. 118–19. D.M.G. Sutherland, *France 1789–1815. Revolution and Counterrevolution*, (London 1985), pp. 79–80.

17. *Diario de las discusiones y actas de las Cortes*, 23 vols., (Cádiz 1811–1813), VIII, p. 279, Argüelles argued that seigneurial jurisdication was incompatible with the principle of equality before the law, (12 September 1811); XVIII, pp. 302–19. Martínez de la Rosa represented Granada in the Ordinary Cortes of 1813–14, and was principal minister in the moderate Liberal cabinet of Feb.–Aug. 1822. He favoured the addition of an upper chamber. See Jean Sarrailh. *Martínez de la Rosa* (Bordeaux 1930).

18. Manuel Ardit, *Els valencians de les Corts de Cadis* (Barcelona 1968), pp. 23–7. Moxó, *La disolución*, pp. 15–16, 38–45, 56. Alberic had been a *señorío* town since

1387. In France in 1789 peasants and sympathetic lawyers argued that the onus of proof of property rights rested with the *seigneurs*. Sutherland, ibid., 100.

19. Antonio-Miguel Bernal, *La lucha por la tierra en la crísis del antiguo régimen*, (Madrid 1979), pp. 74–5, 125–9, 303–5, 334–5. Gonzalo Anes, *El antiguo régimen en España: los Borbones* (Madrid 1976), p. 49, 95. Antonio Domínguez Ortiz, *Sociedad y Estado en el siglo XVIII español* (Barcelona 1976) pp. 345–358. Concepción de Castro, *La revolución liberal y los municipios españoles (1812–1868)*, (Madrid 1979), pp. 41–3.

20. Jordi Nadal, *La población española (siglos xvi a xx)*, (Barcelona 1966), p. 16. Joseph Harrison, *An Economic History of Modern Spain*, (Manchester 1978), p. 13.

21. Manuel Ardit, *Revolución liberal y revuelta campesina. Un ensayo sobre la desintegración del régimen feudal en el País Valenciano (1793–1840)*, (Barcelona 1977), pp. 51–61, 70–1, 81–3, 98–118, 216–18. Domínguez Ortiz, ibid., pp. 417–18. Sutherland, ibid., p. 74, argues with regard to the French peasant risings of 1789–93 that 'almost everywhere the risings were clearly another way of carrying out lawsuits which the villagers had lost or which were pending.'

22. Jaime Vicens Vives, *Cataluña en el siglo xix*, (Madrid 1959), pp. 183–4.

23. Ardit, *Valencians*, pp. 23–7, 31–3, 38–9. In Valencia there was a long tradition of village appeals to the Audiencia for transfer to royal jurisdiction.

24. *Diario* XVIII, pp. 302–19. The population of Galicia was 1.3 million in 1810; the Valencian population quadrupled between 1718 and 1794, and the region had the highest density of rural population in Europe.

25. *Diario* VII, pp. 13, 23, 30, 68–9, 253, 282, 315, 330.

26. For case instances, see Archivo Histórico Nacional (Madrid), Consejos 3588, expediente 15 (*señoríos*), 1814, and Moxó, ibid., pp. 58–61, 193–201, 220–23.

27. *Diario* XVII, 316. Ardit, *Valencians*, pp. 49–52.

28. *Colección de los decretos y ordenes que han expedido las Cortes Generales y Extraordinarias*, 10 vols. (Madrid 1820–23), IV, pp. 80–2. The decree of 8 June 1813 permitted enclosures, removed restrictions on land utilisation, established the right to set up factories and workshops, full liberty of crafts, and removed the obligation of matriculation before the guild authorities. The decree of 4 January 1813 provided for the division and sale of all *terrenos baldíos, realengos, propios*, and *arbitrios*, one-half for sale at public auction, the other half for distribution among loyal soldiers. Bernal, ibid., pp. 81, 129–31, 340, 351. Castro, ibid., pp. 86–8. For rural disturbances in the early 1820s, see 'Contrarrevolución campesina?' in Jaime Torras Elías, *Liberalismo y rebeldía campesina, 1820–1823*, (Barcelona 1976), pp. 7–31.

29. For the development of Liberal support, see Archivo de Palacio (Archive of the Oriente Royal Palace, Madrid). Papeles Reservados de Fernando VII, Tome 21, ff. 68–9., Declaration of the Cádiz Authorities, 1 May 1821; ff. 160–4., Proclamation to the Catalans by the Royalist 'Regency' of Seo de Urgel, 25 October 1822; Tome 67, exp. ix, ff. 214–21., Notice of the Secret Societies Organized in Spain up to 1823.

Revolution and Risorgimento: the Heritage of the French Revolution in 19th Century Italy

M. Broers

The French Revolution and the Italian *Risorgimento* are seminal events in the national histories of their respective countries in modern times; they also have a direct and profound relationship to each other. It is an intense and complex relationship that exists on several levels and is subject to many different interpretations, but the profound impact of the events and example of the French Revolution on the political culture of nineteenth century Italy is undeniable. Essentially, the forms of the Revolution's lasting influence were twofold: the theoretical influence it exercised over the development of the Italian nationalist movement, and the traces it left at local level as a result of the direct participation by Italians in the events of the period 1789–1815. These forms, in their turn, have determined the general outline of this paper.

A: THE THEORETICAL INFLUENCE

The centrality of the Revolution to the development of the *Risorgimento* was elucidated with great clarity by Antonio Gramsci. It is central to his own concept of 'the passive revolution', which emphasizes the importance of 'outside' intervention for the success of any progressive movement in Italy. Gramsci also drew attention to the wider division of opinion about the nature and desirability of the relationship. For Gramsci, the division was clear; it was between the view that modern Italian nationalism was strictly dependent on the French Revolution and could not have come into existence without it, and an opposing range of opinions asserting the autonomous, intrinsically Italian nature of the Risorgimento, insisting that the Revolution diverted Italian nationalism from its true path and falsified its character.[1]

Mazzini was among the most prominent exponents of the latter, negative judgement on the influence of the Revolution, although his acceptance of so many elements of 'Jacobin democracy' can occlude this. Mazzini and his followers embraced the constitutional model of the Year III and, at a more profound level, the concept of national identity as a panacea for the resolution of social, economic, and regional divisions. None of this was regarded by the Mazzinians as the essence of modern nationalism, however. On a functional level the French Revolution of 1789 provided an instructive model, but one which did not merit direct or complete imitation, particularly because between 1815 and 1848 it appeared to have failed within France itself.[2] Ideologically, Mazzini saw the Revolution, 1789–91, as little more than a negative protest, devoid of moral content, rather than the product of a people moved by faith, but by a 'simple reaction to the abuses of the monarchy . . . [and thus] the question of political reform cancels out the real, paramount question – the moral and social question.'[3]

Mazzini's concept of the Revolution, itself, limited its usefulness for the development of any nationalist movement. It could go no further than affirming the liberty of the individual, it could not create nationalist bonds among men, failing to embrace the 'association of men', 'of which liberty is only one element'. By the mid 1830s, the Revolution had become merely a 'tool of purely critical analysis' which had sunk into sterility and decadence: 'the exhaustion of a principle'.[4] The Revolution could not provide a positve nationalist dogma, only the transitional doctrine of individualism. For Mazzini, the skeletal framework of the nation-state emerged from the Revolution, but not its ideological essence. Thus, early nineteenth century radicals did not regard the French Revolution as the fountainhead of modern nationalism, but only as one of several prerequisites for it. To the insurgents of 1848, the Revolution was a thing of the past.

Gioberti rejected the influence of the Revolution from a more moderate perspective in his widely read and influential work, *Del primato morale e civili degli Italiani*, first published in 1843:

> Italy has within itself . . . all the conditions necessary for national and political revival, and to put them into effect, it does not have to hope for an internal revolution, nor [for] either foreign invasion or imitation.[5]

His rejection of the unitary state was even more emphatic:

> the union of power concentrated in the Committee of Public Safety, and of national consensus that inflamed France, had its origins in the radical changes already introduced by the Constituent Assembly which, for its part, had been achieved peacefully, because the state had been united politically for a long time. Now, this is not the case in our country . . . and as for a set of conditions

controlled by a handful of malcontents, it is madness to believe it could succeed against the consensus of public power . . .[6]

The alternative model proposed by Gioberti was a federal Italy co-ordinated by the Pope; his solution to the perceived need for association among Italians was a national identity based on a shared Catholic faith.

Federalism could embrace the powerful local and regional patriotism that actually dominated Italian political culture, just as it did not exclude the emergence of Mazzinian popular democracy at local level. It was a combination of both these elements which produced the most relatively successful of the 1848 revolutions in Italy, that of Daniele Manin in Venice.[7] Manin's was, perhaps, the only truly popular and populist rising of 1848–49, and it was also the one furthest in its ideology from 1789. The Venetians rejected not only the principles of foreign intervention and foreign ideology, but the whole concept of the unitary state founded on the destruction of corporatism. 'Viva San Marco!' stood for a reassertion of traditional privileges as well as new political liberties. By the very nature of their exercise, the radicals of 1848 were intent on driving a wedge between the French Revolution and the new nationalism embodied by the *Risorgimento*.

Implicit in the urgency of the radicals' critique of the Revolution is their recognition of its powerful, central influence on early nineteenth century Italy. This was a *fait accompli* they all accepted, even if they viewed its profound impact as, at best, of limited ideological value, as did Mazzini, or as a deviant force that was antithetical to Italian life, as it was for Gioberti and the traditionalist, reactionary right. Thus there were few Italian political thinkers who took a positive view of the influence of the French Revolution before 1848, but 1848 was itself a turning point in the evolution of nationalist theories. Prior to 1848, radical nationalists had seen the tenets of the Revolution reversed, and they had witnessed the failure of the generation of liberals bred under Napoleon to redress the balance in favour of the Revolution, with the failure of the revolts of 1820–21. However, the *débâcle* of 1848 represented the radicals' own failure and it forced profound ideological changes upon them. Gioberti had to abandon his hopes of a nationalism based on the Papacy, while the military defeats of 1848–49 forced both he and Manin to abandon their belief in the primacy of regionalism. After 1848, they were all driven to embrace the concept of the unitary, revolutionary state, whether under the Savoyard monarchy or a democratic republic, as the only way of overthrowing Austrian rule. They returned to the political theories of *epoca francese*.

B: THE HUMAN INFLUENCE

The history of political ideas is not the history of a people or a period, and the history of nineteenth century Italy is no exception to this. At no time did Mazzini, Gioberti or even Manin shape the course and character of mainstream political events, nor was theirs the sole experience of the influence of the Revolution. To gain a wider perspective on the relationship of the French Revolution to the *Risorgimento*, it is equally important to balance the particular with the abstract, and to approach the problem from a level of history based on individual experience, to juxtapose *mentalité* and ideology.

At the level of personal experience, it would be more accurate to refer to the deep scars left the Revolution, rather than to roots planted in the minds of the Italian political classes, so essentially violent and divisive was the nature of its influence. The most obvious reason for this was the impact of the Revolutionary wars on the Hesperian peninsula reached beyond the transient, if severe, shocks and horrors of war, to engender a civil war between Italians which persisted into the successive generation and, often, well beyond mid-century. To most of the Italian propertied classes, the most poignant and perceptible influence of the French Revolution had more to do with 'the sins of the fathers' than post-revolutionary ideological conflicts.

The presence of the French and Allied armies in the period 1796–1800 politicized a myriad of local and personal conflicts throughout the peninsula, which hitherto had been largely atomized and apolitical in character. When Italians were forced to take sides in a wider, and largely imported, ideological conflict, their own particular antagonisms acquired at once a new scope and intensity. That the mark made by the Revolutionary conflagration took the shape it did, was because it was interacting with a society itself already in crisis. Two features of the politics of *ancien régime* Italy had a powerful influence on the impact made by the Revolution. Municipal life over much of Italy was bitter and factious, often degenerating into violence; in an essentially immobile, subsistence peasant economy, the rivalries within the propertied classes were fierce and enduring exactly because there was no escape from them. Second, with the exception of Habsburg Lombardy, there was nowhere in Hesperia a state strong enough to intervene with sufficient constancy and force to hold these local conflicts in check. Once broadened and politicized, the weak governments of the 1790s and of the Restoration period had little choice but to graft their own political preoccupations onto those of the localities, rather than confront them.

From the vantage point of future generations, that of the direct descendants of the protagonists, there is no doubt that the crucial stage in the development of local and personal conflicts was the Revolutionary period and, quite specifically, the year 1799, when the French client states set up throughout Italy were briefly overthrown and the old order restored until Napoleon's second Italian campaign of 1800 swept them out until 1814. These traumatic swings of the pendulum produced two forms of conflict between Italians that were to leave deep scars on successive generations: the intensification of conflict within the local élites, and the unleashing of popular, particularly peasant violence, in the cause of counter-revolution.

(i) *The Family Feuds*

'The career open to talent' has been seen as one of the permanent achievements bequeathed to modern Europe by the French revolutionaries, but in an Italian context it must be remembered that the counter-revolution could achieve the same release and rapid promotion of talent and that, however fleeting its triumph in 1799, counter-revolution was everywhere triumphant in 1814 and remained so until at least 1848. Equally, it must be remembered that these political purges took place in an otherwise immobile world, and that their results were as permanent as their execution was bloodthirsty and crude.

In his classic study of the revolutionary crisis in Naples,[8] Benedetto Croce discerned the growth of a republican, patriot tradition among many southern families whose members participated in the shortlived Parthenopean Republic and whose attachment to the 'patriot cause' was confirmed in the purges which followed the Bourbon restoration of 1799, a phenomenon known to both sides by the ominous name, *la caccia dei giacobini*. There were over 7,000 *martiri patriotti* in the wake of the restoration in Naples, all of them documented by scholars who were often their relatives, three generations later, under the united kingdom of Italy; their *corpus* of work is itself a tribute to the Revolution as *la longue durée*.[9]

Among the patriot ranks, a fine example is Croce's study of the Poerio family,[10] small landowners and lawyers in Calabria. Giuseppe Poerio was twenty-seven in 1799 and, together with his brother Leopoldo, served the Republic first in their own province, where the family of Giuseppe's fiancée had its estates sacked and permanently confiscated by Cardinal Ruffo's *sanfedisti*, and then in Naples, where the brothers were imprisoned in Sant' Elmo. In the trials that followed, Leopoldo was banished for life and Giuseppe's death sentence was commuted to life in the galleys. Although

Giuseppe was released in 1801, the family's estates had been confiscated and were only recovered in part under Napoleonic rule. Giuseppe said it was his imprisonment that confirmed him in his 'patriot ardour', and he went on to serve the French from 1805 to 1814, becoming *procuratore-generale* of the *Corte di Cassazzione* in 1810. The price for this collaboration was three years in exile, following the restoration of 1815, yet he re-emerged to become one of the most prominent figures of the 1821 revolution, which in turn led to another period of exile which ended only in 1830. A younger brother, Raffaele, led the *Carbonari* in Calabria in 1821, fled to Greece in 1822 where he fought with Byron, and finally joined the French army in 1830. Giuseppe's son, Carlo, fought for the Republic in 1848 and ended his life in the Bourbon galleys.

Perhaps a more typical, less spectacular example is that of Archdeacon Luca Cagnazzi of Bari, in Puglia, described by a descendant as 'a scientist loyal to the throne in 1799, a sworn republican two years later, [who] returned from exile under the Napoleonic régime, a *carbonaro* in 1820 and who – like so many others – first took up arms in 1799'.[11]

Looking beyond the narrow confines of the Revolutionary-Napoleonic period to the nineteenth century as a whole, it is clear that at least until unification, the victors in these local feuds were the counter-revolutionaries. A telling example of the counter-revolution 'opening careers to talent' is the experience of the Pronio family, from the village of Introdacqua, in the Abruzzo, a province in the north of the Kingdom of Naples.[12] Giuseppe Pronio was a notorious outlaw under the *ancien régime*, but in 1799 he put his band at the king's service, and raised and led a peasant militia against the French. Pronio spent the ten years of Napoleonic rule in hiding and exile, but finished his career as a general in the Bourbon army, a rank he gained in 1814. His son, Paolo, died in 1853 with the rank of Field-Marshal, while one of his nephews, the family historian, became archpriest of the provincial capital of Teramo. No reversal of a family's fortunes could be more complete, and so great did their local power become after the Restoration that 'the Pronio district' was excluded from the general disarmament of the kingdom which followed the revolution of 1848. Yet, the story did not end here. Writing in 1905, a descendant noted bitterly:

> After Garibaldi's entry into Naples in 1860 our family was made a target by certain local adversaries, and of harrassment and persecution to the point where my own father was arrested for political motives.[13]

Writing in 1900 about the events of 1799 in Puglia, the historian Francesco Carabelese put this problem in a less particular context with his rhetorical question, 'Does it not seem that 'the Commune' of 1799 inaugurated the wretched and petty life that still – at the distance of a century – . . . twists and warps our municipalities?'[14]

This phenomenon was not confined to the *Mezzogiorno*; in Tuscany, in 1799, the restored government instigated 4,000 trials involving 12,000 families, which led to imprisonment and the confiscation of property,[15] while in Piedmont, the proscription lists drawn up under the regency 1799–1800 comprised 3,157 names.[16] Perhaps the most famous victims of the *caccia dei giacobini* were the Cavour family, who rose to prominence under the French – the future prime minister's godmother was Napoleon's sister, Pauline Borghese – only to be excluded by the post-1814 court in Turin. Members of the family were kept under police surveillance into the 1830s, and Cavour was the first member of his family to hold major political office since 1814, himself propelled to power only by the crisis of 1848–49.[17]

This is the enduring reality of the Revolution as *la longue durée* in the life of nineteenth century Italy. 1799, 1821, 1848 and 1860 spelt the rise and fall of little empires as well as petty states; their memory was kept alive by the zenith and nadir of family fortunes. The experience of the local *notabili* represents the influence of the Revolution as received and transmuted into what Italians call *la società bloccata*, a socio-economic structure the Revolution could enter and disrupt, but not reform or develop. *La società bloccata* embraced a whole society, not just its propertied élite, as did the impact of the Revolution upon it, which was also epitomized by the events of 1799.

(ii) *The Popular Fury*

The counter-revolution of 1799 had a powerful basis of popular support throughout Italy, and it was effected by the masses, both urban and rural, from Ruffo's *sanfediste* armies in Calabria to the peasant risings in the Val d'Aosta. Everywhere, too, the patriot section of the élite was its target, which was both a bloody testimony to patriot isolation within Italian society and a series of events that left deep scars, psychological as much as physical and political, on the patriot clans. Their descendants saw the patriots as proudly, determinedly and properly élitist, and their own writings on the period are marked by a mixture of snobbery and fear; truly, 'a world turned upside down'.

At this point, the historiography of the *epoca francese* becomes, itself, an expression of the Revolution as *la longe durée*, and for Italian historians of the late nineteenth century, it was *Novantanove*, rather than *Quatrevignt-neuf*, that had to be confronted. 1894 had seen the *fasci*, true peasant *jacqueries*, in Sicily; 1897 had seen Crispi, the champion of traditional liberalism, fall from power; finally, 1898–99 had been 'the Red Year' in the cities of the industrial north. Not surprisingly, the writing of historians of these years had an urgency about it when dealing with the tide of popular violence unleashed by the counter-revolution of 1799. In 1903, Serrafino La Sorsa began his account of 1799 in Molfetta, on the Puglian coast, thus:

> The memory of what took place . . . during 1799 has remained alive among our people of the south, as terrible events in which the people [*la plebe*] showed what it was capable of, and with what insolence and audacity it knew how to impose itself on other classes. 1799 is still spoken of as a dismal and savage event which has left an indelible mark on the popular memory.[18]

Writing in 1882 about the *Viva Maria* peasant risings of 1799 in Tuscany, the historian Brigidi described the rebels thus:

> . . . vile and ruthless men, come out of the last dregs of *la plebea*, part of that thriving, violent rabble that is to be found, always and everywhere, in every period of acute social confusion . . . These brutal men, with their horrendous faces, their frightening physionomy, their arms bared, their heads uncovered, dishevelled, with cutlasses in hand . . . the *canaille* . . .[19]

This language has a more direct affinity with De Maistre, Taine, Dickens or Carlyle's views of the Parisian *sans culottes* than with the identification of *le peuple* by most European radicals. Indeed, Brigidi's prose could be that of a French clerical writer on the Commune of 1871, but it is not. Its poignance derives from the fact that it is the work, and the opinion, of a nineteenth century Italian liberal, who sill feels himself linked to the events of 1799, still faced by the same enemies and still under the same threat. That this was so, was because the *Risorgimento* had failed.

C: THE INTELLIGENTSIA BESIEGED

The members Italian intelligentsia of a century ago had no doubts about the centrality of the French Revolution to the *Risorgimento*, nor about the relevance of *Novantanove* to their own lives. The legacy of the Revolution had been one of glorious, costly failure, repeated in 1848, of which they were the troubled heirs, none more so than the *pugliese* La Sorsa: 'For us, the Revolution was ill prepared and immature, it was a dream in a few of the best minds [of the times], that was bloodily aborted – at the hands of the people, themselves –

[the people] infantile and ignorant'.[20] For Carabellese, the struggle was between 'ferocious reaction on one side and the heroic liberalism of the patriots on the other'.[21]

To all of them, the Revolution was the first in a series of defeats or half-won victories that link the 1790s, 1821, 1848 and, if not 1860, then the hard years of peasant rebellion, Papal condemnation and local infighting which confronted the next generation of Italian liberals. Carabellese spoke of '. . . the yeast that began to ferment in 1799 rose for the first time in the first half of the next century; only after the bloody catastrophe of 1848, after so many trials – failed and failed again – did it start on the way to being a concrete, accomplished fact'.[22] The cost and reality of *la Révolution à la longue durée* and the relationship between Revolution and *Risorgimento* was real enough to the local *notabili* in the small towns and remote provinces that made up the reality of nineteenth century Italy: the cost of sustaining those links had been heavy, and calcuable in terms that were all too human. Perhaps the last word of all should belong to Benedetto Croce, who lived to face the threat of Fascism, but who still saw *Novantanove* as the Somme of the Italian intelligentsia. In 1948, he wrote that '. . . my personal sympathies are with the precursors of the new Italy and against the defenders of the old order; they are with the flower of meridional intellect, and against obscurantism'.[23] No descent could be longer, stronger, or more direct.

NOTES

1. A. Gramsci, *Sul Risorgimento* (ed. G. Candeloro), (4 edn., Turin, 1975), pp. 29–30.
2. G. Mazzini, 'Fede e Avvenire' (first published in 1835) in *Opere*, (ed. L. Salvatorelli), (Milan, 1967, two vols.), II, pp. 224-30.
3. Mazzini, 'Fede', *Opere*, II, p. 229.
4. Ibid.
5. V. Gioberti, *Del primato morale e civili degli Italiani*, (first published 1843), (Turin, 1932 edn., 3 vols.), I, p. 94.
6. Gioberti, *Del primato*, I, p. 94.
7. The best account is: P. Ginsborg, *Daniele Manin and the Venetian Revolution of 1848–49*, (Cambridge, 1979).
8. B. Croce, *La Rivoluzione napoletana del 1799*, (Bari, 1948).
9. In addition to Croce's own work, some typical examples are: G. De Nino, *I martiri e perseguitati politici di terra di Bari nel 1799*, (Bari, 1915). L. Conforti, *Il 1799 – La repubblica napoletana e l'anarchia regia: narrazioni, memorie, documenti inediti*, (Avellino, 1890). A. De Pra, 'Alcune vittime potentine nel 1800', *La Lucania*, anno 1, no. 22, (Potenza, July, 1862).
10. B. Croce, *Una Famiglia di patriotti (I Poerio)*, (Bari, 1919).

11. F. Carabellese (ed.), *In Terra di Bari dal 1799 al 1806*, (Trani, 1900), Introduction, p. lvi.

12. L. Coppa-Zuccari, *L'Invasione francese negli Abruzzi. 1798–1810*, (l'Acquila, 1927), 4 vols., vol II, pp. 532–47, letters of the Pronio family held in Arcivio privato di L. Coppa-Zuccari, Rome.

13. Coppa-Zuccari, *L'Invasione*, vol II, p. 537.

14. Carabellese, *In Terra di Bari*, pp. xxxv-xxxvi.

15. G. Drei, *Il Regno d'Etruria 1801–1807*, (Modena, 1935), p. 46, note iv.

16. These lists are analysed in G. Vaccarino, 'L'Inchiesta del 1799 sui giacobini piemontesi', *Rivista Storica Italiana*, lxxvii, (1965), pp. 27–73.

17. The standard account of the family in these years is, R. Romeo, *Cavour e il suo tempo*, (Turin, 1974), vol I.

18. S. La Sorsa, *I Moti Rivoluzionari a Molfetta nei primi mesi del 1799*, (Trani, 1903), p. 5.

19. E.A. Brigidi, *Giacobini e realisti, o Viva Maria: Storia del 1799 in Toscana*, (Siena, 1882), p. 11.

20. La Sorsa, *I Moti*, p. 33.

21. Carabellese, *In Terra di Bari*, p. xxxix.

22. Ibid., p. lvii.

23. Croce, *La Rivoluzione*, p. vii.

The French Revolution and English Literary Radicals: the Case of the *Analytical Review*

Brian Rigby

The *Analytical Review* is generally considered to have been the most radical English Review of the 1790s.[1] The first number appeared in May 1788 and it was published by the Unitarian bookseller and publisher Joseph Johnson, who played such a central role in the literary, intellectual and political activities of English Dissenters and radicals in the late 18th century.[2] The *Analytical Review* became closely identified with all the dissenting and radical debates and causes of the 1790s and came to be seen as a major focus of opposition to the government and of sympathy with the French. In 1798 Johnson was, in fact, charged with selling Gilbert Wakefield's *Reply to the Bishop of Llandaff*, which was deemed to be seditious, and he was imprisoned for six months in February 1799.[3] A copy of the *Analytical Review* for September 1798 was also brought forward as evidence against Johnson.[4] Johnson ceased to be the publisher of the *Analytical Review* in December 1798. The *Analytical* limped on into 1799 with another publisher, but ceased publication after the June issue. The demise of the *Analytical* was met with cries of triumph from the *Anti-Jacobin*, which prided itself on having helped to deliver the 'death-blow', and thereby on having rid the country of one of the chief organs of intellectual opposition.[5] In the eyes of the *Anti-Jacobin*, the *Analytical Review* had symbolised the jacobinical, pro-French stance of the intellectual, dissenting class.

I do not here want to go over this ground in any greater detail. We have set ourselves the enormous task of considering the impact of the French Revolution on European consciousness. I wish to concentrate my small efforts on looking, in perhaps rather precise and localised ways, at how the reviewers in the *Analytical* reacted to and dealt with the Revolution. The *Analytical* was founded in May 1788. It therefore began its life in the immediate pre-revolutionary situation, but its reviewers were people who were already deeply involved in liberal and radical causes, and not least in the campaign of Dissenters to have the Test and Corporation Acts repealed. It is, in fact, a Review which seems precisely to embody that coming together of Englightenment and Dissent which was such a characteristic feature of late 18th-century British intellectual life.[6] In enlightened, dissenting circles, the fight for civil and political liberties and for religious freedoms went closely hand in hand with the quest for scientific truth. Joseph Priestley, who was perhaps Joseph Johnson's principal author, was an exemplary figure in this respect. Among enlightened Dissenters there was a certain openness to continental culture, but this openness was definitely tempered by the puritanical elements in the Dissenters' make-up. The Dissenters were always likely to take offence at what they saw as immorality and sexual licence in the behaviour and in the writings of the French. In addition, though Unitarians like Joseph Priestley were pushing orthodox Christian views to the limit, they nonetheless still could not stomach what they saw as the outright 'infidelity' of many French thinkers. The *Analytical* certainly brings together under one heading attitudes which are reminiscent on the one hand of the freedom and daring of advanced, cosmopolitan intellectual circles, and on the other hand of the narrow-mindedness, parochialism and piety of the local Sunday-school.

When we think of English liberal or radical responses to the Revolution, we inevitably think of an initial idealistic 'enthusiasm', an unreserved welcoming of a new dawn, which is seen as ushering in a new society ruled by reason, truth and justice, a society in which all will be regarded as equal. If, as is generally accepted, the *Analytical Review* is the principal radical Review of the time, then one has to say that one finds little evidence of such an initial response of unreserved enthusiasm. This absence of 'enthusiasm' can, I think, be explained by, among other things, the importance attached by the *Analytical* reviewers to the objectives they set themselves of writing scholarly, analytical reviews. It can also be explained by the rational, philosophical stance that the reviewers on the *Analytical* tended to adopt. By looking a little more closely at these questions, I believe one can add something significant to one's understanding of late 18th-century English Dissenters and radicals and of their response to the French Revolution. To a large degree, what I am highlighting could be termed the philosophical or scholarly resistance to the Revolution on the part of English middle-class, intellectual and literary radicals. This is a resistance to the early stages of the Revolution, and not only to the developments from 1792 onwards, since it is well known that English liberal and radical intellectuals were to withdraw some of their sympathy for the Revolution after the September Massacres, the Terror and the invasion of Switzerland. To highlight the 'resistance' of English Dissenters and literary radicals to the early stages of the Revolution might at first seem a rather paradoxical project, but it is one that I feel to be fully justified by the evidence of the *Analytical Review* and of other writings closely related to the *Analytical*. As well as the *Analytical Review*, I shall also draw on two works which deal with the early stages of the Revolution and which are by two writers intimately involved with the *Analytical*. One is *Letters on the Revolution of France* by the co-founder and co-editor of the *Analytical Review*, Thomas Christie, which was published by Joseph Johnson in 1791.[7] The other is by Mary Wollstonecraft, one of the most regular contributors to the *Analytical*,[8] whose *An Historical and Moral View of the Origin and Progress of the French Revolution and the Effect It Has Produced in Europe* was published by Johnson in 1794.[9] However, in choosing to focus on the philosophical resistance to the Revolution, I am not trying to underestimate the impact that the Revolution ultimately had on this whole generation of English intellectuals. What I am trying to do is simply point out aspects of their moral and intellectual make-up which led them to resist the Revolution in important ways, at the same time as they welcomed it. What I am also trying to do is point out that the very nature of periodical literature, and of the *Analytical Review* in particular, fostered this philosophical resistance.

The first volume of the *Analytical Review* contains a prefatory address 'To the Public', written it seems by Thomas Christie, a young Scottish Unitarian who, as already mentioned, was the co-founder of the *Analytical* with Johnson. The *Analytical Review* saw itself as a scholarly publication, characterised by modesty, sobriety and, perhaps above all, a scrupulous attention to impartiality and objectivity in the reviewing of 'literature',[10] understood in the broadest of senses to cover all published material. What, of course, one must remember is that, although the notoriety of the *Analytical Review* is based on its advanced views upon political and religious matters, it did in fact cover an enormous range of topics,[11] including science, medicine, belles-lettres, fine art, travel and agriculture. This encyclopaedic quality of the *Analytical* is in itself not insignificant, when one is wishing to assess the impact of the Revolution, since it gives one the very strong impression that, however important political developments might be, they still occupy only a very small part of the life of the mind. The fact that the *Analytical* had the character of an encyclopaedia, a repository of all available knowledge, also means that, however palpitatingly alive contemporary political events might be, once they enter into the pages of the *Analytical Review*, the energy of these happenings tends to ebb away under the scholarly, contemplative and analytical treatment. This is, perhaps by definition, true of the periodical press in general, and indeed as a scholarly monthly the *Analytical*

Review is most contemptuous of the daily press, which it sees as incapable of offering the truth on contemporary political events, precisely because it does not have the required intellectual distance from these events.[12]

One of the most famous reviewers for the *Analytical* was the artist Henry Fuseli, who had left Switzerland in the early 1760s to come to England, where he was to be a central figure in the Johnson circle, and one of the most important figures in the literary, artistic and intellectual life of the capital.[13] In his review of Coxe's *Travels in Switzerland*, which appeared in the *Analytical* of December 1789, Fuseli can be seen to be chafing against the scholarly atmosphere within which he was moving, and against the scholarly medium of the *Analytical Review* itself. At this point, Fuseli obviously thought that the momentous events happening in France should shake philosophers and scholars out of their customary routines, their habitual serenity and their exclusive absorption in their own scholarly and scientific pursuits:

> Posterity will learn with equal indignation and astonishment that the philoso-
> pher suffered his mind to evaporate with the steams, and to subside with the
> dregs of a crucible; and that the traveller, heedless of his equals, roamed
> either hemisphere in quest of shores and views, or animals and plants, in an
> age pregnant with the most gigantic efforts of character, shaken with the
> convulsions of old, and the emergence of new empires: whilst an unexampled
> vigour seemed to vibrate from pole to pole through the human mind, and to
> challenge the general sympathy.[14]

One has to say that Fuseli differs quite considerably from most of the other reviewers of the *Analytical*. Whereas this European artist was constantly looking for the release of political, aesthetic, psychological and sexual energies from the constraints of lifeless and encasing forms, the other British reviewers, in their rather stuffy and strait-laced way, were desperately trying to discipline and channel any release of energy, and from the beginning feared the prospect of chaos and anarchy that could result from the destruction of old forms. No doubt Fuseli would at this stage have been willing to call his fellow-reviewers 'tame antiquarians',[15] a charge that he levels in the pages of the *Analytical Review* at certain neo-classical aestheticians. The Dissenters were very suspicious of letting go, of being enthusiastic, of losing rational control. They obviously felt a guilt in this, close to the guilt of shameful sexual excitement:

> Nothing produces conviction like passion, – it seems the ray from heaven, that
> enlightens as it warms. – Yet the effect once over, something like a fear of
> having been betrayed into folly clings to the mind it has most strongly

influenced; and an obscure sense of shame lowers the spirits that were wound up too high.[16]

Fuseli, on the other hand, was extremely interested in investigating and expressing the nature of subconscious libidinal forces, and did not recoil from them in fear or shame.

In May 1795, the *Analytical* carried the review of a book entitled *The Scholar armed against the Errors of the Time*, and this seems to me to be an admirable title that could stand for the attitude adopted by the *Analytical Review* and its reviewers towards the French Revolution. The very first notices in the *Analytical* of items relating to the fall of the Bastille reveal a haughty and dismissive attitude on the part of the reviewer. The notices are cursory and the reviewer seems to show a definite contempt for immediate news and for any attempt to consider recent events at such short notice. He clearly believes that such instant historical interpretation is doomed to be either trivial or wrong, because sufficient time has not elapsed to enable a truly scholarly consideration to take place. In fact, the reviewers constantly refuse to treat the Revolution because it is not already history, and because they believe a worthy intellectual treatment of it is not possible. One reviewer in 1792 for instance is still regretting that the events in France are too alive and, therefore, incapable of being considered in an 'abstract' way:

> The late revolution in France is an event that has engaged the attention of all the surrounding nations, and provoked the inquiries of men of letters in most of the states of Europe. It is almost impossible, however, to consider it as an *abstract question* during the present day, for it is immediately connected with the political sentiments of the times, and is but too apt to take its colouring from the prejudices of the human mind. It will afford a noble subject for the pen of some future historian, and for the contemplation of an enlightened posterity.[17]

In the monthly periodical's suspicion of contemporary events, one sees the firm conviction of the reviewers in the rightness of the rational and scholarly stance towards the world. One does also detect, however, the sense of threat posed to this attitude not only by the engulfing and overwhelming significance of the events in France themselves, but also by the intellectual readiness of others to respond to them, as well as by the greater capacity of other journalistic forms to do so. The French Revolution seems, therefore, to have opened up a gap between daily and periodical literature, and between the scholar and the journalist. One certainly senses all these things in the following extract from a review in 1790 of John Talbot Dillon's *Historical and Critical Memoirs of the General Revolution in France in the Year 1789:*

With a purer and more manly style, and greater time for informing himself, and arranging his matter for the information of others, he would have furnished a more acceptable work to the public. The avidity of both readers and venders of books that promise amusement, conspires too often with the impatience of authors, to pre-occupy the market with unripe and unpalatable fruit, which is attended with this further disadvantage, that the number of customers is thereby lessened to him, who keeps back the produce of his vineyard until the proper season. The custom of anticipating the legitimate compositions of real artists, by the awkward attempts of unqualified persons, cannot be too severely stigmatized, as detrimental to the interest of the republic of letters. If the question comes to be, not *how* an event or object is related or described, but *how soon*; if expedition is to be studied rather than excellence, the journals of common sailors, and the orderly books of adjutants and serjeants, will be more encouraged than the most classical compositions, or the discourses of philosophers.[18]

One can see in this passage how, according to the high-minded scholarly stance, the only book upon political events that is worth writing and reading is one that has been maturing over a long period of time and that has, therefore, all the virtues of intellectual distance, political impartiality, deep reflection and careful composition. The reviewer is clearly contemptuous of a world in which 'expedition' is valued rather than 'excellence'. However, one can also see how this reviewer feels that his elite position of scholar is being threatened by upstart journalists ('unqualified persons'), and that the whole cultural world is going to be severely damaged by such a shift in literary power. The reviewer also makes it clear that it is not only the cultural status of the scholar/philosopher that is threatened by such a shift, but that his economic status is also under considerable attack ('the number of customers is thereby lessened to him, who keeps back the produce of his vineyard until the proper season'). The French Revolution clearly had an impact on the 'philosophic mind' of the *Analytical* reviewers, if only to unsettle them in their scholarly and rational stance. However, they did on the whole remain firmly attached to their preferred self-image as 'cool and dispassionate persons',[19] notable for their candour and discernment, and for their refusal to give in to irrational and immoderate enthusiasms, and to the lure and show of the passing events of the contemporary scene. The scientific and scholarly stance is frequently rendered in the pages of the *Analytical* by optical images, which suggest that, whether the spectator of the contemporary scene is scrutinizing political events and political behaviour through the astronomer's telescope, or through the entomologist's magnifying glass, he is nonetheless adhering to his rational, scholarly position and keeping political events at a philosophical distance:

As in optics, there is a certain field of distinct vision, on either side of which objects become obscure, so in contemplating historical events there is a certain period of time, within which they are viewed with the greatest advantage; and, as it is unquestionably true that, in proportion as events are placed beyond the remote limits of this period they become confused, diminish and at last disappear, it is also true, that those events, which are too recent to lie within its nearer limit are always too much blended with other objects, or too deeply tinged with the colouring of temporary interests to be distinctly and accurately observed.[20]

In the *Analytical Review*, as in the writings of other literary radicals of the late 18th century such as William Godwin, Thomas Holcroft and Mary Wollstonecraft, one finds that the highest value is placed on the individual mind of each person, and perhaps above all on that mind's constancy, firmness and autonomy. The individual mind of the rational and enlightened person is taken to be the unswerving and unbending moral point of reference in a world characterised by oppression, injustice, change and possible anarchy. So many of the reviewers of the *Analytical* give the impression that they themselves are equipped with minds of utmost rectitude and firmness, minds which are already deeply imprinted with the knowledge of what is true, just, and reasonable. It is, in fact, *their* minds which appear to set the standards for events and behaviour in the outside world. Not surprisingly, one finds that many of the reviewers, convinced as they are of their own moral integrity, do not talk as if the Revolution has an impact on their consciousness, because their minds are in no need of moral improvement. Nor do their minds need to be inspired with the vision of what the good and true society might be, since they themselves have already had this vision in relation to their own society. Apart from anything else, there is in such attitudes the deep-rooted conviction (a conviction that English radicals shared with conservatives) that England had already gone a long way towards achieving its own democratic revolution in 1688, and that there was, in any case, some quintessential superiority in the English character and mind. The English were thought to be a manly race of independent citizens with resolute minds. The French, on the other hand, were regarded as almost by definition a race of dependent serfs or effeminate pleasure-seekers, whose minds were incapable of attaining autonomy and moral firmness.[21] For the English literary radicals, the French Revolution was, indeed, a 'revolution in the minds of men',[22] but in their view it was the French who needed this revolution and not so much the English, and certainly not the English Dissenters and radicals, who did not consider themselves to be in need of mental or moral regeneration:

Who is so callous to the interest of humanity as to say it was not a noble regeneration? Who is so benumbed by selfish fears, as not to feel a glow of warmth, at seeing the inhabitants of a vast empire exalted from the lowest state of beastly degradation to a summit, where, contemplating the dawn of freedom, they may breathe the invigorating air of independence, which will give them a new constitution of mind.[23]

It is difficult to avoid the conclusion that, in welcoming the French acquisition of independence and freedom of mind, Mary Wollstonecraft is speaking from an assumption that she and the English were already in possession of them. In pointing to a certain closedness and even self-satisfaction in the minds of English radicals, I am stressing what I see as key features of their mentality which in my view help to explain the response to the French Revolution in the pages of the *Analytical Review*. To highlight a closedness of mind in English radicals of the Revolutionary period might, once more, appear rather paradoxical, since these English literary radicals, in fact, always saw themselves as precisely possessing a spaciousness of mind, in contrast to the narrowness of mind which they constantly attributed to the conservative opponents of the Revolution. What such writers as Mary Wollstonecraft and Thomas Christie[24] were saying at this time was that it needed a spaciousness of mind to understand the magnitude of the French Revolution, and that they themselves already possessed such extensive minds, whereas lesser spirits, particularly on the conservative side of politics, were mentally incapable of grasping the significance of the events.

In December 1794, the *Analytical Review* published a review[25] of Mary Wollstonecraft's *An Historical and Moral View of the Origin and Progress of the French Revolution and the Effect It Has Produced in Europe*. In this review, one sees clearly how the English literary radicals mutually congratulate each other on having the extensive minds with which to understand and explain the Revolution:

In contemplating the French revolution, it is not easy to dilate the mind to a full conception of the magnitude of the event. Narrow intellects, incapable of embracing the whole extent of the subject, are lost amidst a confused mass of facts rising in succession with unexampled rapidity. Feeble minds, born away by the instinctive impression of the moment are overpowered with horror at the barbarities which have blackened the scene, and while they ought to think deeply, can only sigh and lament. The selfish and the bigotted – two pretty numerous classes – can only fix their eyes upon those points of the passing scene, which excite alarm for the safety of the ancient, splendid, and lucrative systems of superstition and tyranny.

It is not from such spectators, that the world is to expect that comprehensive survey of the recent events of France, which can alone lead to just estimate of the present interests of neighbouring nations, or to a judicious accommodation of their public measures to the circumstances of the times. Such enlarged views and wise conclusions can only be the result of a diligent and accurate examination of facts, carried on under the direction of a sound judgment, well exercised in the operation of tracking back effects to their causes, an enlightened understanding, amply supplied with correct ideas on the principles of policy and morals, and a liberal spirit, unconfined by national prejudices and warmed by the steady flame of universal philanthropy.

Furnished with these qualifications for the undertaking in a degree which in a woman may appear to male vanity highly astonishing, Mrs. Wollstonecraft has begun an 'Historical and Moral View of the French Revolution.'[26]

One can see here that there was perhaps a significant disagreement in the ranks of *Analytical* reviewers as to the possibility and desirability of undertaking a serious analysis of contemporary political events. However, it is not by any means a disagreement on scholarly values and scholarly approaches, since the values the reviewer esteems above all in Mary Wollstonecraft's writings are what he considers to be precisely her superior scholarly capacities. She can offer a 'comprehensive survey of the recent events of France' because she is said to have in plenty the scholarly qualities of judiciousness, diligence and accuracy. However, what I am principally stressing here is the fact that these radical commentators do not say that their minds have been enlarged by the Revolution, but pride themselves on already having the extensive and comprehensive minds which are needed to understand it.

Mary Wollstonecraft's account of the Revolution in her *An Historical and Moral View* constantly focusses on the breadth of mind possessed by the English radical commentators and on the narrowness of mind possessed by the French 'actors'. The principal criteria which Mary Wollstonecraft adopts for the judgment of the French participants are those related to mental capacities, and chiefly the 'vigour', 'energy', and spaciousness of the mind. Since, for her, moral and mental capacities are inseparable, spacious minds are inevitably rooted in firm, if enlarged, moral principles. Such minds are capable of true, profound and enduring energy. Conversely, small minds are bereft of any moral depth. They are always controlled by the senses, and according to Mary Wollstonecraft they are only capable of a false, shallow and short-lived form of energy. She talks of Marie-Antoinette's 'empty mind', of 'her little portion of mind', and asserts that she had no 'vigour of mind'.[27] Louis XVI is said to be a 'sensual bigot' without 'firmness of mind'. In fact, she talks of the 'watriness of his head'.[28] The whole aristocratic class is also characterised by its indolence of mind and its pursuit of 'sensual refinement'.[29] However, Mary

Wollstonecraft does not only reproach kings, queens and aristocrats for defects of mind. Having been kept for so long in a state of mental subjection, the French population at large do not have the 'cultivated understanding' necessary to push through political action based on reason and morality.[30] Mary Wollstonecraft constantly regrets that those fighting for political freedoms do not have an enlarged moral and rational conception of their actions, and do not embark on their actions with a clear head. She talks of the people having 'irritated minds' and 'inebriated brains',[31] so far were they from the philosophic calm, lucidity and rational control that she valued. She also speaks of the 'fatal presumption of the headstrong French'.[32] In fact, her whole treatment of the course of the Revolution is governed by her view that, in order for the Revolution to attain its true ends of justice, the French needed to be in 'a more advanced state of reason':[33]

> Contemplating the progress of the revolution, a melancholy reflection is produced by observing, that almost every precipitate event has been the consequence of a tenacity and littleness of mind in the political actors.[34]

At the time of the Revolution the French were, in the eyes of Mary Wollstonecraft, still too much a prey to enthusiasm, which she tended to see as a purely physical or irrational state, and one not sufficiently guided and controlled by the mind:

> This effervescence, so contagious, which is after all only physical sensibility, excited by a commotion of the animal spirits, proves that a considerable length of time is necessary to accustom men to exercise their rights with deliberation.[35]

> The remembrance of their former servitude, and the resentment excited by the late struggle to prove they were men, created in their enthusiastic imaginations such a multitude of horrors, and fantastic images of new dangers, as did not allow them to exercise the full powers of their reason.[36]

If the English literary radicals saw the French Revolution as a battle for the minds and in the minds of Frenchmen, it was also, in their view, a conflict which was played out for the minds and in the minds of English people. According to the literary radicals of the *Analytical*, only those with spacious minds could mentally sort out what was truly happening in France, and only they could resist in their minds the excesses of enthusiasm and violence. What is more, only their minds could, as it were, *resolve* the chaotic image of the Revolution into a steady and focussed picture. Thus we have Thomas Christie lamenting the way in which the Revolution has affected the minds of those English people incapable of ordering the anarchy of impressions thrown up by the Revolution:

The French revolution, I perceive, has at the present moment an unhappy effect on the minds of men in this country. When any mention is made of *reform, improvement*, or *change* of any kind whatever, their feeble or frightened imaginations immediately conjure up the horrors of anarchy, riots, mobs, murders, burnings, etc. The present evil then appears as nothing compared to the future possible mischief, for the objects of reality never bear any proportion to the phantoms of a troubled imagination ... The time of this panic will pass away. Men will recover their reason.[37]

Such literary radicals as Thomas Christie seem above all concerned to avoid any interpretation of the Revolution in exaggerated, apocalyptic terms, and constantly bring matters down to a factual, scholarly, and coolly rational approach. As an epigraph to the title-page of his *Letters on the Revolution of France*, Christie penned the following maxim:

Before men launch forth either into the praise or censure of any system, they ought to be sure that they know *what it is*.

This rather deflationary, factual approach seems very typical of the radicals and Dissenters of the 1790s, and certainly of the group associated with the *Analytical Review*. It corresponds to their deep mistrust, not only of enthusiasm, but also of an aesthetic of sublimity, and of anything excessive in the realms of imagination. To be impressed by the sublime is thought by them to be dangerously close to being duped by the false and the flashy. To be impressed is in itself to risk momentarily abandoning one's critical faculties and the rational control of the self, something which the radicals and Dissenters of the 1790s adamantly refused to do. Here, for instance, is Mary Wollstonecraft refusing to be impressed or taken in by ancient classical tragedy:

The sublime terror, with which they fill the mind, may amuse, may delight; but whence comes the improvement? Besides, uncultivated minds are the most subject to feel astonishment, which is often only another name for sublime sensations.[38]

The refusal to be duped and taken in by the sublime and the sensational seems to have governed much of the dissenting and radical reaction to the French Revolution in the pages of the *Analytical Review* and in associated publications. It is not, I believe, a dimension of radical response which has received much comment. I have dubbed this cautious and measured response the philosophical or scholarly resistance to the Revolution. I think it adds something significant to our perception of the radical response to the Revolution to see in it not the uncritical, enthusiastic welcoming of a new dawn, but the cool and 'analytical' scrutiny of it.

NOTES

1. See for example, D. Roper, *Reviewing before the 'Edinburgh' 1788–1802*, (London: Methuen, 1978), p. 178.

2. On Johnson see for example, G.P. Tyson, *Joseph Johnson: A Liberal Publisher*, (Iowa City: University of Iowa Press, 1979); G.P. Tyson, 'Joseph Johnson an Eighteenth-Century Bookseller', *Studies in Bibliography*, vol. 28, (1975) pp. 1–16; L. Chard, 'Joseph Johnson: Father of the Book Trade', *Bulletin of New York Public Library*, vol. 79 (1975), pp. 51–82; L. Chard, 'Bookseller to Publisher: Joseph Johnson and the English Book Trade, 1760 to 1810', *The Library*, vol. 32 (1977) pp. 138–54; P.G. Mann, 'Death of a London Bookseller', *Keats-Shelley Memorial Bulletin*, vol. 15 (1964) pp. 8–12; J.W. Smyser, 'The Trial and Imprisonment of Joseph Johnson, Bookseller', *Bulletin of New York Public Library*, vol. 78 (1974) pp. 418–35; P.M. Zall, 'The Cool World of Samuel Taylor Coleridge: Joseph Johnson, or the Perils of Publishing', *Wordsworth Circle*, vol. 3 (1972) pp. 25–30. See also, D. Erdman, *Blake Prophet Against Empire*, (Princeton: Princeton University Press, 1969); C. Tomalin, *The Life and Death of Mary Wollstonecraft*, (Harmondsworth: Pelican, 1977).

3. J.W. Smyser, op. cit.

4. G.P. Tyson, op.cit., pp. 160–1.

5. G.P. Tyson, ibid., pp. 166 ff; D. Roper, op. cit., p. 179.

6. See the academic journal *Enlightenment and Dissent*, published at the University College of Wales, Aberystwyth.

7. Thomas Christie, *Letters on the Revolution of France and on the New Constitution . . .*, Part I, (London: J. Johnson, 1791). This was the only part ever written. For further details on Christie, see C. Tomalin, op. cit.

8. On her reviewing for the *Analytical*, see R. Wardle, 'Mary Wollstonecraft, Analytical Reviewer', *PMLA*, vol. 62 (1977) pp. 1000–9; D. Roper, 'Mary Wollstonecraft's Reviews', *Notes and Queries*, vol. 203 (1958) pp. 37–8.

9. All my references to this text are to the reprint edition, edited by J.M. Todd, (New York: Scholars' Facsimiles and Reprints, Delmar, 1975).

10. The full title is: *Analytical Review of History and Literature, Domestic and Foreign*.

11. See D. Roper, op. cit., pp. 37–8, on 'the ideal of comprehensive reviewing'.

12. See also Thomas Christie, *Letters on the Revolution*, op.cit., pp. 142–3, for a violent attack on newspapers.

13. On Fuseli, see E.C. Mason, *The Mind of Henry Fuseli*, (London: R. & KP, 1951).

14. *Analytical*, vol. 5 (Dec. 1789) pp. 463–4. Quoted in Mason, op. cit., pp. 183–4.

15. Quoted in Mason, op. cit., p. 216.

16. M. Wollstonecraft, *An Historical and Moral View*, op. cit., pp. 374–5.

17. *Analytical*, App. to vol. 12 (1792) p. 505.

18. Ibid., App. to vol. 7 (1790) p. 505.

19. Ibid., vol. 8 (1790), pp. 303.

20. Ibid., vol. 20 (1794) p. 350.

21. M. Wollstonecraft, *An Historical and Moral View*, op. cit., pp. 510–11.

22. M. Wollstonecraft, *An Historical and Moral View*, op. cit., p. 396.

23. Ibid., p. 81.

24. T. Christie, *Letters on the Revolution*, op. cit., pp. 133–4.

25. *Analytical*, vol. 20 (1794) pp. 337 ff.

26. Ibid., p. 337.
27. Ibid., pp. 133–4.
28. Ibid., p.136.
29. Ibid., pp. 225–6.
30. Ibid., p. 126.
31. Ibid., pp. 85, 89.
32. Ibid., p. 398.
33. Ibid., p. 319.
34. Ibid., p. 300.
35. Ibid., p. 319.
36. Ibid., p. 350.
37. T. Christie, *Letters on the Revolution*, op. cit., pp. 30–1.
38. M. Wollstonecraft, *An Historical and Moral View*, op. cit., p. 228.

'The French are always at it' – the Impact of the French Revolution on Nineteenth Century English Literature, 1815–1870

Andrew Sanders

In one of Dickens's finest periodical essays, 'A Flight', first published in *Household Words* on 30 August 1851,[1] a traveller describes his trip to Paris by train and steam-packet. The speed of the transition from London to Paris by steampower astonishes the traveller who had been accustomed to the slow discomforts of the stage-coach and the diligence; to be able to complete the journey in a day seems a magic worthy of the fantastic flights of the *Arabian Nights*. At the end of the essay the traveller walks the Paris streets at night, wondering at their brilliance, their colour and their animation. This animation strikes him, as it struck so many other nineteenth-century English travellers, as a sharp contrast to the sobriety, the dullness and the universal sootiness of London. In Paris at night life extended out into the streets and into restaurants and cafes. In London Mrs Grundy made sure that Mr Grundy returned from the City to dine in his suburban villa.

This contrast was more than cultural, and is not to be simply ascribed to Parisian taste or Parisian gas-light. Paris might only be a day's journey away, but it remained the epitome of the foreign. It was also a city that had marked the consciousness of most early Victorians from their childhoods up. It had been the seat of the ogre Bonaparte, the son of a Revolution that had changed everything, and the delight many felt in experiencing Paris was partly tinged with the guilt of tasting forbidden fruits. It was both the city of unaccustomed luxury and pleasure and it had been, almost within living memory, the capital of the bloody Republic. It is scarcely surprising that the daughters of a Tory vicarage, Charlotte and Emily Brontë, chose to perfect their French in Villette, the 'little city' of Brussels, rather than in Paris. The boy Ruskin remembered the city for its soft luxury, for red cushions, shiny polished floors and flowers and shrubs in beds and tubs.[2] This image of comfort never seems to have left him and appears to have tainted his view of European history, a view based on the premise that the 'insolent

104

and festering isolation' of Renaissance luxury had 'attained its utmost height' at Versailles, that symbol of aristocratic oppression.[3] Dickens, the future author of *A Tale of Two Cities*, was, however, swept off his feet by his first view of Paris. He spent two days in the city *en route* for Italy in 1844 and found it 'the most extraordinary place in the world'; his eyes ached and his head grew giddy as 'novelty, novelty, novelty' came swarming before him.[4] Twenty years later he allowed Mrs Lirriper to echo his delight in the 'enchantment'.[5] In the first essay of the *Paris Sketch Book* of 1839 Thackeray describes his entrance to Paris via the Faubourg Saint Denis finding 'a strange contrast to the dark uniformity of a London street . . . here is a thousand times more life and colour'.[6]

But forbidden fruit in the form of Revolutionary excess Paris had once been. If the city had been closed to travellers by war during the infancy of the Victorian generation born between 1805 and 1815, it still contained memories of the horrors which were doubtless recounted to them by their parents. Unlike the earlier English generation that found the 1790s a dawn of bliss, the Victorians who first read Wordsworth's *Prelude* in 1850 had a retrospect shaped by the guillotine and 'those September Massacres' as much as by the Napoleonic threat that had overshadowed their childhoods. The six-year-old Thackeray had glimpsed the Emperor on St. Helena in February 1817 and had been told by his black servant that Bonaparte ate 'three sheep every day, and all the little children he can lay his hands on'.[7] Becky Sharp offends the sheepish Amelia by exclaiming 'Vive la France! Vive l'Empereur! Vive Bonaparte!' as she leaves Miss Pinkerton's Academy at Chiswick for, as Thackeray reminded readers of *Vanity Fair*, the teens of the nineteenth century were days when to say 'Long Live Bonaparte' was as much as to say 'Long Live Lucifer'.[8] But then Becky believes, as Mme Defarge was to do, that 'revenge may be wicked, but its natural'. In England, the Revolution, revenge and all, had come to be seen as wicked *tout court*. The admiration for Revolutionary virtue, the heady Republicanism, the bliss of being young in a heaven with a Parisian accent, was no longer current. Time seemed to have judged the passions of the 1790s and the ideals of the 1800s and to have found them wanting. The Revolution was tainted by Jacobinism and Bonapartism, the one a shorthand for bloodletting, the other for sham. When Thomas Arnold stressed to his pupils that if there was a truth for which he would willingly die it was democracy without Jacobinism he was outlining a nobler way. Robespierre was the anti-model, the 'sincere fanatic in the cause of Republicanism' and 'a solemn warning of what fanaticism may lead to in God's world'.[9] Yet, as Thackeray sensed, Bonapartism was no alternative: 'For what have bastilles been battered down, and king's heads hurled, as a gage of battle, in the face of armed Europe? To have . . . Emperor Stork in place of King Log. O lame conclusion!'[10] If we catch an echo of Carlyle's voice here it should scarcely surprise us, for *The French Revolution* of 1837 is the key work in our understanding of how the maturing generation looked back on the 1790s. For Carlyle, who had been born in the same year as Keats, 1795, his History was a means of analysing and of coming to terms with a disturbing pattern of causes and effects and with past events which seemed to have signal relevance for the present.

In Dickens's essay 'A Flight' a fellow-passenger, whom the narrator nicknames 'Monied Interest', bluntly articulates the threat that recent French history seemed to offer. The French, he believes, are 'no go' as a Nation. When asked why this should be so, he replies that 'that Reign of Terror of theirs was quite enough'. The narrator demands to know if Monied Interest remembers anything that preceded the Reign of Terror, and he adds, in a way that both echoes Carlyle and prefigures *A Tale of Two Cities*, that 'the harvest that is reaped, has sometimes been sown'. Monied Interest reiterates 'as quite enough for him, that the French are revolutionary – "and always at it." '[11] Such xenophonic twaddle was not uncommon in Victorian England, and as we know that Mr Podsnap's attitudes were to some extent based on those of Dickens's friend John Forster it is just possible that Forster is also the source for 'Monied Interest'. Dickens, however, subscribes to Carlyle's suggestion that history, French or English, could form a pattern of repetition, an idea which is stated unequivocally in the final chapter of *A Tale of Two Cities*:

> And yet there is not in France, with its rich variety of soil and climate, a blade, a leaf, a root, a sprig, a peppercorn, which will not grow to maturity under conditions more certain that those that have produced this horror. Crush humanity out of shape once more, under similar hammers, and it will twist itself into the same tortured forms. Sow the same seed of rapacious license and oppression over again, and it will surely yield the same fruit according to its kind.

This has often been dismissed as rhetoric. What Dickens wants to stress is that minds (like those of Manette or Thérèse Defarge) distorted by suffering and injustice wreak revenge according to the twists given to them. In a larger sense, so do societies. Dickens is not simply pointing out to the likes of Monied Interest that the restored Bourbons had learnt nothing and forgotten nothing, or that Louis Philippe's reign was one of a sham only outclassed by that of Napoleon III, but that all systems, sham or otherwise, can serve to distort individuals and individual enterprise. The France of the Old Régime and the France of the Revolution had imposed ideologies; the distinction between those ideologies was only a matter of degree, just as the distinctions between the two cities and the two nations of the novel are matters of degree. Restriction leads to distortion and ill-sown seeds to harvests of whirlwinds. Such 'rhetoric' is Carlylean. The ills of early-Victorian England, its slums, its fevers, its Chartism, or Scrooge's horrid vision of the phantom children Ignorance and Want, all seemed to demand an immediate response lest the future suffer the consequences. The history of France could in this way teach a vital lesson.

Dickens knew, as many of his contemporaries knew, that there was a real enough difference between the histories of England and France. From this sense of difference stems much of the ambiguity that we can note in English reactions to the French Revolution. Implicit in much English thinking, both informed and uninformed, was the idea of progress and that somehow England's destiny, if espoused to gradual progressive reform, might still prove to be distinct. The real question always lay in the problem of how benign progress was to be achieved. Dickens, for example, hailed the 1848 Revolution in France as an English liberal. He wrote enthusiastically to John Forster in the February of that year:

MON AMI, je trouve que j'aime tant la République de France . . . Vive la gloire de France! Vive la République! Vive le peuple! Plus de Royauté! Plus des Bourbons! Plus de Guizot! Mort aux traitres! Faisons couler le sang pour la liberté, la justice, la cause populaire! Jusqu'a cinq heures et demi, adieu mon brave! Recevez l'assurance de ma consideration distinguée, et croyez-moi, CON CITOYEN! votre tout devoue, CITOYEN CHARLES DICKENS[12]

This *is* rhetoric and its school-boy French is gushing rather than explorative, but it does suggest that Dickens was prepared to acknowledge that 1848, and for that matter 1830, had proved to be a very different Revolution from that of 1789–99. These bourgeois revolutions were progressive, and they had swept away the 'sham' regimes that the disciples of Carlyle knew how to despise, but, above all, they were free of the earlier excess. The new France was not slipping back into nightmare. Nevertheless, there was a residual unease. Neither Dickens nor Thackeray could quite grasp the complex nature of French responses to their recent history. In January 1847 Dickens went to see a melodrama called 'The French Revolution' at the Cirque in Paris:

In the first act of which there is the most tremendous representation of a *people* that can be imagined. There are wonderful battles and so forth in the piece but there is a power and massiveness in the Mob, which is positively awful.[13]

Dickens had been in Geneva the year before and had there witnessed a mini-Revolution which had astounded him with its 'moderation and mildness'; the Genevan liberals' appeals to the people had no parallel that he knew of in history 'for their real, good, sterling christianity, and tendency to promote the happiness of mankind'.[14] In Switzerland the Genevans were fighting the 'ignorance, misery and bigotry' which Dickens associated with a petty aristocracy and with the encroaching Jesuitry of the Catholic cantons; the struggle was a miniature rehearsal of a liberal bourgeois challenge to the old order; the new order was Protestant, careful, intelligent and safe. Moreover, it was not a Revolution of mobs, blood and ideas. The French melodrama had dramatised the crowd and the play had reawoken in Dickens a deep-seated worry about mob rule (a fear which he had earlier dramatised in *Barnaby Rudge*). Like many of his English contemporaries Dickens could rejoice in the idea of liberty, but would turn away in horror at the thought of fraternity with the mob.

Thackeray's response to a play of 1849 is equally revealing. In the early September of that year he went to see a vaudeville at the Théâtre des Variétés on the Boulevard Montmartre entitled *Les Caméléons, ou soixante ans en soixante minutes*. The drama showed the history of France, from the Revolution to the present in seven scenes, or, as Thackeray himself described it, it was 'a general satire on the last 60 years':

> Everything is satirized, Louis XVI, the Convention, the Empire, the Restoration, & the Barricades, at wh. these people were murdering each other only yesterday – Its awful – immodest – surpassed my cynicism altogether – and at the end of the piece they pretend to bring in the Author, and a little child who can just speak comes in and sings a satiric song in a feeble tender pipe – wh. seemed to me as impious as the whole of the rest of the piece. They don't care for anything – not religion not bravery not liberty not great men not modesty – Ah Madam, What a great moralist somebody is, and what moighty foine principles entoirely he has![15]

Thackeray's self-deprecatory lapse into Irishisms at the end told his correspondent, Mrs Brookfield, that he was worried about posing too long as the moralist, but he clearly *was* offended by the play which had 'all Paris running to it'. It surpassed even his own questioning cynicism about history, heroes and hero-worship, and the undermining of both past and present crises seems to have puzzled and shocked him. For both Dickens and Thackeray the French were coming to terms with their now very fraught history in ways that were not acceptable to Englishmen tutored by Carlyle. They were, as the title of the vaudeville indicates, inclined to be 'chameleon', unstable, unpredictable, changing colour. The matter of tragedy had been used for burlesque, and the proper study of mankind trivialised. If both writers recognised the disparity between the bloody Paris of the Revolution and the city of delights of their own day, they also felt outsiders. They could apply useful morals to their own country, but English experience in many ways blinkered them to the complex reactions of the nineteenth-century French.

The divisions in French society and within French attitudes to recent national history were at variance with the general Victorian perception of English history as a kind of progressive synthesis. An English Reformation had succeeded, so the Reformation was just; an English Revolution may have produced a Restoration, but it was firmly, and sometimes fondly, held that the constitutional crisis had forever chastened the monarchy and fostered the supremacy of a democratic parliament. When Queen Victoria put on fancy dress for a Court Ball in the fashions of George II's reign, as she did in June 1846, it could be dismissed as a whim of high society. When Napoleon III entertained in the costume of the reign of Louis XV in 1858, or when the Empress Eugénie posed for Winterhalter as Marie Antoinette one can sense the relevance of Dickens's fears voiced in *A Tale of Two Cities* in 1859 that the Revolution was a matter of truly contemporary relevance. Something of the French unease can be detected in the work of a painter proclaimed not only by his fellow-countrymen but hailed too by both Dickens and Thackeray, Paul Delaroche (1797–1856).[16] Delaroche's paintings frequently represent English subjects, but they also seem to reflect on French history. His 'Enfants d'Edouard' ('The Princes in the Tower') (Louvre and Wallace Collection), which was described by Thackeray as 'renowned over Europe' having appeared 'in a hundred different ways in print',[17] might just as well represent Louis XVII in the Temple. His 'Cromwell contemplating the body of Charles I' (Nîmes) could be seen as a comment on the fate of Louis XVI. His huge 'Execution of Lady Jane Grey' (National Gallery) might equally respond to the rather less dignified death of Marie Antoinette. If for Delaroche these English executions, murders, and imprisonments were real enough as historical parallels to more recent events in France, they were also likely to appeal to an international market given the new popularity of two British writers who had classically come to terms with history as literature, Shakespeare and Scott. Disaster, division, usurpation and unrest had been assimilated into a mainstream culture through fictional representation. France's disruptions were too recent, too much like open wounds, hence perhaps an explanation of both the more neutral English dimension to Delaroche's painting and the 'cynicism' of the Théâtre des Variétés. France as yet lacked a

Shakespeare to talk it through its monarchic past, a Scott to reconcile it to its Revolution. What is certain is that the French Revolutionary period had produced precious little literature of distinction.

Carlyle was well aware of his place in the British tradition just as he was aware of his real originality as an historian. He was also appreciative of what Scott had done for the writing of history, the revelation that 'the bygone ages of the world were actually filled by living men, not by protocols, state papers, controversies and abstractions of men'.[18] When he took the French Revolution as his subject he was attempting to explain the event that overshadowed his own century and which haunted its darker imaginings as much as its liberal dreams. Essentially Carlyle views the Revolution as a consequence of the moral, economic, political and philosophical shortcomings of the eighteenth century. His first section, or 'part' of the trilogy, is called 'The Bastille' as if that building somehow symbolises the sham of the *ancien régime*, a sham of oppression as much as a comment on the defunct system inherited by Louis XVI. It is a fortress only in name, a gaol for seven deranged prisoners, which like the kingdom collapses under a determined surge of the third estate. The second part, 'The Constitution', describes the consequences of the victory of the third estate and, moreover, of eighteenth-century philosophical and political ideas. The third part is almost inevitably called 'The Guillotine', for here Carlyle describes the collapse of liberal aspirations under the tyranny of the Jacobins and the Paris mob (for whose politics he uses the shorthand 'sansculottism'). The History ends in 1795 with the quelling of the insurrection of Vendémiaire by the young Napoleon, or, as he was later to sum it up, with 'Anarchic government, if still anarchic, proceeding by softer methods than that of continued insurrection'.[19]

In the last paragraph of the History Carlyle sees his narration as 'our relation', the royal possessive embracing the reader as much as the historian himself. He also poses finally in the role of prophet:

> Yet was our relation a kind of sacred one; doubt not that! For whatsoever once sacred things become hollow jargons, yet while the Voice of Man speaks with Man, has thou not there the living fountain out of which all sacredness sprang, and will yet spring? Man, by the nature of him, is definable as 'an incarnate Word.' Ill stands it with me if I have spoken falsely: thine also it was to hear truly. Farewell.[20]

Carlyle is never averse to archaically theeing and thouing his reader, but here his echoes of the Authorised Version are very self-conscious. History, as he insists elsewhere, is a sacred scripture, and the prophetic historian can use it both to teach and to warn. However much this last paragraph might appeal to modern narratological theorists, it is one of the rarer instances in the History where Carlyle is speaking with a single voice rather than shaping his narrative into a mosaic of many voices. The real originality of *The French Revolution* lies not simply in its extraordinary stylistic inventiveness, but in its cacophony of source echoes, citations from eye-witnesses, memoir-writers, correspondents, pamphlet-writers, newspapers, proclamations and speeches. Carlyle may mock what the voices say, he may play and replay with their words, he may interchange French and English, but he nevertheless relies on the cumulative effect of these voices. Only in his great set-piece descriptions does his own narrative voice dominate. He is scarcely an unprejudiced narrator, but given his conviction that the Revolution constantly teetered on the edge of chaos, he can create fascinating effects out of the self-contradictory and sometimes anarchic nature of his sources. *The French Revolution* is history as nineteenth-century prose epic, not history as analysis.

Carlyle clearly disconcerted as many readers as he impressed. In his review of the book in the *Times* on 3 April 1837 Thackeray found London opinion divided in a 'strange storm of applause and discontent':

> To hear one party you would fancy the author was but a dull madman, indulging in wild vagaries of language and dispensing with common sense and reason, while, according to another, his opinions are little short of inspiration, and his eloquence unbounded as his genius.[21]

Clearly troubled himself by these 'vagaries of language' Thackeray finds himself agreeing with both parties. He ends, though, acknowledging the genius of the argument and of the style of the argument. More interestingly, he draws his own 'timely' and conservative lesson from the prophetic narrative:

> The hottest Radical in England may learn by it that there is something more necessary for him even than his mad liberty – the authority, namely, by which he retains his head on his shoulders and his money in his pocket, which privileges that by-word 'liberty' is often unable to secure for him. It teaches (by as strong examples as ever taught anything) to rulers and to ruled alike moderation, and yet there are so many who would react the same dire tragedy, and repeat the experiment tried in France so fatally . . . Pert quacks at public meetings joke about hereditary legislators, journalists gibe at them, and moody starving labourers, who do not know how to jest, but can hate lustily, are told to curse crowns and coronets as the origin of their woes and their poverty, – and so did the clever French spouters and journalists gibe at royalty, until royalty fell poisoned under their satire; and so did the screaming

hungry French mob curse royalty until they overthrew it: and to what end? To bring tyranny and leave starvation, battering down Bastilles to erect guillotines, and murdering kings to set up emperors in their stead.[22]

Thackeray sees *The French Revolution* as a tract for the times and a survey of modern ills. As he interprets Carlyle's message, revolution from below would lead to universal unhappiness, for, as France demonstrated, the have-nots remain with nothing after toppling those who have too much, and he refers to power as much as to worldly goods. Only in America did a Revolution achieve anything, for there the participants already had an economic stake in their country's future. For Thackeray as much as for Carlyle, class-struggle leads inevitably to class-tyranny. It is easy to guess from this review why Thackeray responded so whole-heartedly to the publication of Macaulay's *History of England* and why he contemplated extending it into the reign of Queen Anne after Macaulay's untimely death. Thackeray is disturbed not simply by Carlyle's bombast, but also by the implications of his subject. Macaulay's observation of the progress of the English Revolution charts a happier and far less violent series of events; it offered an explanation of the democratic destiny of an England blessed above France from the very nature of its parliamentary system and its tested Constitution.

When Dickens noted in his 1859 Preface to *A Tale of Two Cities* that he could not hope to 'add anything to the philosophy of Mr Carlyle's wonderful book' he was assuming that his readers recognised that there *was* a philosophy in *The French Revolution*. Dickens, who once claimed to have read the work five hundred times, evidently subscribed to the theory of history he found in it.[23] Certainly, he shared Carlyle's distaste for all things eighteenth-century and especially for a rigid class-system and a culture based on aristocratic privilege. The absence of any discussion of the principles of the Revolution in his novel may also derive from a reliance on the authority of Carlyle's history (Darnay, for example, may be a principled exile from the *ancien régime*, but he seems to have no opinions as to the validity of its replacement and he returns to France in 1793 only out of a sense of obligation to a former servant). Carlyle is far more impressive as a delineator of anarchy than he is as an analyst of ideas. His intolerance of eighteenth-century intellectuals and theorists is quite glaring. He opens his narrative with a description of the 'Paper Age' at the beginning of the reign of Louis XVI, a Paper Age because it is so far from a Golden Age, but Paper too because a bankrupt economy produces paper money and speculates in shares, but Paper above all because it theorises on paper. It is the age of 'Philosophe-Sentimentalism' and of 'Windbags', and it is, above all, the age of Rousseau and 'Theories of Government! Such have been, and will be; in ages of decadence.'[24] This distaste for all theory, and for the 'Age of Reason' in general, seems to stem from the belief that both together fathered rigidity in a Revolutionary generation. The idea of Liberty, once applied, proved inconsistent with real liberty. This too is reflected in *A Tale of Two Cities* as the 'leprosy of unreality' which infects the party gathered at Monseigneur's levee in Book II Chapter VII. Here we meet 'Projectors who had discovered every kind of remedy for the little evils with which the State was touched except the remedy of setting to work in earnest to root out a single sin' and 'Unbelieving Philosophers' who are 'remodelling the world with words, and making card-towers of Babel to scale the skies with.'

Dickens may have sought, as he later told Bulwer-Lytton that he did, to show Darnay as a representative of 'the time coming in', but he is far from a representative of the late eighteenth-century intellectual ferment.[25] The same could not be said of the central characters in Bulwer's own extraordinary novel *Zanoni* of 1842. In a note – '*Zanoni* Explained' – appended to the 1853 edition of the novel, he types his characters according to their dominant intellectual bent as if they were 'humours' in a Jonson play. Glyndon, the English aristocrat drawn into the circle of mystics at the centre of the story, is described as 'UNSUSTAINED ASPIRATION', for his desire to follow instinct is deterred by his (very English) 'Conventionalism'. The Rosicrucian Zanoni, by contrast, stands for 'Contemplation of the Ideal – IDEALISM. Always necessarily sympathetic'. Despite his fascination with the more spurious mystical ideas of the eighteenth century and with the culture which had variously produced Cagliostro and Mesmer, Bulwer is unswerving in his condemnation of the coming Revolution. He tells us in the second chapter of Book II ('Art, Love and Wonder') that this part of the novel is set in 'the period, when a feverish spirit of change was working its way to that hideous mockery of human aspirations, the Revolution of France'. Once the story moves to the Paris of the Terror in Book VII the point is made even more emphatically:

It roars – the River of Hell, whose first outbreak was chanted as the gush of a channel to Elysium. How burst into blossoming hopes fair hearts that had nourished themselves on diamond dews of the rosy dawn, when Liberty came from dark ocean and the arms of the decrepit Thraldom – Aurora from the bed of Tithon! Hopes! ye have ripened into fruit, and the fruit is gore and ashes . . . wits, philosophers, statesmen, patriots, – dreamers! behold the millenium for which ye dared and laboured.[26]

The Revolution itself represents a rock on which idealism founders, a disaster which nearly destroys the innocent heroine and which claims her husband, Zanoni, Carton-like, in her stead.

Zanoni is, despite its ambitions and its intellectual daring, an awkward, laboured and often turgid book. It is unlikely to enjoy a place even in a drastically revised canon of Eng. Lit., something which could no longer be observed of Fanny Burney's last novel which appeared in its first and only edition to date in 1814. *The Wanderer: Or Female Difficulties* was begun in France in 1802 when the D'Arblays had taken the opportunity provided by the Peace of Amiens to return to Paris. The unfinished manuscript was brought back to England in 1812, with, as the author notes, no problems on either side of the Channel from spies or Customs officials. Like Bulwer, Fanny Burney dramatises her story by contrasting opinions and aspirations. Her discussion of the Revolution is by means of a series of characters, English, French and Anglo-French, all of whom have fled from the Terror. From a standpoint of 1814 she looks back on 'a period, which completely past, can excite no rival sentiments, nor awake any party spirit; yet of which stupendous iniquity and cruelty . . . have left traces that handed down even but traditionally, will be sought with curiosity, though reverted to with horror from generation to generation.'[27] Burney's discussion of her refugees essentially divides between the virtuous Juliet, known under the pseudonym of 'Ellis', the victim of the upheaval in France and of sexism and snobbery in England, and Elinor, an English proto-feminist, infected with Jacobin enthusiasm. The 'Female Difficulties' of the sub-title are effectively those of Juliet, the Wanderer, and Elinor's ideas offer her no consolation or support. Here too we have a contrast of 'sense' and 'sensibility' in which the impulsive Elinor will attempt suicide and will ruin her life over a miscalculated love-affair. She is 'inebriated' with the 'revolutionary beverage', proclaiming that 'this glorious epoch, that lifts our minds from slavery and from nothingness into play and vigour . . . leaves us no longer, as heretofore, merely making believe that we are thinking beings'.[28] Later, Elinor sees France and its Revolution as a phoenix raised from the ashes of an old and consumed world. She rejects religion as much as she rejects convention, though she remains as assured as Shelley in her aristocratic security and superiority. It is the oft-rejected Juliet who hungers and suffers but who is finally vindicated. It is she who judges the now isolated Elinor in the fifth and last volume:

> When Elinor, who possesses many of the finest qualities of the mind, sees the fallacy of her new system; when she finds how vainly she would tread down the barriers of custom and experience, raised by the wisdom of foresight, and

established, after trial, for public utility; she will return to the habits of society, and common life, as one awakening from a dream in which she has acted some strange and improbable part.[29]

This 'awakening', is, one assumes, also that of France, shaking off revolutionary excess and returning to the comity of nations. In this sense Juliet's words uncannily echo a much more famous fictional comment on the distraction of the Revolution, Sydney Carton's vision of a new Paris from the steps of the guillotine.

Carton looks forward to 'a beautiful city and a brilliant people rising from this abyss, and, in their struggles to be truly free, in their triumphs and defeats, through long years to come.' Carton had earlier seen Paris as a city under the enchantment of some evil spirit, and awaiting a new charm to free it. It is an extraordinary twist to the idea of a magic, Arabian Nights' city of 'A Flight', but it does express something of the sense of inconsistency and incongruity that many Victorians felt in comparing the Paris of the present with the Paris of the recent past. Dickens's unease with this historical swing between the 'best of times' and the 'worst of times' may be individual but it was also shared by many other English writers who addressed the sense of disconnection which was readily inspired by a contemplation of the Revolution.

NOTES

1. 'A Flight' was collected with other articles in *Reprinted Pieces* in 1868. Quotations are from *The Uncommercial Traveller and Reprinted Pieces* (Oxford Illustrated Dickens), pp. 474–84.

2. John Ruskin, *Praeterita. The Works of John Ruskin* (Library Edition) ed. E.T. Cook and A. Wedderburn (39 vols. 1903–12), Vol. 35 pp. 104–5.

3. *The Stones of Venice, The Works of John Ruskin* (Library Edition), Vol. 11, p. 80.

4. Letter of 7 August 1844, *The Letters of Charles Dickens* (Pilgrim Edition), Vol. 4, (ed. Kathleen Tillotson), p. 166.

5. *Mrs Lirriper's Legacy* (1864), *Christmas Stories* (Oxford Illustrated Dickens), p. 422.

6. *The Paris Sketch Book* (1840), (The Oxford Thackeray ed. George Saintsbury), p. 10.

7. Quoted by Gordon N. Ray in his *Thackeray: The Uses of Adversity 1811–1846* (1955), p. 66.

8. W.M. Thackeray, *Vanity Fair* (1846–7), Chapter 2.

9. Arthur Penryn Stanley, *Life of Thomas Arnold DD* (Popular Edition 1904), p. 409.

10. *Paris Sketch Book*, p. 137.

11. 'A Flight', p. 477.

12. Letter of 29 February 1848. *The Letters of Charles Dickens* (Pilgrim Edition), Vol. 5 (ed. Graham Storey and K.J. Fielding), pp. 256–7.
13. Ibid., pp. 19–20.
14. Ibid., p. 20.
15. Letter of 4–6 September 1849. *The Letters and Private Papers of William Makepeace Thackeray* (Collected and Edited by Gordon N. Ray), Vol. 2, p. 588.
16. Dickens admired his fresco in the Palais des Beaux Arts as 'the greatest work of art in the world' (Pilgrim *Letters* 5. p. 37). Thackeray praised Delaroche's draughtmanship in *The Paris Sketch Book*, p. 51.
17. *The Paris Sketch Book*, p. 51.
18. Thomas Carlyle, 'Sir Walter Scott', *Critical and Miscellaneous Essays* (1899), Vol. 4, p. 77.
19. This 'summary' was added to the 2-volume edition of 1857.
20. Thomas Carlyle, *The French Revolution* (2 Vols. 1857). Vol. 2, p. 376.
21. W.M. Thackeray, *The Yellowplush Papers and Early Miscellanies* (Oxford Thackeray), pp. 67–78.
22. Ibid., p. 67.
23. Letter of July 1851. *The Letters of Charles Dickens* (Nonesuch Edition), Vol. 2, p. 335.
24. *French Revolution* (1857 ed.) Vol. 1, pp. 31, 39, 43.
25. Letter of 5 June 1860. Nonesuch *Letters*, Vol. 3, p. 162.
26. Edward Bulwer-Lytton *Zanoni* (New Knebworth Edition), pp. 362–3.
27. Fanny Burney, *The Wanderer: Or, Female Difficulties*, 5 vols. (1814), 'Dedication to Dr. Burney', pp. xiii-xiv.
28. Ibid., Vol. 1, pp. 1, 18.
29. Ibid., Vol. 5, pp. 370–371.

The French Revolution in Spain and the Art of Goya

N. Glendinning

Few Spaniards were positively in favour of the French Revolution at the time of its occurrence. The enthusiastic reception of men like the Abbé Marchena and Santiago Miguel Rubín de Celis seems to have been exceptional,[1] and the Spanish Government's response was predictably negative, long before the lives of the French Bourbons were at stake. The Conde de Floridablanca, the chief minister, expressed his reservations in a much quoted letter to the Spanish ambassador in Paris, the Count Fernán-Núñez: 'I fear these developments and sympathise with the good king [of France] and his ministers. I also sympathise with the French people, fickle and frivolous and impulsive as they are. It is said that the Age of Enlightenment has made men aware of their rights. But it has also deprived them of true happiness, peace of mind, the safety of their persons and the security of their families. We are not in favour of so much Enlightenment in Spain, nor of the effects that come in its train: opposition through actions, and spoken and written words, to legitimate authority'.[2]

Despite the sense that an anti-revolutionary stance was generally maintained in Spain, Goya himself has long been associated with subversive and, to some extent, revolutionary attitudes. Initially it was thought that such a position was a natural consequence of the artist's class background and his supposedly peasant origins. And although the factual basis for this view has long since been called into question – his mother's family, the Lucientes, were rural *hidalgos* or petty nobles, and his father's on the fringes of the urban professional classes with a certain potential for upwards mobility – the idea of a revolutionary Goya persists. There have been serious assessments of the ideological implications of Goya's work that have shown the artist in a convincingly democratic light. Some fiction about him has fleshed out a similar line imaginatively, and his portrait group of *The Family of Charles IV* has often been thought to mock the Spanish monarchy. Although this is a view that not all critics share, there is every reason to look at the impact of the French Revolution on Goya's world again.

The consequences of the Spanish Government's fear of the Revolution are well known. Censorship of the press and a reactivated Inquisition helped Floridablanca to put in place what he himself called a *cordon sanitaire* to protect the country from political fevers in the 1790s.[3] Already in 1789 the Inquisition declared the revolutionary ideas of the French criminally heretical. A Royal Order of January 1790 banned all 'books, papers, engravings, boxes, fans, and other items which refer to or represent the revolutions which have occurred in France'. This was followed by other edicts against seditious writing in September 1791. The censors were wary of indirect sources of ideological contagion as well as direct ones. In December 1791, for instance, the *Diario de Física de París*, a scientific periodical, was prohibited. The edict suggested that advocates of the separation of political powers were not content with blatantly inflammatory publications, but also 'spread their maxims and ideas in works that are apparently unconnected with Religion, Morals and Politics'.[4] As the revolutionary process developed, controls were tightened. A close watch was kept on books being printed in Spain, as well as on the manuscripts submitted to the Council of Castile for a licence to publish. In November 1793, José Colón de Larreátegui wrote to complain about a translation of a *Life of Gustavus of Sweden* currently at press in Madrid. He stated that the work was 'opposed to all monarchical government, to hereditary monarchy, to the power of kings and to the obedience of vassals'.[5] The work was duly seized and its publication prevented.

During the period of the war between France and Spain from 1793–1796, there were still moments when the King's ministers felt threatened by dissident views deriving from France. And after the war a number of factors led to a recrudescence of censorship measures. In January 1798 there was an edict to ensure that banned books were physically removed from the premises of booksellers, and 'conversations in bookshops attacking the political constitution of Spain' were also forbidden.[6] Then two Royal Orders in June and July 1799 were designed to ensure that priests did not refer 'to French forms of Government', or related matters, in sermons.[7] A marked rise in the cases of capital punishment in Madrid at the end of the decade reinforces the broad sense of a crisis in law and order.[8] Fear of influential reformers is reflected in the removal from power, and condemnation to exile or imprisonment, of politicians like Jovellanos and Saavedra, both of whom were painted by Goya at that time.

The *cordon sanitaire*, in politics as in public health, is evidence of an epidemic, but does not guarantee freedom from infection. The measures taken by the government tend to suggest that radical ideas and revolutionary attitudes had indeed penetrated into Spain in the wake of the French upheaval. There is archival evidence to support this view; evidence, furthermore, that revolutionary ideology did not take long to reach people of different social classes in Spain. At the present time there is information about a number of minor revolutionary episodes in Spain in the 1790s, some clearly inspired by the French model. There was a disturbance in the Rioja area in August 1793, for instance.[9] Some fifty people took to the streets in a village called Alesanco and marched to the neighbouring town of Torrecilla (now San Isidoro near Nájera in the province of Logroño). They carried clubs and other weapons, proclaimed 'French freedom and equality', and also wanted a representative body like the French Constituent Assembly of 1789 since they shouted 'Asamblea'. The rioters were almost certainly peasant in background, although the son of a pharmaceutical chemist ('boticario') was amongst the accused later. The fact that the orchards and vineyards of wealthier members of the community were attacked and fruit robbed suggests that a combination of class feeling and hunger lay at the root of the disturbances, while the relative proximity of the French border explains the bouquet of French ideology. Another known revolutionary effort inspired by the French example in Spain in the 1790s was very different in character. It was planned by middle-class intellectuals under the leadership of a writer on educational topics called Juan Antonio Picornell.[10] His group, which was active in 1795, made efforts to buy support in rural communities, although the base of their revolutionary conspiracy was in Madrid itself. Disillusionment with Charles IV was by that time well established and there was disquiet at Godoy's style of life and manipulation of power in the capital. Picornell no doubt hoped to build on the growing urban opposition and resentment towards Godoy and the sense of unsolved economic problems in rural areas.

These two revolutionary attempts give evidence of an ideological awareness that is missing in other Spanish disturbances in the 1790s. But there is other testimony in relation to the radical debate in Madrid and elsewhere at the period. Discussions in intellectual circles were recorded by Manuel Belgrano, for instance, and the impact of the French Revolution is reported in his *Autobiography*. 'I was in Spain in 1789,' the Argentinian general writes, 'and the French Revolution led to changes in ideas there too, particularly amongst men of letters with whom I was acquainted. In consequence ideas of freedom, equality and property had a great impact on me. I protested at the tyranny of those who opposed the rights of man, given by God and Nature in the first place, and confirmed by society subsequently. When I completed my studies, around 1793,

theories of political economy were rife in Spain'.[11] Additional
evidence that the ideology behind the French Revolution reached
further than the bourgeoisie in Spain, comes from documents dated
November 1794, signed by a French Dominican living in exile in
Madrid, Jean-Jacques Dauga.[12] Dauga wrote to Godoy with helpful
suggestions deriving from his experience of the French situation. He
warned the Spanish Government against complacency and recom-
mended steps to raise money, improve security and enhance the royal
image in Spain. He implied that court expenditure had been strongly
criticised in Spain (as in pre-revolutionary France) and that open
discussion of libertarian ideas had already made considerable
headway in the Peninsula, more especially in Madrid. He advocated a
periodical publication for religious and political propaganda to offset
ideas being advanced at gatherings in the Puerta del Sol and the Calle
de Montera. Antidotes were evidently still required eight years later
when Gregorio González Azaola spoke of 'the need to eradicate a
thousand false ideas, adopted without due consideration during the
Revolution; the necessity to refute once and for all the audacious
opinions on complex questions of morality and politics, which have
spread through the whole of Europe during the last few years,
encouraging the overthrow or destabilisation of ruling monarchs'.[13]

Of the views mentioned so far, only those of González Azaola come
directly from a person close to Goya's circle. At the period in question
he was Professor of Chemistry to the royal pages, and in 1811 he was
to write the first serious review of Goya's *Caprichos*. France's change of
attitude to religion with the Concordat of 1801 appears to have
rendered Spain's neighbour respectable in his eyes. Other
acquaintances of Goya undoubtedly shared a partly favourable view
of revolutionary France.

Only one of Goya's friends, Leandro Fernández de Moratín, was a
direct witness of any part of the Revolution. During his period in
Paris in 1792 he saw the disturbances in the capital on the 9th
August.[14] The following day Moratín visited the Tuileries, found
buildings sacked, and statues of Louis XIV and XV pulled down. In
some of the streets he saw heads on pikes and his diary records his
feelings of terror. Moratín was undoubtedly a source of information
and radical ideas for Goya in the 1790s and early 1800s. His writing is
both implicitly and explicitly against tyranny. He criticized egois-
tical parents in his plays and was indignant about the poor in Naples,
whose deplorable state stemmed from the fact that they were the
'property' of the rich and powerful. In his account of his stay in
London, Moratín reports attending a banquet for 'Friends of the
Freedom of the Press'; he also collected satirical prints that mocked
the British Royal Family, recorded English appeals for constitutional
reform, and read Tom Paine's *Rights of Man*.[15]

Moratín was probably more responsive to French ideology than most other close friends of Goya in the 1790s. In 1793 he had visited a Jacobin club in Lucerne according to his *Diary*, and in 1808 he was to be a supporter of Joseph Buonaparte and the revolutionary possibilities of his regime. Jovellanos, on the other hand, an influential patron as well as a friend of Goya, was rather more cautious. He wrote critical comments in relation to the Revolution in France in his diaries and his letters and wanted a more gradual and peaceful change in Spain.[16] He was confident, in fact, of the ultimate ability of Reason and Enlightenment, through the channels of education, to achieve the right climate for political reform and economic progress. At the same time Jovellanos was certainly shocked by the despotic aspects of Godoy's regime and the corruption that accompanied it. Equally he wanted to broaden land ownership, had no time for the idle nobility, and was worried by the impact of taxation on the poor. In a satire he warned nobles that they might see their land revert to 'infame behetría' (meaning either 'primitive confusion' or the medieval system whereby the common people could select their own overlords).[17] Yet it is by no means clear that Jovellanos was prepared to eliminate class structures altogether.

On the fringes of Goya's circle, if not among his closest friends, there were certainly some who supported the ideals of the French Revolution. The most obvious case is that of the poet Manuel Quintana, who played an important political role during the Peninsular War. Quintana gave Goya a copy of his poems, and in about 1805 wrote an ode to him. Poet and artist were both connected with the Duchess of Alba's circle, and the two of them put pen to paper to celebrate her adoption of a negro girl: Goya in a drawing and Quintana in verse. Since both are likely to have spent time in the Albas' summer palace at Piedrahita in the province of Avila, there is every reason to suppose that Goya and Quintana knew one another reasonably well, even if there is no evidence at present that their friendship was intimate.

Quintana's writings reveal the positive character of his response to the French Revolution. In 1810 in Cadiz he recalled the cry of liberty on the banks of the Seine twenty years previously. 'The heart of good people everywhere', he wrote 'beat with joy as it heard the beneficial echoes of that precious cry. How could one not but feel delight at the banner of Goodness raised in the wind, driving vice and all the abuses and errors of degraded humanity before it'.[18] But Quintana did not wait twenty years before expressing his views about radical change in France. And several poems written in the late 1790s and early 1800s reflect his response. The first of these was the ode addressed to the leader of an uprising against Charles

V in the sixteenth century, 'Juan de Padilla'. This poem praised the
pursuit of 'honour, constancy and liberty', criticised despotism, and
celebrated the sense of brotherhood and freedom of the sixteenth-
century rebels. The figure of Padilla subsequently returned in
another poem by Quintana in which he again expressed sympathy
towards revolutionary ideas: 'El Panteón del Escorial' (April 1805).
But the clearest echo of French ideology occurs in Quintana's 'Ode
on the Invention of the Printing Press'. Written in 1800 the poem
was published in a bowdlerized version in 1802, and only circulated
in print in its original form in 1808.[19] In it the major contribution of
the press falls in the area of politics and morality: the destruction of
tyranny and slavery, and the introduction of Liberty and Equality.

Despite efforts to keep it out, information about the facts of the
French Revolution and the strands in its ideology spread in Spain.
In Goya's circle there were those who opposed revolution such as
Jovellanos, and others like Moratín and Quintana who spoke in
favour of radical change and revolutionary principles when the
relaxation of censorship allowed. The position of a third group,
including González Azaola, is more difficult to determine. By
implication, however, they probably supported some aspects of the
French Revolution while rejecting others.

It is time to turn briefly to another potential source of social and
political ideology to which Goya certainly had access: publications
of the period in Spain that express Liberal views, some of them
close to revolutionary ideas deriving from France. Of special
interest in the present context are changing attitudes to the
monarchy itself, opposition to the privileges and power of the
aristocracy, conceptions of equality and human rights, and generally dissident postures.

So far as the monarchy is concerned in Spain, there is a
perceptible shift in attitude in works of literature between the 1770s
and the 1790s.[20] In writers active in the 1770s there is moral
criticism of the conduct of monarchs, criticism of kings whose
personal ambition is detrimental to their people, and some questioning of the traditional view that kings ruled by Divine Right and
could do no wrong. In a play by Jovellanos from that period there is
criticism of the king's advisers, and a quarrel with royal edicts that
introduce laws imperfectly related to national character and not in
accord with 'l'esprit des lois'.[21] On the other hand, there is
certainly condemnation of *popular* uprisings against bad monarchs,
even if dramatists uphold the right of *aristocrats* to draw attention to
their ruler's moral shortcomings. By contrast, plays of the 1790s
and notably those of Cienfuegos are more sharply critical of
monarchs of a despotic, ambitious and aggressive type. There is a
greater concern for the will of the people, and an underlying sense

of the importance of public opinion in relation to political conduct. Public opinion, indeed, was a relatively new concept so far as Spain was concerned at the period. The term seems to have arrived there in the modern sense (presumably on the basis of French usage) precisely in the 1790s. Another striking development in Cienfuegos' plays at the end of the century is the contrast in his *Pítaco* (1799), between a ruler who is elected (wise, unambitious, and concerned for the general good) and a hereditary monarch (who believes in absolute power, the achievement of personal wealth and other ambitions).[22] No work reflects more clearly the growing importance of the collective will and the desire for new constitutional structures.

The broader issue of rights and privileges surfaces more frequently in legal and economic texts than in literary discourse. There are particularly interesting overtones in the debate on torture in Spain, since *hidalgos* and aristocrats were exempt from torture there.[23] The question of aristocratic privileges also arises in the area of taxation, because nobles were exempt from certain taxes. A particularly cogent assault was made on their privileges by Vicente Alcalá Galiano in a Discourse written for the Economic Society in Segovia in 1783. Alcalá Galiano argued that the rich should pay more than the poor in the future. 'Are not the lives and estates of those of you who are Nobles much more consciously protected by the State than those of the poor?' he asks. 'Do you not benefit from a thousand privileges and exemptions, whilst the less fortunate suffer an equal number of tax and other burdens? Do you not enjoy the better paid posts in the country? Are you not almost entirely free from punishment in the minor criminal offences? And finally, are not the sacred balances of Astrea constantly tilted in your favour on account of your social status?'[24]

There is a deep sense of injustice and inequity in this attack on privilege. It is more radical than the criticism of absentee landowners and of those aristocrats who are not useful to society, which is common in Spanish literature in the second half of the eighteenth century.

A desire for greater social equality is also reflected in literature at the period, more particularly in an anonymous Utopian narrative published in Spain in 1790. This was the *Treatise on the Columbian Monarchy (Tratado sobre la monarquía columbina)* – Columbian from pigeon, not from Columbus – which was printed in a periodical called the *Semanario erudito* that commenced publication in 1787.[25] A number of friends of Goya were subscribers, including in Madrid Jovellanos, Antonio Valdés y Bazán and Tadeo Bravo de Rivero, and in Cadiz, Sebastián Martínez. This fiction is more particularly worth mentioning in the present context because it contains an ironic reference to revolution as a means of changing society.

The *Treatise* is a mixture of Utopian narrative and beast fable. The setting is the kingdom of birds, rather than men, and the anonymous author contrasts the peace-loving, sociable nature of the doves with the aggressive self-interest of birds of prey. The latter have introduced hierarchy as well as aggression into bird society and are clearly identified with the aristocracy.

The doves' solution to their problems, as slaves and victims of predatory hawks and falcons, is migration. They fly to some woods near the City of the Sun ruled over by the Phoenix, from whose kingdom birds of prey were excluded. Initial chapters describe minor as well as major ideological conflicts, but the socio-political core of the story comes in Chapter 3, when the constitution of the new kingdom is promulgated. There were to be no classes or privileges, no property, no legal institutions, very few laws and even fewer lawyers. But there would be religious beliefs, and education. Parents were to be chiefly responsible for the latter, and they were also to be answerable for the crimes of their offspring. Education was to be social and religious (or ethical), and would not involve other branches of learning. The most serious crime would be disrespect for parents.

Evidently there are conservative elements in this Utopian programme. The authority of Gods and Fathers is not called into question. Ultimately, however, there is an underlying pessimism about human nature and society that leads to an ironic ending. In the last chapter, five hundred years on, the doves suddenly become lax, enjoy too much freedom and turn presumptuous. Finally, in the wake of the death of the Phoenix, birds of prey are readmitted by the new ruler. The more powerful birds re-establish aristocratic privileges, gain control of land belonging to the doves, build up legal institutions, academies and universities, reintroduce taxes. An innocent bird, who feels that happiness can only be achieved by destroying all these structures and institutions, is put to death.

Goya clearly lived in an environment in which many establishments and hierarchies were questioned. What was his own position?

Of obvious interest in the present context are those of his paintings which focus on class differences. Some of them place the rich and poor side by side in apparent harmony, and seem to make no comment. Others view the same juxtaposition with an evident irony, that certainly draws attention to class differences and implies a sense of injustice. The early tapestry cartoons, above all, provide examples of the uncritical, non-egalitarian posture, and they were produced by the artist when he was dependent on royal patronage and executing works of art designed for palace apartments. These had to follow the conventions of the genre and create an image of a

Plate 1   *Winter* Tapestry cartoon, 1786–87
Madrid, Prado Museum

All works reproduced are by Francisco de Goya (1746–1828)

Plate 4 *Pr Liberal?* (For being a liberal?) Sepia wash, *c.* 1814–20

Plate 2 *Caprichos 39 Asta su Abuelo* (Back to his grandfather), 1797–98

Si son de otro linage

Plate 3 *Disasters of War* 61 *Si son de otro linage* (They belong to a different class) *c.* 1812–15

Contra el bien general.

Plate 5 *Disasters of War* 71 *Contra el bien general* (Against the common good) *c.* 1815–20

Plate 6 *Disasters of War 74 Esto es lo peor!* (This is the worst of all!) *c.* 1815–20

Plate 7 *Disasters of War* 78 *Se defiende bien* (He defends himself well) *c.* 1815–20

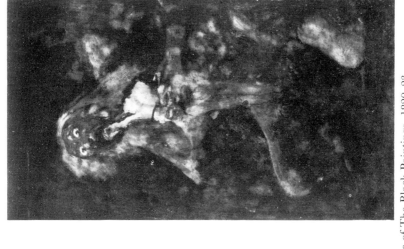

Plates 8 and 9 *Judith* and *Saturn* from the series of 'The Black Paintings, 1820–23
Madrid, Prado Museum
Reproduced from nineteenth-century photographs

Plate 10   *The Holy Office* from the series of The Black Paintings, 1820–23
Madrid, Prado Museum

happy and carefree working population, designed to reassure a benevolent despot. In one of the early tapestry cartoons called *The Blind Guitar Player*, a small upper-class group – a man, a woman and two children – mingle with working-class people, listening to a blind man singing and playing the guitar. In this instance, a classical pyramid structure binds rich and poor together, and here, as elsewhere, labourers sell their wares and the wealthy buy.[26] But a change in approach occurs in the late 1780s that is particularly apparent in the cycle of the seasons that Goya produced in 1786 and 1787. In *Spring* the group of women wear quite elegant dress, in a style that might be appropriate to a farmer's family of the middle-class kind. The man in the background seems lower in social class to judge from his dress, yet he is by no means excluded from the group. There is no attempt to stress the hard work involved in country life, and the same is true of *Summer*, a harvesting scene, in which nearly everyone is resting from their labours. In both *Spring* and *Summer*, pyramid arrangements hold the groups together; there is no sense of class differences that might give rise to conflict. In *Autumn*, on the other hand, there is a clear distinction between the sense of leisure and plenty in the foreground – composed of comfortably middle-class figures, it would seem – and the labour of those bending over their work behind. The girl with the basket of grapes links the two worlds. She is less well dressed than those in front of her and carries a burden, which they do not. In the *Winter* scene (Plate 1) – considered original in its approach to the subject by Goya's contemporaries[27] – all those shown belong to the same class, as in the *Summer* design. But the harshness of winter is emphasized by Goya, whereas the norm for the depiction of the season was to show how its discomfort and misery could be alleviated by wearing furs, sitting by the fire, or skating on ice.

What attitude, if any, is implied by the artist here? Perhaps primarily sympathy for those that were members of the 'useful classes',[28] in Spain, and a realistic recognition of the conditions in which they lived, that other artists working for the tapestry factory seem to have avoided. Possibly, in Goya's case, the specific date at which he worked on the seasons may have led him to a fresh perception of rural problems. There were crop failures in 1786, and these were followed by heavy snowfalls and flooding during the winter and the spring of the following year. Furthermore, the price of wheat and barley was unusually high. Cabarrús reported individuals dying of starvation close to his country residence at the time.[29]

In the 1790s Goya translates this new awareness into criticism of privilege in the rural context in his satirical prints. This certainly seems to be the implication of *Capricho* 42, in which country people of the labouring classes carry asses on their backs. The manuscript caption in one of the proofs reads 'Cómo suben los borricos' (How asses mount, or rise in the world),[30] and the final caption 'Tú que no puedes' is definitely ironic. The phrase in question is half a Spanish proverb – it requires the words 'llévame a cuestas' to complete it – which is normally used to mock those who attempt something foolish. Literally the proverb means: 'Carry me on your back, since you are incapable of doing so!'. Goya's contemporaries thought that the plate referred to the unfair distribution of the burden of taxation which had been attacked, as we have already seen, by progressive thinkers like Vicente Alcalá Galiano.[31] The implication is that working people have to carry the whole weight of society (and 'the real asses') on their backs. Goya's own commentary is more ambiguous.[32] In translation it runs 'Wouldn't you say that these gentlemen are asses', or conceivably, 'Wouldn't you say that these gentlemen are privileged'. The idea of representing noblemen as asses occurs in another plate too, No. 39 in the series, 'Asta su abuelo' ('Back to his grandparents') (Plate 2). In that instance, a noble who is also an ass, checks his family tree to make sure there is no illegitimacy, manual labour, Jewish or Moorish blood, to lower his status. He is able to establish the genuineness of his assininity 'on all four sides', as the Spanish say: namely, back to the grandparents on both sides of the family, as formal proofs of nobility required in Spain.

But Goya's strongest criticism of class divisions was made in the context of the Peninsular War. This was hardly surprising, since the mood of the times and the greater freedom of the press encouraged the debate of topics that had previously been censored. Articles on liberty and equality appeared in 1809 in the *Semanario patriótico*,[33] and the expectations of the mass of the people involved in the struggle against the French were recognised in print in relation to land ownership. There is evidence that the lower classes themselves brought pressure for the redistribution of wealth at the period. A guerrilla band in Andalusia, led by Andrés Ortiz (nicknamed The Shepherd), invaded one of the Duke of Osuna's estates with his flock.[34] According to the Duke's administrator, Ortiz had claimed 'that there were no dukes or rich people any more; the land belonged to everybody; and all the cash [that the administrator held] should be distributed forthwith'. Even though Goya, in occupied Madrid, was cut off for much of the time from progressive Spanish publications, there were periods of nationalist control in the capital which stimulated awareness of these developments. In the Madrid Gazette of 26 September 1812, for instance, the author of a discourse on Public Spirit imagined the People asking the following question: 'Is the existence of privileged individuals and classes bad for the state?' The answer given was 'It is extremely bad; since it results in the absence of equality before the law, and there can be no civic virtues'. The author went on to recommend discussions of the constitution in social gatherings, workshops and even taverns.

Goya turned to openly political themes during the war. He is believed to have produced at least one painting to celebrate the constitution, and others of a patriotic nature for public display. But more significant for the present purposes are a number of etchings he made, probably in 1812 or 1813, as part of the *Disasters of War* series. Their central theme is famine, and the different way in which different social classes coped with it. The price of grain gradually increased in the capital in the course of 1812 and crisis point was reached in May that year. A total of 4,038 people died in that month alone.[35] There was fever as well as famine, and Goya's wife was one of those who died.[36]

Goya's view of the crisis highlights in a number of plates the contrast between bourgeois survivors – some of them perhaps officers in the Spanish forces raised to fight for Joseph Buonaparte – and the poor who succumb. A particularly strong series of etchings shows hungry, ill-clothed and exhausted families begging in the foreground. Well-fed, well-dressed bourgeois walk by on the other side, and Goya's captions point up the inhuman character of their neglect. The caption of *Disasters* 54, for example, is addressed to the poor: 'There's no point in calling out' ('Clamores en vano'); and in *Disasters* 55, the caption reflects the feelings of the poor themselves: 'The worst thing is to have to beg' ('Lo peor es pedir'). In this last case, the preliminary drawing underlines the egoism of the bourgeoisie even more strongly; and the caption of *Disasters* 58 either identifies with the poor again or represents ironically the critical and insensitive voice of the bourgeoisie: 'No hay que dar voces' ('You shouldn't cry out' or 'We mustn't cry out'). Finally *Disasters* 61, 'Si son de otro linage' ('They belong to a different class') (Plate 3), adds to the visual irony a caption that emphasizes the unfeeling nature of the affluent. Here too Goya, ironically, uses a bourgeois voice in the caption.

Apart from these observations on inequality and unjust distribution of wealth, Goya raises two other topics that deserve a mention: critical attitudes to the monarchy and the church. The latter is soon dealt with, for there seems to be no connection with the religious issues raised by the French Revolution in Goya's work. The crucial questions were the wealth and possessions of the church (including church lands), and the religious orders. Goya's drawings and etchings certainly contain anti-clerical elements, and mockery of the monastic orders more particularly. There is irony at the expense of the cult of images, and attacks are made on the inhumanity of the Inquisition and on the church for supporting the absolutist regime of Ferdinand VII (Plates 4 and 5). But none of this amounts to a revolutionary stance. Anti-clericalism is common-place in religious countries, and attacks on the Inquisition, or doubts about the values of monastic life, occurred frequently in enlightened and liberal circles in Spain in Goya's time. They had no need of external stimulus.

Attitudes to the monarchy, on the other hand, are a different matter. In the 1790s, for instance, there is clear evidence that Goya shared his contemporaries' dislike for the relationship between the favourite Godoy, and Charles IV and María Luisa.[37] Some of Goya's contemporaries thought that there were references to a sexual relationship between Godoy and the queen in one of the *Caprichos* (No. 5), and they held that other plates were connected with the sexual or political immorality of the favourite (Nos. 56 and 72).[38] Yet there is little to suggest that Goya was against the institution of monarchy in a political sense, although he was critical of specific members of the royal family. Some of Goya's contem-poraries thought that *Capricho* 2 criticized the deceptive nature of royal marriages,[39] and that No. 63, which shows two beasts carrying repulsive humans on their backs, satirized monarchs or leading politicians.[40] The validity of these interpretations, however, is impossible to prove, although the very existence of commentaries of such a radical nature is, in itself, significant.

More interesting, in reality, are Goya's coded comments on the Spanish monarchy in the Ferdinand VII period. These are to be found in the *Disasters of War* series and in plates which can definitely be clearly linked with Giambattista Casti's political allegory *Gli animali parlanti* (The talking animals).[41] Nos. 74 and 78 are the clearest examples. *Disasters* 74 ('Esto es lo peor!', 'This is the worst of all') (Plate 6) is the key to the Casti connection, since it contains a direct quotation from Casti written down by the wolf within it. Casti, in the passage in question, blames society in general for allowing monarchs to wage war to satisfy their own personal ambitions. Goya gives the quotation an ironic sense ('Miserable humanity, you are to blame') by making Casti's wolf write it, while a member of a religious order holds the inkwell. Since Casti's wolf represents a minister in an absolutist regime, absolutism itself is 'the worst thing of all' – a clear allusion to the position adopted by Ferdinand VII between 1814 and 1820, when Liberal friends of Goya, like Quintana, were imprisoned, and the Inquisition was active once again. No. 78 ('He defends himself well') (Plate 7) appears to take the horse figure from Casti, who uses the animal as a proponent of constitutional monarchy. If Goya was indeed following Casti here, the horse, like the Liberals in Spain, has to fight against the supporters of absolutism (i.e. the wolves), while the revolutionary dogs look on. The plate seems to imply clear respect for the Spanish Liberals on Goya's part. As for the more extreme positions to right and left, Goya appears to favour the revolutionaries more than the absolutists.

One last plate in the *Disasters of War* could be related to questions of monarchy: No. 69 'Nada. Ello dirá' ('Nothing. It speaks for itself'). There is a possible connection between this plate and seventeenth-century emblems about the inevitability of judgment after death.[42] The high and mighty will be weighed in the balance as well as the humble and meek. It is certainly possible to see the corpse in Goya's etching as a royal cadaver with a crown-like object in its left hand. The balances dimly visible in the background tilt, and the 'king' is, by implication, found wanting. 'Nothing' is either the monarch's contribution to society, or the 'nothingness' to which kings return after their brief reign on earth. In Spain, the idea of coming from nothing and returning to nothing was specifically applied to Napoleon during the Peninsular War period, but an older tradition applied it to rulers in general. There is also the remote possibility of an echo from the French Revolution here. A comment on revolutionary justice at the time of the trial of Louis XVI in 1792 ran as follows: 'The people do not try like courts of justice, they cast lightning; they do not condemn kings, they plunge them back into oblivion'.[43] It is conceivable that this view is reflected in *Disasters* 69.

In relation to Goya's stance in later work, Professor Paulson has recently found evidence of a counter-revolutionary posture,[44] in the figures of Saturn and Judith (Plates 8 and 9) in the Black Paintings. These use the imagery of decapitation associated with the French Revolution and emphasize its horror in a way that implies an essentially pessimistic vision of human society, Hobbesian in character. However, these late paintings are not without their satirical touches – in the Inquisition scene, for instance, called *The Holy Office* (Plate 10) – and this, in turn, would suggest that Goya's interest in political protest and social change had not entirely disappeared. The kernel of anger can still be sensed in this late work, and it is not, in fact, easy to eliminate the progressive element from any stage of Goya's career. It is difficult, perhaps, to say how much of Goya's ideology derives from the Spanish Liberal posture, evolving in his own time in the circles in which he moved, and how much from a broader and more radical European tradition. But Goya's wish to see change in his society remained strong, and strands in the movement for reform that he supported are clearly related to the spirit of the French Revolution.

NOTES

1. Miguel Rubín de Celis' *Discurso sobre los principios de una constitución libre* and two works by the abbé Marchena, *A la nación española* and *Inpromptu d'un espagnol* (1792), were republished by Antonio Elorza in *Pan y toros y otros papeles sediciosos de fines del siglo XVIII*, Madrid, 1971.

2. Quoted by Cayetano Alcázar Molina, in *El conde de Floridablanca*, Madrid, n.d., p. 29.

3. cf. Floridablanca's 'Informe' dated 1791 (Archivo Histórico Nacional = AHN, Estado, Legajo 3959, N° 41), reproduced by Gonzalo Anes as an appendix to his essay 'La revolución francesa y España. Algunos datos y documentos', in *Economía e 'Ilustración'*, Barcelona, 1969, pp. 184–186.

4. cf. Juan Antonio Llorente, *Historia crítica de la Inquisición*, Madrid, 1822, p. 114; Severo Aguirre, *Prontuario alfabético y cronológico . . . de las instrucciones, ordenanzas, reglamentos, pragmáticos, y demás reales resoluciones no recopiladas, expedidas hasta el año de 1792 inclusive*, Madrid, 1793, p. 217.

5. AHN, Estado, Legajo 3239, N° 53.

6. cf. *Novísima recopilación de las leyes de España*, Madrid, 1829, VI, p. 424. See also Richard Herr, *The Eighteenth-Century Revolution in Spain*, Princeton, 1958, p. 364.

7. *Novísima recopilación . . .*, ed. cit., VI, p. 429.

8. The statistics provided by Mariano de la Lama y Noriega in his *Memoria histórica del piadoso instituto de la Real Archicofradía de Caridad y Paz y Catálogo de los hermanos asistidos por ella*, Madrid, 1868, refer to twenty executions between 1797 and 1799, and only ten between 1790 and 1796.

9. cf. Gonzalo Anes, op. cit., pp. 176–177 and 193–197.

10. cf. Gonzalo Anes, op. cit., and Iris Zavala, *El texto en la historia*, Madrid, 1981, pp. 199 ff.: 'Picornell y la Revolución de San Blas, 1795'.

11. Museo Histórico Nacional, *Memorias y autobiografías*, I, Buenos Aires, 1910, p. 92.

12. AHN, Estado, Legajo 3022 ('Projet d'utilité publique') and 3022, N° 16 ('Mémoire'). The covering letter to Godoy is dated 28 November 1794.

13. Ibid., 'Projet' pp. 17 ff.; also AHN, Estado, Legajo 3239, N° 36.

14. Leandro Fernández de Moratín, *Diario (Mayo 1780 – Marzo 1808)*, ed. René y Mireille Andioc, Madrid, 1968, p. 85.

15. cf. Nigel Glendinning, 'Tendencias liberales en la literatura española de fines del siglo XVIII', in *Dieciocho*, 9 (1986), pp. 147–48.

16. *Diarios de Jovellanos*, ed. Julio Somoza, Oviedo, 1953–1955, I, pp. 436, 483 and 489. In the letters Jovellanos' opposition to revolution is most explicit in those to Alexander Jardine written on 21 May 1794 and 3 June 1794 (cf. Gaspar Melchor de Jovellanos, *Obras completas*, II, Correspondencia 1, Oviedo, 1985, pp. 634–37 and 642–3).

17. The phrase quoted comes at the end of Jovellanos' 'Sátira segunda a Arnesto' in a passage that was omitted when the poem was first published in 1787 in *El Censor*. The translations of the phrase are based on the entries under 'behetría' in the *Diccionario de la Real Academia Española* (1832 ed.).

18. cf. Albert Dérozier, *Manuel Josef Quintana et la naissance du libéralisme en Espagne*, II, Paris, 1970, p. 610 'Discours adressé aux députés des Cortes . . . Cadix, 14 Septembre 1810').

19. Dérozier published the two versions in his edition of Quintana's poems (Clásicos Castalia, 1969). See also Nigel Glendinning, 'Tendencias liberales . . .', *Dieciocho*, 9 (1986), p. 142.
20. Nigel Glendinning, 'Tendencias liberales . . .', p. 140.
21. The play in question is the 'comédie larmoyante' entitled *El delincuente honrado*.
22. cf. Nigel Glendinning, 'Tendencias liberales . . .', pp. 143–6. The history of the concept of public opinion in Spain was outlined in Nigel Glendinning, 'Cambios en el concepto de la opinión pública', *Nueva revista de filología hispánica*, XXXIII (1984), pp. 157–64.
23. There are illuminating differences of approach in Alfonso de Azevedo and Manuel de Lardizábal. The former, writing in Latin on the subject of torture in 1770, uses the exemption of nobles as an argument in favour of eliminating torture altogether. He argues that if those with power, knowledge and authority are exempt, what is the point of torturing lesser mortals? It is the powerful rather than the weak who are most likely to be able to harm society. Lardizábal is more anxious to preserve differences between the classes (cf. *Discurso de las penas*, Madrid, 1782, p. 144), but he recognises the need to modify privileges which run contrary to the legal interests of society as a whole (op. cit., p. 282).
24. cf. Nigel Glendinning, *Historia de la literatura española. El siglo XVIII*, Barcelona, 1986, p. 105.
25. cf. Pedro Alvarez de Miranda, *Tratado sobre la monarquía columbina (una utopía antiilustrada del siglo XVIII)*, Madrid, 1980, pp. VIII–IX.
26. This tapestry cartoon had to be modified by Goya. It is generally thought that his original design coincided with an etching he made on the same subject. This shows a man driving an ox-cart on the left. This detail was eliminated from the revised version of the cartoon, and replaced by the figure of a man fishing in a pond by a tree. The exchange of an individual relaxing for a man engaged in work is striking. Presumably Goya's superiors at the Tapestry Factory thought that the foreground scene should exemplify leisure activity. Melons are for sale in the background on the right in both versions of the subject.
27. Nigel Glendinning, *Goya and his Critics*, New Haven-London, 1977, pp. 50–51.
28. 'Useful classes' is one of the terms used in Spain in the late eighteenth century for agricultural and craft workers.
29. cf. *Actas y memorias de la Real Sociedad Económica de los amigos del país de la provincia de Segovia*, IV, Segovia, 1793, pp. 320 ff. The prices of wheat, barley and rye are quoted for the years 1746–1793. See also Conde de Cabarrús, *Cartas sobre los obstáculos que la naturaleza, la opinión y las leyes oponen a la felicidad pública*, Madrid, 1820, pp. 161–162.
30. cf. Valerian von Loga, *Francisco de Goya* (Meister der Graphik, IV), Leipzig, n.d., Plate 20. I believe the caption to be in Goya's handwriting.
31. The Ayala and Biblioteca Nacional MS commentaries coincide in saying that 'the useful [or working] classes bear the whole burden of society or the real asses on their backs'. The Biblioteca Nacional MS states that they also 'carry the whole weight of the state taxes'.
32. Goya's commentary reads '¿Quién no dirá que estos caballeros son caballerías?'. The Royal Academy dictionary suggests that 'caballerías' can mean

privileges. In this and in other cases I refer to the Prado MS, which is in Goya's handwriting, as 'Goya's commentary'. Since the artist made a copy of this text for the Duke of Wellington, he obviously considered it authoritative. René Andioc has recently made a convincing case for the involvement of Leandro Fernández de Moratín in the preparation of the commentary in question. I believe, nevertheless, that Goya had a hand in it too.

33. *Semanario patriótico*, Nos 18, 19 and 22 (25 May, 1 June and 22 June 1809).

34. cf. Condesa de Yebes, *La condesa-duquesa de Benavente. Una vida en unas cartas*, Madrid, 1955, p. 234.

35. The figures are given in a manuscript 'Report made to Sir H. Wellesley by a society of Spanish Patriots at Madrid' dated 19 July 1812. The document in question is in the Vaughan Papers at All Souls' College, Oxford.

36. Goya's wife, Josefa, died on 20 June 1812.

37. Two satirical etchings made by Goya at the same period as the *Caprichos (The Old Woman and her gallants*, and *Dream of Lying and Inconstancy)* can be connected with the relationship between the Queen and Godoy.

38. cf. the Ayala manuscript commentary in Edith Helman, *Trasmundo de Goya*, Madrid, 1963, pp. 221, 234 and 239.

39. Ibid., p. 219.

40. According to the Bibloteca Nacional manuscript commentary the figures were like 'the kings and principal magistrates [or law-givers] of nations' (cf. *Trasmundo de Goya*, p. 237).

41. cf. Nigel Glendinning, 'A Solution to the Enigma of Goya's 'Emphatic Caprices'', *Apollo*, CVII, N° 193 (1978), pp. 186–91.

42. cf. Nigel Glendinning, 'Goya and Van Veen. An emblematic source for some of Goya's late drawings, *The Burlington Magazine*, CXIX, No. 893 (1977), pp. 568–70.

43. Marc Bouloiseau, *The Jacobin Republic 1792–1794*, Cambridge, 1983, p. 55.

44. Ronald Paulson, *Representations of Revolution (1789–1820)*, New Haven-London, 1983, pp. 361 ff., and especially p. 370. Paulson rightly recognises the ambiguous character of Goya's images, and the balance between progressive and regressive attitudes in his work.

France during the French Revolution through German eyes

T.C.W. Blanning

I

Everyone will have their own image of German visitors to Paris. For many it will be the Wehrmacht goose-stepping their way down the Champs-Elysées in 1940, or perhaps the celebrated photograph of Adolf Hitler gazing at the Eiffel Tower. For myself, the clearest memory is aural rather than visual – the never-to-be-forgotten sound of a mob of drunken German conscripts on leave rampaging down the Avenue Kléber in the early hours singing lustily 'Wir scheissen auf die Bundeswehr'. Paris was also, of course, the target for German soldiers during the revolutionary period. In 1792 the invading Austro-Prussian armies thought they were embarking on a gentle stroll; in the event it took them twenty-two years and untold casualties before they could indulge in their first victory-parade in the French capital.

In the meantime, Paris had been visited by a large number of German civilians, all attracted by the Revolution, and it is they who are the subject of this paper. Throughout the eighteenth century Paris had been the favourite foreign destination for well-heeled German tourists, more accessible, more fashionable and more fun than the only other possible rival – Rome. The terminal crisis of old regime France, especially when dramatised by the fall of the Bastille, both increased this influx and broadened its social base. It also gave it an ideological flavour, for most German visitors took the decision to visit revolutionary Paris because they were sympathetic to the Revolution. Fortunately they lived up to the German stereotype of earnest scholarship by recording diligently what they saw and – more important – what they thought about what they saw. Back home there proved to be an insatiable market for news about the Revolution, so the visitors obliged, in books, reports for the press and in private correspondence.[1]

The existence of this material is, of course, well known and has been used extensively by historians writing about relations between Germany and the French Revolution – by Gooch, Droz and Epstein, for example.[2] I can hardly hope to add much of significance in the course of this short paper. All I propose to do is to draw attention to three aspects of German reports from Paris during the revolutionary-Napoleonic period which perhaps have not been given the attention they deserve.

My first suggestion is, I fear, likely to be dismissed by the historians of France present without much ado. It is that the German observers might actually have had something of value to say about what was happening inside France. Hitherto, so far as I am aware, their accounts have been regarded as valuable evidence of their own opinions and – by extension – of collective German attitudes towards the Revolution, but their accounts have not been taken seriously on their own terms. It is not so much that they have been tested and found wanting, rather that they have been ignored. As we shall see later, the Germans did have a perspective which was special, not to say peculiar, but that does not invalidate their eye-witness accounts altogether. Coming from quite a different political culture, these Germans were sometimes struck by phenomena which seemed so natural to the natives that it was never deemed worthy of comment – but which, with the advantage of hindsight, we can now see to have been important.

A good example was provided by the Prussian composer Johann Friedrich Reichardt, who carefully described the dimensions of the Manège – the vast former riding school in which the National Assembly met – and drew attention to the consequences: this was no debating chamber but *a continuous political rally*.[3] His account makes it clear that the physical circumstances within which the National Assembly's deliberations occurred exercised a decisive influence on the style of revolutionary politics. There could hardly be a more stark contrast than between the cavernous Manège, with its seething public galleries, and the tiny, intimate chambers of the contemporary British Parliament, where the right even to report its proceedings had only recently been established. The French way was much more open, more public, more democratic, and much less socially exclusive. Thanks to pressure from the clubs, the press and the presence of the public, the National Assembly was much more responsive to its constituents' aspirations, needs and fears. But, as Reichardt found, it was also much less pluralist and much more susceptible to demagoguery, much more inclined to seek simple answers to complex questions. The headlong rush to war during the spring of 1792, for example, from which so many of the Revolution's problems and even its eventual demise stemmed, was made possible in large measure by the Brissotin orators' skilful exploitation of the demagogic potential of the Manège.[4] As Reichardt's experiences in March 1792 suggested – and as the events of the next few months were to confirm – the formal freedom the deputies had wrested from the old regime was in danger of being negated by their new masters. It is worth remembering that when the Parisian crowd marched to Versailles in the October Days of 1789, it took prisoner and brought back to Paris not only the royal family but also the National Assembly.

II

Although the German travellers could be illuminating about the situation in France, what they say about it reveals most, of course, about their own country and its culture. In particular – and this is the second point I want to make – their response to the Revolution is a timely reminder of the special character of the German Enlightenment. There has been a bull market in Aufklärung studies during the past twenty years or so, fuelled in part by the belief that they can contribute to the resolution of present-day problems, especially those relating to social and political emancipation.[5] With anything smacking of German nationalism under a cloud, the wild men of the Sturm und Drang have been pushed to one side, in favour of the rational, cosmopolitan Aufklärer, demonstrably part of the mainstream of European culture. Indeed, one recent account has argued against even using the words 'Aufklärung' and 'Aufklärer', because to do so distances the German version from its essentially similar counterparts in Western Europe.[6]

There is something in this, but far too much has been made of it. Of course there were striking similarities between Enlightenment thinkers in Germany and France (and elsewhere), but to downgrade the even more obtrusive differences is to elevate form at the expense of substance. Among other things, the concern of the Aufklärer with metaphysics in general and religion in particular led them to stress morality rather than material welfare and duties rather than rights.[7] This gave their thinking a strongly ethical flavour which accounts for the priggish, schoolmarmish flavour of so much of their writing. Moreover, this preoccupation with questions of morality was not diluted by the self-conscious cosmopolitanism of the Aufklärung. On the contrary, the most important enlightened thinker of the first half of the century – Christian Wolff – had stressed that a man's rights depended on the way in which he exercised his duties and that the end of the state was not the *bonheur* of its citizens but their moral perfection.[8] This ethical approach to politics was then powerfully reinforced during the decade before the outbreak of the Revolution by the reception of the philosophy of Kant, whose lapidary phrase – 'True politics cannot take a step without first rendering homage to morality' – was the watchword of all those Aufklärer who saw in the French Revolution the triumph of philosophy.[9]

There were plenty of them. Indeed, the reason why so many German Aufklärer responded so favourably to the events of 1789 was that, like Georg Forster, they believed 'it is glorious to see what philosophy has ripened in the brain and realised in the state'.[10] Even the later arch-conservative Friedrich Gentz saw in the Revolution the first practical triumph of philosophy.[11] The first to report back was Johann Heinrich Campe, who arrived in Paris on 9 August 1789 and recorded the following observation at the end of his first day there:

> What divine inspiration was it then that taught the so-called mob to behave with such unselfish generosity, in so orderly, so discerning, so heroic a fashion? The inspiration was there in advance, created by destiny despite all the attempts by evil despots to prevent it; and the names of this inspiration were – culture and enlightenment.[12]

For those lucky enough to be in Paris during the heady days of 1789, there was a strong sense of witnessing a truly world-historical moment and a correspondingly strong sense of optimism. Another of the early visitors, Konrad Engelbert Oelsner wrote at about the same time that the events in France had demonstrated that philosophy was the fundamental 'invisible but active force' which carried all before it'.[13]

This sort of millenarian approach was all very well, so long as the Revolution meant simply tearing down the most obvious abuses of the old regime, but it left these starry-eyed Germans ill-prepared for the political rough-and-tumble which became increasingly obtrusive. In their political vocabulary the word 'power' was conspicuous by its absence and when they saw it at work, red in tooth and claw, they did not like it. They were bewildered by the revolutionaries' sense of priorities – this was not the way to go about things, they thought. Instead of arguing about the distribution of power and struggling to obtain it, the revolutionaries should have been concentrating on the moral education of the French people. To suppose that such formal changes as a new constitution could create a valid new order was to turn the proper sequence the wrong way round – it was putting the political cart before the ethical horse.

The most eloquent exponent of this point of view was Georg Forster, who had sacrificed everything in the cause of the Revolution by collaborating with the French occupation regime in Mainz. In his last anguished letters to his wife, written from Paris in the course of 1793, he revealed that although a committed revolutionary in principle, he was essentially at odds with the Revolution as it had manifested itself in France. In one letter after another he stressed that all that mattered was personal morality. It was the only true basis of politics and 'for that reason I laugh at the visions of those well-meaning fanatics who conjure up for themselves a utopia in which a free constitution will mean that there will be nothing but good, wise, and happy people'.[14] The only true form of liberty, and the only kind worth having, was 'intellectual freedom' [*Geistesfreiheit*] and what he called 'external liberty' could at best be only a means to it.[15]

These German moralists were, of course, aware that there was an insurmountable problem of timing here. As Reichardt put it, the French political theorists were right to claim that without an improvement in the constitution there could be no improvement in public morality – but it was equally the case that without an improvement in public morality, there could be no improvement in the constitution.[16] This was a dilemma which could not be resolved and could only end in disillusionment. Ten years later, Reichardt paid another visit to Paris and mused on what a disaster the Revolution had been, for France and for Europe: if only all those wantonly squandered energies had been used to improve education, aesthetic appreciation and the establishment of national monuments in the style of the Greeks and the Romans! Then a splendid example would have been set for mankind; in the event, everything had run into the sand and he was sick to the heart when he remembered how enthusiastic he had been for the great cause at the beginning and how everything had been spoilt by human wickedness.[17]

That was the conclusion of most, if not all of the early enthusiasts: the cause had been great, because it had been the cause of enlightened philosophy, but the men called to serve it had proved immoral and so had dragged it down with them. Forster himself was thoroughly disillusioned by the revolutionaries he met and observed at work in the summer of 1793, prompting him to draw the characteristic conclusion that liberty unsupported by morality was only license.[18] As the years passed, this kind of criticism could only grow in intensity. In A.G.F. Rebmann's view, the revolution had fallen prey almost at once to a gang of opportunists. He complained that 'a mob of total and utter moral degenerates – and there are more of them, alas, in France than in many other countries – saw in the Revolution simply the opportunity to deceive all the rest and to make their fortunes by pillage, corruption and infamies of every kind'.[19]

III

With Rebmann's observation that France contained more moral degenerates than many other countries, we move to the third and final aspect of the German visitors' reaction to the Revolution I wish to consider: nationalism. Once a source of pride, German nationalism has been so discredited by the atrocities committed in its name between 1933 and 1945 that the recent historiography has post-dated its emergence and has underestimated its strength. It is now argued that true nationalism began to develop only during the revolutionary-Napoleonic period, in the short-term as a reaction to the French occupation and in the long-term as part of a process of modernisation. What one finds earlier is just particularist attachment to a specific principality or region (*Landes-patriotismus*).[20] This view, of course, is closely linked to the heavy emphasis on the cosmopolitanism of the German Enlightenment and its allegedly bourgeois character.

Yet even a cursory review of the periodical press of the eighteenth century reveals a strong and growing nationalism. Moreover, it was not just cultural nationalism. In an article entitled simply 'Germany', published in 1774 in his own periodical *German Chronicle*, C.F.D. Schubart rejoiced not only that German culture was now the envy of foreigners but also that Prussian military might now gave the law to Europe.[21]

The response of the German travellers to what they found in France during and after 1789 provides additional and powerful evidence that a keen sense of nationality, fed by pride and Francophobia, existed prior to the Revolution – even among those who admired it. One line often taken was that the French had been utterly repellent under the old regime but had now been regenerated. Through their rejoicing at this welcome development can be seen their original image of the French national character. A particularly good example was supplied by Johann Heinrich Campe in 1789, who wrote that the offensive arrogance, folly, vulgarity and frivolity which had so disfigured the French in the past had been banished by the Revolution.[22]

Unfortunately, it was not long before disillusionment set in. As it became clear that the French Revolution was not a moral crusade but a struggle for political power, the old xenophobia reared its ugly head again. A week after his arrival in Paris at the end of March 1793, Georg Forster could still find something pleasant to say about the French. He wrote to his wife: 'I am no more edified by the character of the French than those who hate and despise them, but together with their faults and shortcomings I can also see their good points, and I don't regard any nation as ideal'.[23] Only a few days later, after commenting that at a distance everything had seemed quite different from the deeply depressing reality, he was revising that assessment downwards:

The [French] nation is what it has always been – frivolous and fickle, without stability, without warmth, without love, without truth – It possesses only wit and fancy, with no heart and with no feeling ... Virtue and integrity have become so rare in this depraved nation that at least we know there is no form of evil we cannot expect.[24]

A strong sense of moral disapproval thunders out from one account after another, as any specific shortcoming on the part of an individual is generalised into an attack on the whole French national character. The fastidious Wilhelm von Humboldt, for example, was moved to adverse generalisation by such trivia as having to watch some clumsy table-manners, or by observing the agreeable but in his view over-cultivated landscape of the Ile de France or even by meeting an ill-favoured woman: after an unflattering description of Madame Condorcet, he commented: 'In other words, all in all very French and the absolute opposite of the ideal'.[25] It would be disheartening to quote one indictment after another – there is a limit to one's tolerance of such diatribes as that of Joseph Görres: 'Egoism is their idol, intrigue their sole endeavour, hedonism their only occupation'.[26] Repetition is also unnecessary, for there was a stereotype which was presented time and again. According to this, the French were incorrigibly frivolous, light-hearted, irreligious, sensual, restless, volatile, passionate, fickle, theatrical and superficial.[27] In short, they were just not serious.

Of course it is not unusual for travellers to find that, far from broadening the mind, exposure to foreign culture only exacerbates prejudice. Such very different visitors as Wilhelm von Humboldt, Joseph Görres or Friedrich Schlegel were not the first or the last to find their cosmopolitanism making way for nationalism.[28] However good their knowledge of the French language may have been, problems of comprehension could still arise. Even Wilhelm von Humboldt, perhaps the most distinguished linguist of his age, found it difficult to fathom the patois shouted at him by a group of peasants as he passed them in his carriage; only such familiar words as *'bougre'* and *'foutre'* indicated that they were not being polite.[29]

Especially after the outbreak of war in 1792, nationalist sensibilities were inflamed long before Paris was reached by the experience of the occupied territories. Travelling through the Rhineland en route for Paris in 1801, Heinrich von Kleist recorded the following impressions with characteristic intemperance:

Fields devastated, vineyards laid waste, whole villages just piles of ashes, castles plunged into the Rhine – Oh, if a *single* individual's conscience had to bear such a burden of crime, it would surely collapse, crushed by the load –

but a whole nation never has to blush. It can divide the guilt up among 30,000,000 people, with the result that each inhabitant of France can bear a tiny portion without difficulty. In Halberstadt Gleim made me promise to return to my fatherland a *German*. That is a promise it is not going to be difficult to keep.[30]

Not many Germans arrived in Paris with minds as closed as Kleist's, but many had been alienated from the revolutionary ethos by the sight of the Revolution in action along the way. Karl Gustav von Brinckmann's account of conditions on the left-bank of the Rhine was just as depressing, while Joseph Görres and Rudolf Eickemeyer went to Paris with the express purpose of protesting against the exploitation of the occupied territories.[31] Routes through the Low Countries had a similar effect. A.G.F. Rebmann was upset by what he saw in the Netherlands, now the Batavian Republic, where it was clear to him that the wrong people had got to the top.[32] F.J.L. Meyer was disillusioned by his experiences in Belgium, now annexed to France:

'We do not want to be free' – this unyielding declaration has dogged my footsteps through this country. And I am still hearing it. It seems to echo from the melancholy walls of Belgium's depopulated towns and especially from this desolate Brussels . . . Oh, believe me, they have paid dearly, very dearly, for the so-called gift of this high-sounding word [liberty].[33]

On arrival in Paris, the Germans were often – if not invariably – shocked by a city so much larger and so much more sophisticated than anything they had experienced before. Once again their strong sense of morality was brought into play, as they professed at least to be outraged by the hedonism they found. Writing of his journey to Paris in 1796, A.G.F. Rebmann exclaimed: 'I had thought that I was approaching the temple of liberty, but in fact I entered – its brothel!'.[34] This fascination with the seamy side of 'this cesspit covered with flowers' (Joseph Görres), 'the city of childishness, folly and frivolity' (Johann Friedrich Cotta), 'this modern Babylon' (Count Gustav von Schlabrendorff) recurs again and again, as in Heinrich von Kleist's excited description of the Palais Royal: 'there is no sensual need which cannot be satisfied here to the point of nausea, no virtue which is not derided, no infamy which is not committed as a matter of principle'.[35] So Rebmann warned German supporters of the Revolution not to visit Paris, for disillusionment was certain; he himself had found true republicanism only among the German expatriates there.[36] He was not the only one to huddle together with his fellow-countrymen for moral edification. When trying to persuade his brother August Wilhelm to join him in Paris, Friedrich Schlegel made a familiar distinction between the real and the superficial: 'everyone who comes from Germany, in other words from the real world and not just from the world of appearances, will be heartily welcome, no matter what his name is'.[37]

The other side of the coin to these hostile accounts of the French and their capital, of course, were the virtues attributed tb the rival German stereotype. The Germans may have been slower, perhaps even ponderous, it was maintained, but thanks to their Protestantism and their superior education, they were also deemed to be much more profound, more reflective, more religious and better disciplined.[38] Hence the exasperating air of condescension which informs their pronouncements on the Revolution. It had been necessary in France, they opined, because the political system had been so despotic and public morality so corrupt. In the German states, however, cultural advance introduced by reform from above had brought the benefits which the unfortunate French were having to seize from below. So Johann Heinrich Campe prefaced his reports from Paris with a fulsome tribute to his German prince, the duke of Brunswick, who had given for free the 'order, security and rational liberty' which the French were having to buy with their blood.[39]

The hostile view of the French derived in part from the German visitors' unshakeable confidence in the superiority of their culture, a conviction which long antedated the outbreak of the Revolution. The French were allowed a certain talent for mathematics, chemistry and rhetoric, but their music, theatre and literature were dismissed as third-rate.[40] French culture, observed Karl Gustav von Brinckmann, was rather like a French stove, which lit the room with dancing, shimmering flames – but did not heat it.[41] Above all, what passed for philosophy in France was dismissed as unworthy of the name. It was with a mixture of amusement and indignation that Wilhelm von Humboldt listened to Sieyès telling him complacently that German metaphysics was to true metaphysics as astrology was to astronomy. Humboldt (for whom the difference between French and German metaphysics was a constant preoccupation during his stay in Paris in 1798) commented that Sieyès simply could not understand German philosophy.[42]

There could be no clearer demonstration of the singularity of these German visitors' approach to the Revolution than their complacent belief that the French were just seeking to implement in the world of appearances what they themselves had achieved already in the much more important world of philosophy. As Joseph Görres put it: 'During the past ten years there has occurred a revolution in Germany which has achieved as much for humanity by theory as France has by practice – and by that I mean the reformation of philosophy carried out by Kant'.[43] What was now needed was an amalgamation of the two, to create a new humanity, truly regenerated within and without. Referring to 'that other revolution, intellectual and philosophical, which Kant, the immortal Kant, has provoked in our beliefs and our principles', Wyttenbach observed: 'It is a blessing for humanity that the two revolutions, the French and the German, have been produced simultaneously'.[44] So a particularly popular analogy was the relationship between Greece and Rome – France had conquered Germany militarily, but would now succumb to her superior culture.[45]

In the event, it was German military force to which the French succumbed: 'Babylon has fallen!' trumpeted Joseph Görres' periodical *Reinischer Merkur* in April 1814.[46] Görres' own political odyssey during these years personifies what had happened to the German intelligentsia as a whole. A supporter of the Revolution from the start – he visited the revolutionary club at Mainz at the tender age of sixteen – he was eager to collaborate with the French regime established in his native Rhineland during the 1790s. It was his gradual discovery that his understanding of apparently simple concepts such as liberty and equality was essentially different from that of his new masters which changed him from cosmopolitan Francophile into a nationalist Francophobe. And in this process his journey to Paris in 1799 played a crucial role.[47] Yet Görres remained a liberal; as much at odds with the Restoration as he had been with the Revolution.

He was not alone in that either. Some of the Germans I have been considering – notably Gentz, Kleist and Schlegel – certainly ended up in the conservative camp, but most of the others adhered to the enlightened principles of their youth, sadder and wiser perhaps but still loyal to ideals of *Aufklärung, Recht* and *Bildung.* Significantly, none of those concepts can be translated satisfactorily into another language. They stemmed from a German cultural tradition, they educated the German intelligentsia and they determined that the events of 1789 would remain the French Revolution and not the revolution in France.

NOTES

1. For a useful bibliographical introduction, see Hammer, 'Deutsche Revolutionsreisende in Paris' in Jürgen Voss (ed.), *Deutschland und die französische Revolution. 17. deutsch-französisches Historikerkolloquium des Deutschen Historischen Instituts Paris (Bad Homburg 29 September – 2 Oktober 1981)*, Beiheft der Francia, vol. 12, Munich and Zürich, 1983.

2. G.P. Gooch, *Germany and the French Revolution*, London, 1920; reprinted 1965. Jacques Droz, *L'Allemagne et la Révolution française*, Paris, 1949. Klaus Epstein, *The Genesis of German Conservatism*, Princeton, 1966.

3. Johann Friedrich Reichardt, *Vetraute Briefe aus Paris 1792*, ed. Rolf Weber, Berlin, 1980, pp. 108–11.

4. T.C.W. Blanning, *The Origins of the French Revolutionary Wars*, London, 1986, p. 112.

5. For some acute remarks on the historiography of the Aufklärung, see Joachim Whaley, 'Enlightenment and History in Germany', *The Historical Journal*, 31, 1 (1988), pp. 195–9.

6. Jonathan B. Knudsen, *Justus Möser and the German Enlightenment*, Cambridge, 1986, p. 4.

7. I have discussed the peculiarity of the German Enlightenment in 'The German Problem in the Eighteenth Century', which forms the first part of my *Reform and Revolution in Mainz, 1743–1803*, Cambridge, 1974. The author of the most recent – and best – general study of the Aufklärung, Horst Möller, is also well aware of the special characteristics of the movement – *Vernunft und Kritik. Deutsche Aufklärung im 17. und 18. Jahrhundert*, Frankfurt am Main, 1986, *passim*.

8. Droz, *L'Allemagne et la Révolution française*, pp. 153–4.

9. Ibid., pp. 166–9.

10. Forster to Heyne, *Sämtliche Schriften*, vol. viii, Leipzig, 1843, p. 274. Also quoted in Gooch, *Germany and the French Revolution*, p. 40.

11. Ibid.

12. Johann Heinrich Campe, *Briefe aus Paris zur Zeit der Revolution geschrieben*, ed., Hans-Wolf Jäger, Hildesheim, 1977, p. 102.

13. Alfred Stern, 'Charles Engelbert Oelsner: notice biographique, accompagnée de fragments de ses mémoires relatifs à l'histoire de la Révolution française', *Revue Historique*, 63 (1897), p. 83. For Oelsner's view on the relationship between the Revolution and the Aufklärung, see also Klaus Deinet, *Konrad Engelbert Oelsner und die Französische Revolution*, Munich and Vienna, 1981, p. 28.

14. Forster, *Sämtliche Schriften*, vol. IX, p. 19.

15. Ibid., p. 36.

16. Reichardt, *Vertraute Briefe aus Paris 1792*, p. 224.

17. Johann Friedrich Reichardt, *Vertraute Briefe aus Paris 1802/3*, ed. Rolf Weber, Berlin, 1981, p. 263.

18. Forster, *Sämtliche Schriften*, vol. IX, p. 48.

19. Rainer Kawa, *Georg Friedrich Rebmann (1768–1824). Studien zu Leben und Werk eines deutschen Jakobiners* Bonn, 1980, p. 355.

20. See, for example, Hans-Ulrich Wehler, *Deutsche Gesellschaftsgeschichte*, vol. I: *1700–1815*, Munich 1987, ch. 5 and the huge amount of literature cited in his footnotes. For a crude example of the view that German nationalism dates only from 1813, see Axel Kuhn (ed.), *Linksrheinische deutsche Jakobiner*, Stuttgart, 1978, p. 21, a particularly choice example of the wishful thinking school of neo-Jacobin historiography.

21. Christian Friedrich Daniel Schubart (ed.), *Deutsche Chronik auf das Jahr 1774*, Augsburg, 1774; reprinted, Heidelberg, 1975, pp. 5–6.

22. Campe, *Briefe aus Paris*, p. 17.

23. Forster, *Sämtliche Schriften*, vol. VIII, p. 5.

24. Ibid., pp. 7, 15.
25. Wilhelm von Humboldt, *Materialen, Gesammelte Schriften*, vol. 14, Berlin, 1922, p. 463.
26. Joseph von Görres, *Gesammelte Briefe*, ed. Marie Görres, 3 vols, Munich, 1858, vol. I, p. 8.
27. See, for example, the views recorded in Droz, *Cisrhénans*, p. 23; Siegfried Streller (ed.), *Heinrich von Kleist: Werke und Briefe in vier Bänden*, vol. IV: *Briefe*, Berlin and Weimar, 1978, pp. 260–2; Kawa, *Rebmann*, pp. 352, 392; Reichardt, *Vertraute Briefe aus Paris 1792*, pp. 220–2; Friedrich Schlegel, 'Reise nach Frankreich', *Europa. Eine Zeitschrift*, vol. I, 1 (1803), pp. 28–9.
28. Albert Leitzmann (ed.), *Wilhelm von Humboldts Briefe an Christian Gottfried Körner* Berlin, 1940, pp. 53–4; J.N. Sepp, *Görres und seine Zeitgenossen 1776–1848* Nördlingen, 1877, p. 62; Friedrich Schlegel, 'Reise nach Frankreich', *passim*.
29. Wilhelm von Humboldt, 'Tagebuch der Reise nach Spanien 1799-1800', *Wilhelm von Humboldts Tagebücher*, ed. Albert Leitzmann, vol. II: *1799–1835*, *Wilhelm von Humboldts Gesammelte Schriften*, vol. XV, Berlin, 1918, p. 54.
30. Streller (ed.), *Heinrich von Kleist: Werke und Briefe*, IV, pp. 247–8.
31. Caroline von Wolzogen, *Literarischer Nachlass der Frau Caroline von Wolzogen*, 2 vols, Leipzig, 1848–9, II, pp. 264–5; *Johann Joseph von Görres, Resultate meiner Sendung nach Paris*, Koblenz, 1800. On the Görres-Eickemeyer mission, see T.C.W. Blanning, *The French Revolution in Germany. Occupation and Resistance in the Rhineland 1792–1802*, Oxford, 1983, pp. 281–3.
32. Kawa, *Rebmann*, p. 347.
33. Friedrich Lorenz Meyer, *Briefe aus der Hauptstadt und dem Innern Frankriechs*, 2 vols, Tübingen, 1802/1803, II, p. 3.
34. Kawa, *Rebmann*, p. 352.
35. Görres, *Gesammelte Briefe*, p. 6; Dorothea Kuhn (ed.), *Goethe und Cotta: Briefwechsel 1797–1832*, 4 vols, Stuttgart, 1979–83, vol. I, p. 62; Wolzogen, *Literarischer Nachlass*, vol. II, p. 73; Streller (ed.), *Heinrich von Kleist: Werke und Briefe*, IV, p. 250. The brothel metaphor was also employed by Konrad Engelbert Oelsner to describe Paris – Alfred Stern, 'Konrad Engelbert Oelsner's Briefe und Tagebücher. Eine vergessene Quelle der Geschichte der Französischen Revolution', *Deutsche Zeitschrift für Geschichtswissenschaft*, 3 (1980), p. 102.
36. Karl-Georg Faber, 'Johann Andreas Georg Friedrich Rebmann', *Pfälzische Lebensbilder*, vol. I, ed. Kurt Baumann, Speyer, 1964, p. 202; Kawa, *Rebmann*, p. 352.
37. Oskar F. Walzel (ed.), *Friedrich Schlegels Briefe an seinen Bruder August Wilhelm*, Berlin, 1980, p. 523. For similar remarks about good company only being found among the German community in Paris, see Rudolf Unger (ed.), *Briefe von Dorothea und Friedrich Schlegel an die Familie Paulus* (Berlin, 1913), p. 8; Wilhelm von Humboldt, *Briefe an Christine Reinhard-Reimarus*, ed. Arndt Schreiber, Heidelberg, 1956, p. 110; Reichardt, *Vertraute Briefe aus Paris 1802/03*, pp. 258–9. Georg Forster even found himself driven to seek the company of British expatriates – *Sämtliche Schriften*, vol. IX, p. 11.
38. Kawa, *Rebmann*, p. 392; Droz, *Cisrhénans*, p. 23; Friedrich Schlegel, 'Ueber die Pariser Kunst-Ausstellung vom Jahre XI', *Europa, Eine Zeitschrift*, vol. I, 1 (1803), p. 105.
39. Campe, *Briefe aus Paris*, pp. iii, 102. There is an abbreviated translation in

Gooch, *Germany and the French Revolution* p. 43. For other contemporary comments on there being no need for a revolution in Germany, see Blanning, *Reform and Revolution in Mainz*, p. 310.

40. For example, Reichardt, *Vertraute Briefe aus Paris 1802/3*, p. 259; Friedrich Schlegel, 'Literatur', *Europa. Eine Zeitschrift*, vol. I, i (1803), p. 60.
41. Wolzogen, *Literarischer Nachlass*, vol. II, p. 267.
42. Humboldt, *Materialen*, p. 483.
43. Droz, *Cisrhénans*, p. 38.
44. Ibid., p. 39.
45. Ibid.
46. *Rheinischer Merkur*, no. 38, 6 April 1814.
47. Sepp, *Görres und seine Zeitgenossen*, p. 62.

Goethe and the French Revolution

Hans Reiss

What is one to do when asked to lecture on this subject which, like virtually any subject whose title begins with 'Goethe and . . .', has been dealt with often before.[1] The simplest way would be to turn down the invitation. But there are other well-trodden routes of escape. For instance, an impenetrable piece intelligible to the initiated only could be produced which would confirm Goethe's own observation: 'The Germans – and not only the Germans – have the gift of making scholarship inaccessible'.[2]

There is yet another route of escape – to provide one hour's filibuster explaining why one has to clear the ground without ever coming to the subject itself at all. You may well, with some justice, think that I am well advanced on that road.

Therefore, let me stick my neck out instead and attempt to say something new, one of the few justifications for any lecture. My contention is as follows: Goethe, as is well known, was all along opposed to the French Revolution and it is generally agreed that his political views were influenced by his reading of Justus Möser[3] who was a consistent critic of the Enlightenment and the French Revolution and has been called the German counterpart of Edmund Burke.[4] While in no way denying his affinity with Möser's thought I shall maintain that Goethe's attitude was also determined by the Enlightenment. How can this be so? Does this contention not involve a contradiction? For were the revolutionaries not inspired by the ideas of the Enlightenment and even its German version, the *Aufklärung*? How could Enlightenment thought, therefore, make Goethe turn against the Revolution? It is this paradox which I want to explain.

Of course, Goethe owed much to Möser. Möser, who emphasised the historical approach to, and the value of tradition in, political and social life, was distrustful of the rhetoric of Englightenment thinkers and French revolutionaries. He attacked Kant, whom Marx has, with some justice, called *the* philosopher of the French Revolution,[5] and held that it was wrong to base arguments on high presuppositions, on abstract principles of reason since they were bound to do violence to practical life.[6] For Goethe, too, general

146

principles were the source of endless trouble. As one of his aphorisms runs:

General concepts and great conceit always cause ghastly disasters (H.A., XII, 471)

The Revolution disturbed Goethe deeply. Unfortunately, hardly any contemporary evidence about his attitude has survived. The only significant remark made in a letter to his friend Jacobi of 3 March 1790 is cryptic rather than informative. After having stated that he was as well as anyone could be he wrote:

That the French Revolution has also been a revolution for me you can well imagine.

Momentous words, indeed! But unfortunately they do not tell what sort of mental revolution he had experienced.

Why is there so little evidence? Goethe despised empty rhetoric and any kind of pretence.[7] He also wanted to avoid being misunderstood by the public, and often preferred silence to speech on matters which were important to him. Therefore, he did not want to talk about the Revolution and the politics engendered by it.[8] He stuck to his intention. To cite one instance only: in his *Tag-und Jahreshefte* or *Annalen*, the continuation of his autobiography (*Dichtung und Wahrheit*) written after the end of the Revolution and its Napoleonic aftermath, he admitted that the Necklace affair almost drove him out of his mind because he realised how it had destabilised the régime in France and consequently threatened the whole European order (H.A., X, 433). Indeed, he was so disturbed, he asserts that his friends began to fear for his sanity. But there are no contemporary documents testifying to that inner anguish.

We have therefore to turn to his imaginative works, to dramas like *Egmont*, *Iphigenie auf Tauris* and *Torquato Tasso* to appraise his attitude to politics in the years immediately preceding the Revolution and to other works to appreciate his response to the Revolution itself before the campaign in France of 1792.

Egmont, completed in 1787, reveals a basic ambiguity of outlook. On the one hand, it is made plain that it is wrong for rulers to ride roughshod over established rights and local customs; on the other, the intellectual case for reform from above is also set out, though reforms should never be imposed by force. No extreme measures, let alone resort to revolution, are advocated. The end of the play has been hailed as anticipating the Revolution in France since it appears to champion the revolt in the Netherlands. But this is a wrong reading, if only because the end is ambiguous. While it can refer to the liberation of the Netherlands from foreign tyranny along the lines laid down by Enlightenment thought, it can also allude to the restoration of ancient rights in the Southern Netherlands which stayed under Spanish overlordship, but regained their ancient regional constitutions.[9]

Egmont emphasises the power and significance of customs and traditions. But Goethe never believed that all customs and traditions ought to be respected. If they had not proved their mettle they ought indeed to be discarded. *Iphigenie auf Tauris*, a play infused with the spirit of the Enlightenment,[10] reminds us that barbaric customs, such as the ritual sacrifice of human beings, the solving of political problems by strife or murder, are evil.[11] They must be replaced by a humane approach to politics. To act in accordance with enlightened thought means to reject 'theological' politics which scorn the exercise of independent indivdual judgment, permit barbaric deeds and justify them as the necessary means to achieve traditional ends.

In *Torquato Tasso* Goethe shows how conventional attitudes become inadequate and even harmful, if challenged by a sensitive individual. Tasso, a poet of stature, has no choice but to assert his right to write poetry and live his life as impelled by his genius and personality. The Establishment, personified by the Duke of Ferrara and his court, fails to understand his needs and unwittingly sets up obstacles to his inner development and to the writing of his poetry. Its members have perhaps little choice if they wish to, as they virtually have to, preserve the *status quo*. Their power resides in their doing so. For the Duke as a Renaissance prince – and it was little different in the 18th century – a great poet, such as Tasso, is no more than a useful ornament that augments the court's glory. Tasso is treated as if he were a minor and lacked the maturity to make his own decisions. In the court's view, to accept patronage entails surrendering rights. Obligations to one's patron must needs curtail an individual's freedom. Tasso does not at first quarrel with this view, explicitly stating that man is not born to be free and that there can be no greater happiness than to serve a prince whom one esteems:

Doch glaube nicht, daß mir
Der Freiheit wilder Trieb den Busen blähe.
Der Mensch ist nicht geboren, frei zu sein
Und für den Edlen ist kein schöner Glück,
Als einem Fürsten, den er ehrt, zu dienen –

But do not believe that freedom's wild urge distends my breast. Man is not born to be free, and for a noble man there is no greater happiness than to serve a prince whom he esteems

Yet the claims of his individuality and of his genius make Tasso challenge the constraint forced upon him by convention and political prudence. The need to assert his individuality inevitably leads to conflict and, since the powers-that-be are stronger, to defeat. Tasso suffers, but does not rebel, for he never fully rejects the social order in which he has grown up and in which he has acquired fame. His attitude to the existing social order remains ambivalent, but as a poet Tasso can transcend the ensuing suffering by writing poetry. He can thus indirectly make an impact on public opinion and bring about a reappraisal of attitudes of mind.

These three plays, all completed a year or so before 1789, during Goethe's stay in Italy, urge us then to reconsider our views on politics and society, but in none of them is resort to violence advocated, let alone a clarion-call to revolution sounded. Individuals matter, but so does the tradition. These dramas are far too complex works to permit simple interpretations, they speak of complexity of character and action of which the *simplificateurs*, to use Jacob Burckhardt's term, of the Revolution were unaware, revealing a lack of insight that displays their shortcomings and the perils caused by their actions.

In a later major play *Die natürliche Tochter*, written in 1803, Goethe, as he expressly stated (cf. H.A., V, 477), sought to sum up his experience of the Revolution. In this play the king is too weak to govern justly. Consequently, his rule is undermined and domestic strife prevails. The ruling class is divided: the Duke's son intrigues against his father when he fears that his inheritance may be jeopardised by the Duke's legitimising his natural daughter. Eugenie, the heroine of the play. For political reasons, cruelty and deceit are practised and excused on pragmatic grounds. Humane feelings yield to force. Injustice prevails by way of secret machinations and is upheld by a clandestine royal decree. A future breakdown of society envisaging a collapse of the social and political order is forecast. Yet the play, despite all the unjust deeds which are perpetrated, ends on a note of hope. Eugenie who had, by way of subterfuge and force, been removed from her father and the court will, by giving up the privileges of birth and marrying someone of lower rank, a bourgeois judge, be able to prepare herself for future fruitful action in the public domain.

Die natürliche Tochter makes it plain that for Goethe moral faults, as evidenced by the weakness, the ineptitude and injustice of rulers, brought about unrest and revolution. To use moral criteria for judging people and events is in keeping with Enlightenment thought. For kings who fail to rule with strength and justice forfeit the right to rule. In later years Goethe put it neatly into a quatrain:

'Warum denn wie mit einem Besen
Wird so ein König hinausgekehrt?'
Wären's Könige gewesen,
Sie stünden noch alle unversehrt.

'Why is such a king swept away with a broom' Had they been genuine kings, all of them would still be unharmed.

Goethe – and he is very much in tune with *Aufklärung* thought – expected professionalism, or at least serious and consistent dedication to their task, from rulers. He abhorred bungling.[12] For him, as for Plato, government is a task requiring professional expertise and moral conviction. Hereditary rulers had the opportunity, denied to others, of being brought up to learn what their obligations were and how to carry them out. There is no substitute for experience. To leave politics to the untutored, uninformed, and inexperienced many is folly. He was strongly opposed to the democratic strand in Enlightenment thought. He distrusted majority rule; for he thought that it brought about the rule of a few leaders who, without an obligation to established customs and beliefs, would ruthlessly exploit political opportunities for their own benefit and glory, and trim their sails to the wind, attracting a following of weak men, who would go along with anything, as well as a mob which followed suit heedlessly.[13] There would, he was convinced, always be rulers and subjects. As he wrote to his fellow-Weimar privy councillor C.G. Voigt on 10 September 1792: 'the more we get about in the world, the more we recognise that man is born to servitude.'[14] To pretend otherwise was bound to provoke social instability and public disorder. These views are in accordance with that strand of Enlightenment thought which advocated rule by enlightened monarchs, a strand which betrays an only partially enlightened attitude of mind, for it unduly limits the individual's freedom by depriving him of his independence. However, Goethe did not side uncritically with enlightened absolutism.[14a] Neither professionalism nor an enlightened approach to politics is enough. In his drama *Torquato Tasso* the Duke of Ferrara's secretary of state, Antonio Montecatini, has to learn this truth after having failed to appreciate Tasso's needs. And Goethe himself on his visit to Berlin in 1778 disliked the machine-like state which Prussia had become under the rule of Frederick the Great, the prototype of an enlightened monarch.

Misuse of power is a form of arrogance or conceit. So is any kind of pretence. Goethe inveighs against charlatanism in politics or any other sphere of life. From his youth onwards he alerted his readers to the misdeeds of impostors. In his early satirical play *Satyros*, a charlatan who uses religious language to pursue his own selfish ends and satisfy his lust, succeeds in bamboozling many foolish and gullible people by extravagant claims before his pretence is finally exposed. The mob is easily taken in, and pretentious men, not legitimised by training and experience, would seize power during a revolution. Like Plato, he found demagogues repulsive and dangerous. Moreover, he believed that charlatanism was inherent in the very claims of the revolutionaries. For they clamoured for and promised both freedom and equality for all men. But as Goethe asserts, 'Legislators or revolutionaries who simultaneously promise equality and freedom are dreamers or charlatans'.[15] In the *Venezianische Epigramme* composed in 1790 as a result of a visit to Venice on which he had accompanied the Dowager Duchess Amalia of Saxe-Weimar he specifically attacked those who advocated freedom for all and sundry; for they did not realise what it entails to be at everyone's beck and call!

Alle Freiheitsapostel: sie waren mir immer zuwider,
Willkür sucht doch nur jeder am Ende, für sich,
Willst du alle viele befrein, so wag es, vielen zu dienen
Wie gefährlich das sei, willst du denn wissen? Versuch es.

(H.A., I, 179)

All apostles of freedom: I always found them repugnant.
Arbitrary power for himself – that's what everyone is seeking.
If you wish to set many free you must dare to serve many.
How dangerous that is, you want to know? Just try it out.

The self-styled champions of freedom are self-seekers. They want arbitrary power for themselves. To set the multitude free only leads to enslavement; for to have many masters leads to lawlessness, to anarchy. Or as Kant, the philosopher of the *Aufklärung*, observed, 'the rule of the many (which he called 'democracy', using that term in a sense different from modern usage) establishes an executive power through which all the citizens make decisions about (and indeed against) the single individual without his consent, so that decisions are made by all the people and yet not by all the people, and this means that the general will is in contradiction with itself, and thus also with freedom'.[16] It is in fact 'despotism' under another name for the mob, so Goethe noticed, quickly becomes tyrannical:

Frankreichs traurig Geschick, die Großen mögen's bedenken!
Aber bedenken fürwahr sollen es Kleine noch mehr,
Große gingen zu Grunde: doch wer beschützte die Menge
Gegen die Menge? Da war Menge der Menge Tyrann.

(H.A., I, 180)

France's sad fate, the great men of the world should ponder it!
But the ordinary folk should ponder it even more,
Top people perished, but who protected the crowd against the crowd?
The crowd tyrannised the crowd.

The individual would, so Goethe thought, be submerged in the crowd. Personal development, self-cultivation, would become impossible. Good intentions were not enough. Lack of realism due to 'Schwärmerei', that is undue enthusiasm, spells disaster. Monarchs had been untrue to their calling and used false coinage, the revolutionaries did no better; they misused their mind by spreading lies and nonsense. (cf. H.A., I, 180).

To apply the wrong criteria amounts to mistaking false coinage for the genuine stuff. The public ought not to be deceived. Rulers should possess integrity and speak and act truthfully (cf. H.A., I, 180). Impostors stir up trouble. They encourage men to abandon commonsense. Their actions defy principles of reason and impair humane values. Empirical observation and sound judgement are abandoned. Superstitions and wild fancies are rife, even supernatural powers are invoked. All that was anathema to the Enlightenment, and not only to Goethe, for the Enlightenment, as its name indicates, wanted to cast the clear and harsh light of reason and experience on human thought and conduct.

In the early 1790s Goethe wrote three plays; generally agreed to be minor ones, inspired by the Revolution and its preludes. In all three of these plays (which are nowadays hardly ever performed) impostors cause harm. Since these plays are comedies the damage is, predictably, contained and the tables, for our entertainment, are turned on the culprits. In *Der Großkophta*, a play doubtless inspired by the Necklace affair and Cagliostro and dealing with the political situation before the Revolution,[17] the folly of gullibility among highly-placed personages is ridiculed, but the deceivers themselves are shown not to be immune to deceit; for we are meant also to laugh at the deceived deceivers. In *Der Bürgergeneral* the would-be revolutionary, whose name 'Schnaps' indicates his intoxication with his own verbiage, disturbs domestic harmony and peace by his pseudo-revolutionary antics, but the poverty, indeed, absurdity of his case cannot mask his own greed and quest for humdrum satisfactions, trivial in contrast to his professed high aims. In *Die Aufgeregten* the peasants are incited by a demagogue to ask for alleged ancient rights which allegedly once existed. Their demands are not scorned by the reigning countess. She has just returned from revolutionary France and learnt the need for just and benign rule so that revolutionary uprisings can be avoided. Therefore, she shows understanding for the people's needs, since she has grasped what damage, bad rule and disregard for ancient rights can do. She restores those rights which her peasants are entitled to, but no more. The demagogue claiming an aristocratic title to which he has no right is shown up for vaunting false ideals and using empty verbiage. In each play charlatanism, by making false promises and trumpeting forth unrealisable demands, is shown to be the cause of much evil.

Goethe then took charlatanism most seriously. His reaction to it can be gauged by his appraisal for the Necklace affair which, as we have seen, disturbed him beyond measure. For he saw the writing on the wall. The French monarchy was found wanting, and Goethe feared dire consequences for the European political order if the most powerful country in continental Europe was ruined by a political upheaval. By letting the affair erupt the French crown had lost respect. The rotten core of the French court was revealed, visible for all those who had eyes to see. What monarchs had built up over centuries would be destroyed within a short span of time. How keenly Goethe felt the dangers of charlatanism is revealed by his interest in and concern about the rise of Cagliostro. He first alludes to his awareness of dangers threatening political stability in France in a letter to Lavater of 22 June 1781, written eight years before the Revolution and four years before the Necklace affair. In this letter he speaks of subterranean movements threatening the established order with collapse. How compelling the phenomenon of Cagliostro was becomes apparent when we read in *Italienische Reise* (H.A., XI, 254–264) of his visit in disguise to Cagliostro's mother in Palermo.

Why did Goethe single out the activities of Cagliostro and the Necklace affair as portent of disasters to come? The reason can be surmised only. False claims of talent or genius appear to have touched him in the raw, perhaps because he knew himself surrounded by pretenders, fellow-*Sturm und Drang* writers who claimed to have genius without possessing it and because he felt the need, in contrast, to assert his own genius. In his old age he was appalled by the poetic dilettantism which flourished at that time.

The author of the *Die Leiden des jungen Werthers* knew how close the kinship between genius and fraudulence was. Werther is not a fraud, of course, but his claim to artistic genius and to be following in the footsteps of Christ is spurious.[18]

To feel repelled by all types of frauds and impostors is also a feature of Enlightenment thought; for the Enlightenment, particularly in its German variety, the *Aufklärung*, was a movement that cultivated seriousness – the strong professorial contingent and the many secularised descendants of Protestant parsons among the *Aufklärer* saw to that.

There is another reason why Goethe found false prophets repulsive. Language itself, so he was convinced, was profoundly ambiguous, and therefore forms of speech could be deliberately misused. When false prophets employ religious language, for instance, they tend to use clichés to conceal their lack of intellectual and spiritual substance. Many of Goethe's early plays are directed against purveyors of spurious values.[19] Goethe even goes so far as to speak in one of the *Venezianische Epigramme* of the kinship between the artist and the charlatan:[20]

Denn Gaukler und Dichter
Sind gar nahe verwandt, suchen and finden sich gleich.

(G.A., I, 232)

For charlatans and poets are too closely related They seek and find each other straightaway.

Goethe is, in his dislike and distrust of 'Schwärmerei', particularly in the sphere of religion, in tune with Enlightenment thought. For the Enlightenment emphasised the need for objective criteria, for clarity, commonsense and judgement based on empirical evidence and practical experience, and charlatanism, whether deliberately employed by evil men or unwittingly by victims of enthusiasm and credulity, turns its back on this enlightened way of looking at the world.

Tolerance was another idea central to Enlightenment thought which Goethe saw violated by the Revolution. It was, as he said in *Dichtung und Wahrheit*, the motto of the age before 1789 (H.A., IX, 512). But the French revolutionaries spurned it. Dogmatism prevailed, an attitude of mind which a philosopher of the Enlightenment like Kant also detested. The revolutionaries were intolerant; for they believed that their doctrines were exclusively right, they claimed a monopoly of virtue. That intransigent stance aroused intolerance in others, it bred hatred – and from hatred strife, disorder and even war sprang. Hatred is evil. Yet the revolutionaries fanned hatred; their hatred for the ancien régime was repaid in kind by the emigrés and their German allies. It was the task of cultured men to bridge the gulf between opposing views, however fervently held. Literature ought to promote that kind of attitude. In *Unterhaltungen deutscher Ausgewanderter* Goethe shows how it could be done. The telling of stories is resorted to because it allows one to ignore the political differences of the day, ensuring civility of speech and conduct. Thoughtless idealism without regard for the feeling of others is likely to cause offence, even unhappiness and distress. Hatred is hostile to art and science; in later life Goethe regretted that the atmosphere created by the Revolution made him indulge in scientific polemics.[21] Goethe's rejection of the French Revolution, then, reflects the consistent moral attitude to public and private life which is one of the main characteristics of *Aufklärung* thought. In his creative work Goethe of course avoids moralising. He knew it to be inimical to art and to be counter-productive, yet he also believed that literature had a moral content and that moral consequences could and would necessarily flow from genuine works of art. As he said in *Dichtung und Wahrheit*:

> A good work of art can and will make a moral impact, but to demand that an artist work with a moral end in mind would amount to spoiling his craft. (H.A., 9, 539)

Freedom from hatred and the spreading of tolerance were necessary to ensuring good public order and private contentment. In the verse epic *Hermann und Dorothea* the heroine Dorothea is not filled with hatred for the French, even though she had lost her home and belongings as a result of the French annexation of the left bank of the Rhine. Even the disappointment with the Revolution suffered by her deceased fiancé does not prevent her from recalling his genuine feeling for the aims of the revolutionaries with respect. Instead of feeding on hatred she returns all her energy to the task of helping others. Because she does that, her beauty is enhanced and she gains Hermann's love and a home.

To demand an orderly society governed according to generally accepted principles of law was one of the major planks of the Enlightenment. For anarchy spells disaster. It prevents self-cultivation, the study of science and the writing of poetry. The due process of law must therefore be respected. Goethe's striking words, often misunderstood, expressed in *Belagerung von Mainz* of 1793 (published only in 1823) that 'he would rather commit an injustice than tolerate disorder' (H.A., X, 391) reveals not that he was supporting despotic rule, but rather that he defended the principle inherent in English common law and central to Enlightenment legal doctrine, namely that it is better to acquit a guilty man than to convict an innocent one.[22] For he risked his own life in order to prevent the lynching of an alleged supporter of the French revolutionary forces which were leaving Mayence after their defeat.

Order can be disturbed not only by political but also by economic action. Goethe, who had for some years been in charge of Weimar finance, having been called in to clear up a mess caused by an inefficient administrator, knew well that financial prudence is the basis of good government. Enlightenment thought demands fiscal responsibility from rulers or government. The profligacy of courts and their extravagance which Goethe, to some extent, had also personally experienced, is pilloried in the first act of *Faust II* where he strikingly depicts the cost of monetary inflation.

Fiscal profligacy leads to inflation and threatens to destroy the social fabric. The failure of successive French kings and their ministers to put the country's finances right is generally agreed to have been a major cause, if not the major cause, of the outbreak of the Revolution.[23] The scene in *Faust II* where the Emperor follows Mephistopheles's advice and needlessly prints money, may allude to the Ancien Régime's financial calamities, but it does so merely because it is one instance of inflationary fiscal policy. For Goethe himself, as his *Campagne in Frankreich* reveals, knew that inflation was not merely a prerogative of kings. For the infamous *assignats*, those bonds that became so quickly worthless, were issued by the revolutionaries. And it was a sign that the emigrés had forfeited their rights and privileges when they forged the *assignats* in the callous and unfounded hope that Louis XVI, once restored to the throne, would pay for the lot (H.A., 10, 200). As if he ever had been able to repay his debts! Thus, Goethe's objection to the financial malpractices of the Revolution as well as of the French monarchy is in tune with Enlightenment thought, always opposed to financial profligacy.

If Goethe was hostile to the Revolution in France, but, as he told Eckermann on 4 January 1824, recognised its 'necessity', he utterly rejected its spread to Germany. To impose foreign practice and ideas on the Germans conflicted with his Möserian respect for local and regional customs and political tradition. Moreover, he felt that there was no need for a revolution in Germany because reforms which had been impossible in France had, he believed, already taken place or were still in train. Indeed, many German rulers were imbued with ideas of the Enlightenment. Sound reforms could, so he thought, come from above only and German rulers might well carry them out, provided agitation and undue demands were kept in check. The spirit of Enlightenment could, if at times only dimly, be perceived to be at work in Germany. The French revolutionaries threatened it just as Lutheranism had done in the sixteenth century (H.A., I, 211). Goethe himself had initiated reforms in Weimar: for instance he had reduced the army by one third, abolished the whole artillery of two officers and eight men by transferring them to other duties, reformed finances and done much to improve road building and mining. Thus, from an Enlightenment point of view he objected to the practice of the revolutionaries just as much as he objected to the excesses of enlightened absolutism. Both were immoderate. Political excess of any kind runs counter to genuine Enlightenment thought; for it produces tyranny which violates individual freedom. His concern was never merely personal, but always related to the world around him. His aim was to see things as they are and not to be influenced by wild fancies or ideology. Thus, he regarded any attempt to bring about a major social or political upheaval with scepticism. The price of revolution was likely to be too high. His urge to be objective made him take that view and believe in the efficacy of gradual change which, so he was convinced, was in tune with nature.

Whether Goethe was right in his appraisal of the German political scene is a moot point and depends on what view is taken of the Empire, whether it is seen as a going concern, as some historians think, or whether it is believed to have been rotting away, falling like an overripe fruit to the assault of the French armies. Goethe undoubtedly accepted in his youth the Empire as it existed: for he never was a revolutionary demanding the overthrow of the existing order, and once the Empire was gone he first accepted the Napoleonic reorganisation of Europe and later the Restoration: for he feared the anarchy brought about by the Revolution itself more than anything else. For revolution ran counter to his view of nature which profoundly shaped his thought. As a natural scientist, he was a Neptunist, not a Plutonist, as *Faust II* makes plain; that is, he believed that the earth had come into being by slow evolution rather than by sudden eruption. Therefore, by way of analogy, evolution, and not revolution, was appropriate to nature and society. Both Enlightenment thinkers and Goethe focussed attention on nature, but Goethe almost invariably interpreted nature differently from most Enlightenment thinkers: for he saw it as a dynamic and organic force while the Enlightenment thinkers viewed it more often than not as an abstract entity. But Goethe, however much he was indebted to Möser, accepted many ideas arising from the school of Natural Law, and integrated them into his vision of a humane society.

Throughout his life Goethe's concern was with the individual whom he saw not as an isolated entity, but as a member of society. However, he believed it to be imperative that an individual should not be impeded by convention when seeking to develop his individual talent. On the other hand, he considered respect for social traditions, provided they are healthy, to be equally important. The Revolution, by its very violence, interfered with the natural rhythm of social change. In Germany a revolution would not usher in progress but set the clock back, for it would curtail individual freedom which Goethe sought to develop by means of his work.

Moreover, Goethe's work makes us aware of genuine issues which arise again and again and which all of us are capable of grasping and experiencing. At the same time, he makes us look for practical, sensible responses. That intention was at the core of his attitude to the French Revolution. If we sum up this attitude in a few words which can, as always with imaginative writings, be no more than tentative, it is as follows: however critical Goethe was of the Revolution, his response was practical, combining a conservative Möserian attitude with liberal, even radical Enlightenment views. That practical approach stood him in good stead. It brought out the full measure of his creative power.

NOTES

1. There are many studies of this subject. For instance, Claude David, 'Goethe und die französische Revolution', in Richard Brinkmann et. al., *Deutsche Literatur und französische Revolution. Sieben Studien*, Kleine Vandenhoek Reihe, No, 1965, Göttingen 1964, pp. 63–86; G.P. Gooch, *Germany and the French Revolution*, London 1920, pp. 174–207; J. Droz, *L'Allemagne et la Révolution*, Paris 1949, pp. 213–320; Wilhelm Mommsen, *Goethes politische Anschauungen*, Stuttgart 1948, pp. 91–118.

2. Goethe, *Werke*, Hamburger Ausgabe, Hamburg 1949–64 (further abbreviated as H.A.), XII, 427.

3. There are many studies in which this relationship is examined: cf. above all G. Kass, *Möser und Goethe* (diss.) Göttingen 1909/Berlin 1909 for a thorough analysis; cf. also Jonathan B. Knudsen, *Justus Möser and the German Enlightenment*, Cambridge 1986, who believes that Möser basically belonged to the Enlightenment; although there are some affinities he overstates his case. cf. my review, *Neue Zürcher Zeitung* No. 121, 27 May 1987, p. 28.

4. cf. David, p. 64 who points out that Burke is rather surprisingly never mentioned in Goethe's work.

5. Marx in Marx/Engels, *Historische Kritische Gesamtausgabe*, Frankfurt 1927, I, 254.

6. cf. Justus Möser, 'Über Theorie und Praxis' (first published 1797/98) in *Sämtliche Werke. Historische-Kritische Ausgabe*, Oldenburg, n.d., X, pp. 141–157.

7. cf. letter to F.H. Jacobi, 7 July 1793.

8. cf. my article 'Zu Goethes *Belagerung von Mainz. Einige Überlegungen*', in E. Huber-Thomas/Ghemela Adler (eds.) *Romantik und Moderne. Neue Beiträge aus Forschung und Lehre, Festschrift für Helmut Motekat*, Frankfurt/Main, Berne, New York, 1986, pp. 402f. where this problem is discussed.

9. H.A. XII, p. 433. cf. also my article 'Möser, Goethe and the *Aufklärung*. The Holy Roman Empire in *Götz von Berlichingen* and *Egmont*', *Deutsche Vierteljahrsschrift für Literaturwissenschaft und Geistesgeschichte*, XL, 1986, pp. 609–41, for a discussion of how this attitude is reflected in *Egmont*.

10. cf. my forthcoming essay, 'Theological politics in *Iphigenie auf Tauris*', in *Patterns of Change: German Drama and the European Tradition. Festschrift for Ronald Peacock*.

11. Goethe, *Werke*, Artemis-Gedenkausgabe (further abbreviated as G.A.) II, p. 413.

12. cf. Hans Rudolf Vaget, *Dilettantismus und Meisterschaft. Zum Problem des Dilettantismus bei Goethe: Praxis, Theorie und Zeitkritik*, Winkler Studien, Munich 1971, pp. 97 ff. who points out that Goethe became increasingly critical of

dilettantism if it was turned into 'Pfuscherei'.

13. Conversation with Eckermann, 27 April 1825.
14. cf. Friedrich Sengle, 'Die didaktischen und kulturkritischen Elemente in 'West-Östlicher Divan'', *Oxford German Studies*, XII, 1981, particularly p. 72.
14a. I am indebted to T.J. Reed who made this point in a lecture at the University or London Institute of Germanic Studies on 14 January 1988 entitled 'Coming of Age in Prussia and Swabia: Kant, Schiller and the Duke', and who emphasised that Enlightened absolutism fell short of the goal of Enlightenment as defined by Kant in *Beantwortung der Frage: Was is Aufklärung? (Answer to the Question: What is Enlightenment?)*'
15. *Goethe-Jahrbuch*, XXIII, 1901, p. 17.
16. For a discussion of Kant's politics cf. my edition, *Kant's Political Writings*, Cambridge 1970, particularly pp. 29 ff. The quotation (ibid., p. 101) is found in *Zum Ewigen Frieden (On Perpetual Peace)*. cf. also my book, *Kants Politisches Denken*, Berne/Frankfurt 1977.
17. Walter Müller-Seidel, 'Deutsche Klassik and Französische Revolution', *Die Geschichtlichkeit der deutschen Klassik. Literatur und Denkformen um 1800*, Stuttgart 1983, who points out that *Der Groß-Cophta* does not deal with the Revolution itself, but with the political conditions which preceded it.
18. cf. *Goethe's Novels*, London 1969, p. 27. cf. also my *Goethes Romane*, Berne and Munich 1963, p. 21, where this aspect of Werther's character is discussed.
19. Victor Lange, 'The Language of the Poet Goethe 1772–1774' in Curt von Faber et. al. (eds.), *Wächter und Hüter. Festschrift für Hermann J. Weigand zum 17 November 1957*, New Haven, Conn 1957, p. 72.
20. This whole question is discussed by Wolfdietrich Rasch in his article 'Die Gauklerin Bettine. Zu Goethes *Venetianischen Epigrammen*' in Stanley A. Corngold et al. (eds.). *Aspekte der Goethezeit*, Göttingen 1977, pp. 115–36.
21. cf. my article, 'Goethe's *Campagne in Frankreich*. Some reflections', *Publications of the English Goethe Society*, N.S., LIII, 1984, pp. 120 ff. for an elaboration of this point (forthcoming German version 'Goethes *Campagne in Frankreich*. Einige Uberlegungen', *Goethe-Jahrbuch*, CIV, 1987).
22. cf. Stefan Korányi, *Goethe: Autobiographie und Wissenschaft*. Studie über seine Schrift 'Campagne in Frankreich' (unpublished M.A. diss.), Munich 1986, p. 101. Cf. also Goethe, *Die Schriften zur Naturwissenschaft*, Leopoldina Ausgabe, Weimar, 1947 ff., I, 5, pp. 193 ff.
23a. cf. John R. Williams, *Goethe's Faust*, London, 1987, pp. 127 f. who discusses this aspect in some detail.
23. cf. my article, 'Belagerung von Mainz . . .', pp. 415 ff.
24. cf. Alfred Cobban, *A History of Modern France*, I, p. 14 who says so explicity.
25. Conversation with Eckermann, 24 January 1824.
26. cf. David, pp. 82 ff. who also emphasises this point.
27. cf. Hans Rudolf Vaget, 'Liebe und Grundeigentum in Wilhelm Meisters Lehrjahren: Zur Physiognomie des Adels bei Goethe', in Peter Uwe Hohendahl/Paul Lützeler (eds.) *Legitimationskrise des deutschen Adels*, Stuttgart, 1979, pp. 137–57. cf. also Karl-Heinz Hahn, 'Adel und Bügertum im Spiegel Goethescher Dichtungen zwischen 1790 und 1810 unter besonderer Berücksichtigung von *Wilhelm Meisters Lehrjahren*, *Goethe-Jahrbuch*, 95, 1978, pp. 150–62, both of whom discuss the political implications of the novel, in particular the relationship between nobility and bourgeoisie.

On Rousseau's, Robespierre's and Kant's Criteria of Moral Action

S. Körner

It is a generally accepted position of political history that Rousseau's ideas played an important role in shaping the course of the French Revolution. Historians of ideas, in particular historians of philosophy, similarly agree that Rousseau's conception of human nature and morality caused a revolution in Kant's mind, which in turn greatly influenced post-Kantian philosophical thought. Among the evidence for the Rousseauistic aspects of these two revolutions are clear acknowledgments by Robespierre and by Kant of their deep indebtedness to Rousseau. The purpose of the present essay is a characterization, comparison and critique of Rousseau's, Robespierre's and Kant's criteria of moral action. It will in particular be argued that Rousseau and – to a lesser extent – Kant overestimate the consensus which results from the correct application of these criteria by different people and that they thereby pave the way for an unwarranted moral dogmatism.

The essay begins with an account of Rousseau's conception of the general will as a criterion of morality (I). After a consideration of its interpretation and application by Robespierre (II), it is compared and contrasted with the Kantian criterion of moral action, as based on the categorical imperative (III). A critical discussion of both criteria leads to some brief concluding remarks on the relation between moral universalizability and moral disagreement (IV).

I

On Rousseau's conception of the general will as a criterion of morality
Whatever the state of nature may have been, the morality of human beings is according to Rousseau based on their social life. A clear statement of this relation is found at the beginning of the *Discourse on Political Economy*, where the body politic is described as 'possessed of a will . . . which constitutes for all members of the State the rule of what is just and unjust'.[1] The assumption that the general will exists does not imply the knowledge of its content. Nor does it

follow that there exists an unfailing method of discovering it. While 'the general will is always right', it does for example 'not follow that the deliberations of the people are equally correct'[2], or that 'the judgment which guides it' is 'always enlightened'.[3] Who then has access to the content of the general will? According to Rousseau it is those legislators who while rightly relying on their judgment and 'having no right of legislation'[4], '. . . have recourse to divine intervention and credit the gods with their own wisdom, in order that the peoples submitting to the laws of the state as to those of nature . . . might obey freely, and bear with docility the yoke of the public happiness'[5]. Yet in putting forward his own political and moral theory Rousseau does not appeal to higher authority, but relies on argument and a rhetoric which Kant and many others have found difficult to resist. In order to arrive at a critical understanding of Rousseau's conception of individual and political morality it is useful to distinguish between on the one hand his general method for discovering a nation's will or his general criteria of moral action and on the other hand some more specific guidelines which he uses in applying his general method or criteria.

The most important feature of a moral law is its twofold universality *i.e.* that it 'considers subjects *en masse* and actions in the abstract, and never a particular person or action' and thus 'unites universality of will with universality of object'.[6] In so far as the will of a person is part of the general will, *i.e.* part of the source or creator of law, the person is a citizen; and in so far as the person is governed by law, the person is a subject. Clearly not all human beings, *e.g.* infants and those suffering from serious mental handicaps, are capable of being citizens in Rousseau's sense. Yet Rousseau also has no doubt in excluding women from citizenship since 'however lightly we may regard the disadvantages peculiar to women . . . they necessarily occasion intervals of inaction . . .'.[7] In this respect he not only disagrees with many later political thinkers, but also with Plato who, one may assume, was aware of these disadvantages.

The attempt of different human beings, to 'unite universality of will with universality of object' may lead to different results, in particular to the formulation of different laws. One obvious way to reduce this variety – and one of which Rousseau was aware – is to require that what is willed is practicable. Yet the combined requirements of universality and of practicability still allow for a great many mutually incompatible, sincerely made and selfless choices. This, it seems, is the reason why Rousseau supplements his definition of the general will and his distinction between the general will and the self-interested 'will of all' by some more specific guide-lines for discovering the former. Among them is a rather crude utilitarian recipe. Since, 'the will of all takes private interest into account and is no more than a sum of particular wills' one has to 'take away from these same wills the pluses and minuses that cancel one another', with the result that 'the general will remains as the sum of the differences'.[8] Another guide-line, which is applicable to assemblies, consists in the observation that 'the nearer opinion approaches unanimity, the greater is the dominance of the general will' and 'long debates, dissensions, and tumult proclaim the ascending of particular interests and the decline of the State'.[9] The last example of a guide-line for ascertaining the correct content of the general will is a demographic preference, which today would seem dubious to politicians of all shades of opinion. It is, other things being equal, the preference for that 'government under which, without external aids, without naturalization or colonies, the citizens increase and multiply most . . .'.[10]

Turning to the constitutional and other legal rules the morality of which Rousseau inferred from his definition of the general will and his guide-lines for discovering it, it is important to distinguish the historical question about the inferences which he drew from his premises and the logical question about the validity of these inferences. The general will chooses according to Rousseau between various forms of government – in particular democratic, aristocratic and monarchic forms, depending on certain natural conditions in which the subjects of the government find themselves, *e.g.* the size of the state, its natural wealth, the degree of complexity of its citizens' manners. An exception is representative democracy, which Rousseau rejects without qualification as a relic of the 'iniquitous and absurd system' of feudal government, which 'degrades humanity and dishonours the name of man'. He, therefore, regards the people of England as free 'only during the election of members of parliament' after which 'slavery overtakes it'.[11]

Yet whatever government is chosen, it must protect the public welfare, which Rousseau conceives very much after the fashion of those political theorists who argue for a welfare state. Thus, while every government must protect the right to private property, it must also 'prevent extreme inequality of fortune; not by taking away wealth from its possessors, but by depriving all men of the means to accumulate it'.[12] It must in addition safeguard the subsistence of the subjects,[13] provide for public education,[14] guarantee a sufficient fund for the maintenance of magistrates,[15] introduce a system of progressive taxation and do so only with the consent of the people.[16] Two further aspects of Rousseau's vision of social justice played an important part in the French Revolution, namely his attitudes to religion and to revolution. As regards the former, he argues that 'each citizen should have a religion' which 'will make him love his duty'. It implies belief in the 'existence of a mighty, intelligent and beneficent Divinity' as one of its main positive dogmas and one negative dogma namely 'intolerance', which he regards as characteristic of 'the religions of the Lamas and of the Japanese' as well as of 'Roman Christianity'.[17] Rousseau is clearly opposed to revolution, which, he holds, can be prevented 'by periodical assemblies' of the citizens 'which need no formal summoning' and which have the power to change the form of government, in particular any form of hereditary government. Yet he admits that in some cases the distinction between 'a regular and legitimate act' and 'a seditious tumult' may be very difficult to make and – it may be added – controversial.[18]

Some of Rousseau's views – in particular the exclusion of women from active citizenship, the rejection of representative democracy and the need for a civil religion – have seemed unacceptable to some of his contemporaries, to some leaders of the French Revolution and to some later political theorists. Yet such a difference of conviction did not always prevent them from continuing to consider themselves as his followers and as bound to excuse their master's apparent misreadings of the general will. The difficulty of reconciling their convictions with those of Rousseau was overcome even by those of his followers who held that during a revolution, intended to create a state conforming to the general will, its content may be accessible only to a small minority of the people, which may become even a minority of one.

II

On Robespierre's application of Rousseau's criterion of morality
Robespierre regarded himself as a faithful disciple of Rousseau and is so regarded by many historians of the French Revolution. Thus J.M. Thompson holds that Robespierre 'refused to move from the pure doctrine of Rousseau' and calls him the deputy not 'merely of Arras, but the deputy for Rousseau', who towards the end of his life was convinced that he 'stood alone in apostolic succession to Rousseau'.[21] If he misunderstood Rousseau, the fault was not entirely his own – especially as he had to interpret the people's general will in circumstances which, it can be argued, Rousseau had not considered. He certainly agreed with most of Rouseau's ideas about the content of the social contract. Where his agreement with Rousseau's understanding of the general will is open to serious doubts, is his attitude towards the means of realizing the form of government which the general will would find suitable in the political situation of the French people during Robespierre's life-

time. His 'Proposed Declaration of the Rights of Man and Citizen' is to a large extent a synopsis of Rousseau's political theory.[22] The outlined constitution contains – apart from a general guarantee to all men of equal rights for the preservation of their existence and liberty – the following Rousseauistic proposals among others: the rights of peaceable assembly; freedom of the press; a guaranteed subsistence minimum; progressive taxation; placing education within the reach of all citizens; the right of the people to change its government and to recall its representatives, when it pleases; payment of public functionaries. It also condemns war and declares that 'who ever oppresses a single nation declares himself the enemy of all'. This last proposal is, it can be reasonably argued, in the spirit of Rousseau. So is Robespierre's civil religion and cult of the supreme being, which find expression in the introduction of the Declaration, proclaimed 'in the presence of the Universe and before the eyes of the Immortal Legislator'.

While Rousseau may have implicitly admitted and justified certain kinds of revolutionary action, he would not have agreed with the following article of the Declaration or the terror which it justified for Robespierre. 'When the government violates the right of the people, insurrection is the most sacred of rights and the most indispensable of duties for the people and every portion thereof'. It is here not necessary to describe in detail the terror which Robespierre regarded as justified. Its nature finds, it seems, adequate expression in the following words: 'If the basis of popular government in time of peace is virtue, its basis in time of revolution is virtue and terror – virtue, without which terror is disastrous, and terror, without which virtue is powerless'.[23]

It is now possible to compare the essential features of Rousseau's and Robespierre's moral theories. They both accept the doctrine of the primacy of social over individual morality. More precisely, they imply that a social practicability or institution (e.g. a legal system) is moral if, and only if, it is based on the general will; and that an individual action or set of actions is moral if, and only if, (1) it contributes to the realization or preservation of a practicability based on the general will and (2) does *not conflict* with the content of the general will. They also agree that a form of government as characterized in Rousseau's *Social Contract* is a practicability, i.e. that *there exists* a set of cooperative actions, by which this practicability can be realized. How far, if at all, they agree that the terror of which Robespierre approved can be justified as not conflicting with the general will and, hence, as moral, remains a controversial issue. That this should be so constitutes part of the evidence that the correct application of Rousseau's criterion of morality may yield mutually incompatible answers.

III

From Rousseau's general will to Kant's categorical imperative
Kant acknowledges Rousseau's profound influence on his thinking.
He compares Rousseau's understanding of humanity with New-
ton's scientific discoveries and expresses his gratitude to Rousseau
for correcting the mistaken view of humanity which he had before
reading his works.[19] In his moral and political philosophy Kant
accepts Rousseau's distinction between the moral will of human
beings and their individual desires, directed towards the realization
of their self-interest. He also on the whole accepts Rousseau's
characterization of the moral will as considering 'subjects *en masse*
and actions in the abstract' and as uniting 'universality of will with
universality of object' (see I above). Yet, as is made clear in Kant's
ethical and political writings, he considers it necessary to modify
Rousseau's account in two important respects. First, the universal
character of the moral will and the way in which it gives rise to
specific duties must be made clearer. Second, whereas Rousseau's
conception of the general will, as primarily 'the will of the people'
implies that individual morality has its source in a morally acceptable social organization, Kant holds, on the contrary, that a morally
acceptable social organization and, hence, a morally acceptable
legal system must be based on a moral law which is binding on any
human being *qua human being*. It follows that for Kant there is no
need to assume that a society has a will of its own.

Kant's criterion of a moral action is the categorical imperative,
which in the *Foundations of the Metaphysics of Morals* is formulated as
follows: 'Act only according to that maxim through which you can
at the same time will that it should become a universal law.'[20] Kant
assumes that every action, which can be judged to be moral or
immoral, realizes a maxim, i.e. a subjective rule of which the agent
is aware or which he, at least, implicitly accepts. A maxim is like a
legal rule in that it describes a situation and a course of action in
general terms, that is to say without referring to a particular agent.
It differs from a legal rule in that the agent himself has decided on
the course of action which is appropriate in the described situation.
Examples are the maxim not to repay a debt when punishment for
not repaying it can be avoided; or the maxim to relieve human
suffering whenever possible. The maxim – and the action realizing
it – is moral if, and only if, its acceptor *can will* it to become a
universal law.

To assert that a maxim *can be* willed (i.e. freely willed) by its
acceptor to become a universal law, is not to assert a mere logical
possibility. It also implies: (1) that what is being willed by the

acceptor of the maxim is a practicability, i.e. that 'ought implies *can*' (see *Kritik d. praktischen Vernunft*, Part I §6); (2) that the acceptor's will is sincere, e.g. that although he may be able to pretend to will a certain kind of fraudulent promise to become permissible by a universal law, he cannot really will this; (3) that if one person can sincerely will a certain maxim to become a universal law, then every other person considering this maxim cannot but also will this maxim to become a universal law. That is to say that whoever applies the categorical imperative correctly, must arrive at the same result. Just as Rousseau held that the general will is always right, although the deliberations of the people may fail to discover it, so Kant is committed to the view that there is only one correct application of the categorical imperative, although even a wholly sincere person may fail to apply it correctly. To make this point is not to deny that discovering the content of the general will is likely to prove more difficult than applying the categorical imperative.

In order to make the transition from individual to social morality two questions have to be answered. First, what kind of legal system is most likely to help rather than hinder those who are bound by it to act morally rather than immorally? Second, how can such a system be realized or, if already in existence, preserved by individual or cooperative actions which are not immoral (which for a follower of Kant either conform to the categorical imperative or, at least, are not inconsistent with it). Kant's general answer to the first question consists in asserting the fundamental principles that every member of society is as a human being free; as a subject equal to every other member of society; and as a citizen independent, in the sense of being a 'co-legislator' (*Mitgesetzgeber*).[24]

These principles are in agreement with the letter and spirit of Rousseau's theory, as are some of Kant's more specific proposals. Thus he agrees with Rousseau's exclusion of women from active citizenship, *i.e.* their exclusion from the class of co-legislators. Indeed Kant's class of co-legislators is even narrower than Rousseau's, since he excludes everybody 'whose existence (food and protection) depends on the disposition of others', such as apprentices of merchants or craftsmen or servants who are not servants of the state.[25] He similarly agrees with Rousseau's conception of a civil religion which acknowledges a supreme being but opposes any intolerant fetishism or clericalism (*Pfaffentum*).[26]

Probably the most serious disagreement between Kant and Rousseau concerns representative democracy, which Rousseau, as has been mentioned earlier, wholly rejects. Kant, on the other hand, is equally convinced that 'every true republic is and cannot be other than a representative system of the people so that its rights are taken care of through its representatives.'[27]

The fact that Kant barely discusses certain issues which seem of the utmost importance to Rousseau and *vice versa*, does not necessarily imply a disagreement, but may with some plausibility be interpreted as a matter of emphasis or as a difference in ranking the importance of various morally acceptable political choices. Thus Kant hardly, if at all, considers those features of government which are characteristic of modern welfare states and which Rousseau regarded as fundamental. Among them are a guaranteed subsistence minimum for all citizens, a progressive system of taxation and a public system of education. Kant on the other hand devoted much thought to the problem of international peace, which he regarded not as a mere idea, but as a practicability.[28] While Rousseau never discussed the problem systematically, it might well be argued that when Robespierre included his own conviction about the need for international peace in his proposed declaration of the rights of man and citizen, he was acting in the spirit of Rousseau. (See II)

Turning to the question of the morally acceptable actions through which a morally acceptable form of government is to be realized, we find Rousseau and Kant in close agreement on the central issue of revolutionary action. Rousseau is in principle opposed to revolution, although he might have admitted the need for some revolutionary actions in exceptional cases (see I). However, he would not have approved of the regime of terror and would have rejected Robespierre's attempts at justifying it. Kant's rejection of revolutionary action is complete and unambiguous. 'There exists' according to him 'no rightful (*rechtmässig*) resistance of the people against the legislative head of the state ... no right of sedition (*seditio*) or, still less, a right of rebellion (*rebellio*)'. While Kant admits that 'a change of a defective constitution may at times be necessary' it can 'rightfully be brought about only by the sovereign, that is to say, through *reform* and not by the people and, hence, by revolution'. Yet once a revolution has been successful in bringing about a new form of government, sedition or rebellion against it is no less excluded than the rebellion to which it owes its existence.[29] Thus Kant's political and moral theory contains no justification of a French counter-revolution. Indeed, Kant held that Louis XVI voluntarily surrendered his sovereign power to the Third Estate.[30]

It is worth noting that Kant's rejection of revolutionary action does not prevent the possibility of two sets of border-line cases. The first may arise for a person who has to decide whether a certain sequence of actions constitutes the revolutionary overthrow of a sovereign (and is, therefore, immoral) or whether it constitutes the voluntary abdication of the sovereign (and is, therefore, not immoral). The second set of border-line cases may arise for a person who has to decide whether a certain sequence of actions constitutes a counter-revolution (which is immoral) or the successful prevention of a revolution (which is not immoral).

IV

Some critical remarks on Rousseau's and Kant's criteria of moral action
In the context of this essay the following theses of Rousseau are of central importance. First, there exists in every society a general will which is the will of the society and which differs from the will of its members in such a way that in the case of a conflict between the general will and the will of one or more individuals, the general will is supreme. Second, the general will is universal in the sense that 'it considers subjects *en masse* and actions in the abstract' (see I). Third, what is being willed by the general will is not a mere possibility, but a practicability or, at least, an ideal which is capable of being approximated by individual or cooperative actions. Fourth, the general will is unique in the sense that it wills what is moral for society as a whole and for each of its members. The applicability of these theses, i.e. the supremacy-, the universality-, the practicability- and the uniqueness-thesis, to an action guarantees its morality.

To the four Rousseauistic theses there correspond four Kantian theses. Their greater clarity is due to Kant's relying on the application of the categorical imperative to actions or, more precisely, to their maxims rather than on some ill defined method of discovering the content of a will belonging to a society, which *qua* society is assumed to have a personality of its own. The following are the Kantian versions of the four theses. First, according to the Kantian supremacy-thesis every person is aware of the difference between acting in conformity with the morally good will, as determined by the categorical imperative, and acting in conformity with mere desires. The person, moreover, knows that in the case of a conflict between the morally good will and other desires the morally good will is supreme. Second, according to the Kantian thesis of universality the good will is universal in the sense that it can will the maxims of certain actions (namely the moral actions) to become universal laws. Third, according to the Kantian practicability-thesis what is willed by the good will is necessarily practicable (*i.e. ought* implies *can*). Fourth, according to the Kantian uniqueness-thesis the good will is unique in the sense that it is the same for everybody, *i.e.* that anybody's correct application of the categorical imperative to the same action (as characterized by its maxim) yields one and the same result.

The supremacy- and the practicability-theses are hardly con-troversial. They are in one form or other accepted by all moral philosophers and by common sense. The supremacy of moral over all other human attitudes does not, of course, mean that human actions always conform to the former. It can be – but need not here be – explained in terms of a stratification of practical attitudes, i.e. by pointing out that practical attitudes may be the object of practical attitudes and that moral attitudes, while having other practical attitudes as their objects, are not themselves the objects of other practical attitudes.[31] Since moral attitudes are a species of practical attitudes, a person's attitude cannot be moral unless the person believes it to be practicable. The thesis that a moral attitude is necessarily *believed* to be practicable is, of course, weaker than the Kantian practicability-thesis according to which any moral attitude is necessarily practicable.

In the case of the universality- and the uniqueness-thesis diffi-culties arise both for Rousseau's and for Kant's moral theory. A major difficulty stems from their shared assumption that the universality-thesis implies the uniqueness-thesis. This is so because according to Rousseau the correct reading of the general will cannot yield incompatible results and because the same holds according to Kant for the correct application of the categorical imperative. Yet in considering some moral disagreements, for example the disagreement between Kant and Rousseau about representative government, their respective methods of deciding the issue are of no help. Again, attempts by one follower of Rousseau or Kant to show that another, whose moral convictions he does not share, has misapplied his master's criterion may lead to accusations of self-deception or of an inability to grasp what is intuitively self-evident. The appeal to a self-evident intuition is particularly frequent in ethics. There, as in other fields, it proves either superfluous or useless: superfluous if the interlocutors are in agreement, useless if they are not. In cases of a morally inspired political struggle the uniqueness-thesis may lend support to the use of terror, as became clear during the French Revolution.[32]

The following very brief remarks are intended to indicate how the thesis that moral attitudes are universal can be freed from the mistaken implication that two persons cannot have two incompat-ible practical attitudes, both of which can be reasonably judged to be moral attitudes.[33] The so revised principle of universality can be expressed in a variety of equivalent ways. The following version of the principle has been chosen in order to facilitate its comparison with the Kantian and, indirectly, with the Rousseauistic criterion of morality: Act only according to that maxim through which not only you, *but also every other rational human being*, can will that it should become a universal law. This formulation is meant to underline that two people may correctly universalize two incompatible maxims – *provided* that each of them considers the other capable of a change of will, resulting in their agreement, in particular on the basis of argument. That moral arguments may be the reason, not only for a person's abandoning an immoral for a moral conviction, but also one moral conviction for another which is incompatible with it, is highly relevant to the political issues raised by Rousseau, Robespierre and Kant. It provides strong support for the establishment and continuance of democratic government, of institutions which promote free discussion and, most important, of political tolerance.

NOTES

1. Jean Jacques Rousseau, *The Social Contract and Discourses*, translated with an introduction by G.D.H. Cole (1913) pp. 236–7.
2. Op. cit., p. 22.
3. Op. cit., p. 31.
4. Op. cit., p. 33.
5. Op. cit., p. 34.
6. Op. cit., p. 30 and p. 80.
7. Op. cit., p. 234.
8. Op. cit., p. 23.
9. Op. cit., p. 87.
10. Op. cit., p. 69.
11. Op. cit., p. 78.
12. Op. cit., p. 250.
13. Op. cit., p. 254.
14. Op. cit., p. 252.
15. Op. cit., p. 256.
16. Op. cit., p. 261.
17. Op. cit., p. 114 and p. 111.
18. Op. cit., p. 83.
19. Kant, Akademie edition Vol. XX, p. 58 and p. 44.
20. Kant, *Foundations of the Metaphysics of Morals*, Akademie edition vol. 4 p. 421.
21. J.M. Thompson, 'Robespierre' in *Leaders of the French Revolution* (1929).
22. For the text of the declaration see G. Rudé, *Robespierre* (1967) pp. 54–57.
23. J.M. Thompson, 'Robespiere' in *Leaders of the French Revolution* (1929) p. 231.
24. Kant, *Über den Gemeinspruch: Das mag in der Theorie richtig sein, taugt aber nicht für die Praxis*, Akademie edition Vol. VIII p. 290f.
25. Kant, *Metaphysische Anfangsgründe der Rechtslehre*, part 2 Section 1, Akademie edition vol. VI, p. 314.
26. Kant, *Religion innerhalb der Grenzen der blossen Vernunft*, Akademie edition vol. VI, pp. 175 ff.
27. Kant, *Die Metaphysik der Sitten, Rechtslehre*, 52, Akademie edition vol. VI. p. 341.

28. Op. cit., p. 386.
29. Op. cit., p. 318ff.
30. Hans Reiss, *Kant's Political Writings* (1970) p. 30, and Akademie edition vol. XIX p. 595, No. 8055.
31. S. Körner, *Experience and Conduct* (1976), ch. VII.
32. For an illuminating account of the way in which during the French Revolution 'the ultrademocratic ideal of unlimited popular sovereignty evolved into a pattern of coercion' see J.L. Talmon, *The Origins of Totalitarian Democracy* (1952).
33. For a detailed discussion see *Experience and Conduct*, ch. XI.

Grillparzer and the French Revolution

A. Grenville

My subject here is an undoubted, but unjustly neglected, master-piece by the undoubted master of the Austrian drama, Franz Grillparzer (1791–1872). Grillparzer was born and grew up during the revolutionary and Napoleonic period; and the best years of his life were spent during the years 1815–48, under the shadow of the reactionary backlash against the great revolutionary experiment. His great historical drama *Ein Bruderzwist in Habsburg (Fraternal Strife in the House of Habsburg)* was begun in 1824, but only completed in 1848, and he continued to revise it into the 1850s. *Ein Bruderzwist in Habsburg* is a masterpiece because it interweaves the surface level of the power-political motives and ambitions of individuals with the deeper level of historical and ideological forces, and fuses the two together into the dynamic of the historical process in an almost Shakespearean manner.

Grillparzer was born roughly half-way between two other great German historical dramatists, Schiller and Büchner. I would rate him superior to both in one respect: his ability to convey the historical process itself. Schiller tends to soar above history to ethical and philosophical concerns. Büchner, by contrast, already claims to have discovered laws operating beneath the surface of history;[1] his *Dantons Tod (Danton's Death)* is moving towards that view of history as a social science where the individual specificity proper to historical situations and agents is blurred by a deterministic emphasis on 'deeper structural forces'. Between his two great fellow-dramatists, Grillparzer's play stands firmly on the living reality of the historical process, in its depiction of the conflict between revolutionary forces and an established, absolutist order. Like many of the best historical dramas, this play about the early seventeenth century is clearly also relevant to the time at which it was written.[2] The political conflicts within the imperial Habsburg House on the eve of the Thirty Years War in *Ein Bruderzwist in Habsburg* mirror those that Grillparzer saw as besetting Austria as it struggled to come to terms with the ideological and political legacy of the French Revolution.

The aim here is to analyse Grillparzer's drama in the light of its historical context, the period of restoration that followed the upheavals of the revolutionary and Napoleonic wars. The contention here is that Grillparzer's treatment of his subject was decisively influenced by the ideological conflict between, on the one hand, the conservative, absolutist, legitimist order of the monarchical restoration and, on the other, the radical forces of constitutional democracy and revolutionary nationalism that had been unleashed in Europe by the French Revolution. *Ein Bruderzwist in Habsburg* should be seen as Grillparzer's attempt to grapple with the ideological aftermath of the French Revolution, to dramatise the clash of conservative and radical ideologies that was its political heritage.[3]

There can be little doubt that in broad outline the Austrian Grillparzer saw the era 1815–48 as dominated by ideological conflicts deriving from the French Revolution. No state was threatened more fundamentally than the Austrian Empire by the revolutionary forces of liberalism and nationalism that had taken the European stage in 1789. As a bastion of conservatism and autocracy, the Austrian Empire was bound to resist the spread of constitutional liberalism and egalitarian democracy by all available means; the constitutional principles of popular sovereignty, the liberty and equality associated with 1789, were totally incompatible with the resolutely anti-democratic absolutism of the Habsburg Empire. The memory of the French people governing themselves through an elected assembly of their own representatives was a constant and mortal threat to the Austria of Metternich and Franz I. But the French Revolution had not only provided a democratic alternative to dynastic monarchism; it had also demonstrated to the other nationalities of Europe the model of the French nation governing itself in full consciousness of its national unity, integrity and independence, and this powerfully stimulated the national awakening of other national groups. More than any other state in Europe, the Habsburg *Vielvölkerstaat*, the state of many nationalities, was threatened in its very existence by revolutionary nationalism; for the triumph of the principle of free self-determination for each national group would have spelt the disintegration of the Habsburg Empire into its various constituent nationalities.

To counter this threat of dissolution, Grillparzer was forced back on the dynastically legitimated imperial House, whose traditional unifying function provided the last barrier against disintegration and chaos. This is reflected in the lone stance of the Emperor Rudolf II in *Bruderzwist* as the solitary defender of order against the forces bent on war and conflict. Rudolf II is supported by and identified with no single group; he represents the common good of the all-embracing whole, and his authority depends solely on the aura of sacrosanct legitimacy emanating from his imperial office. Rudolf's embattled position therefore represents precisely what the Austrian patriot Grillparzer saw as the last defence of the monarchy against disintegration: the integrating force holding together a supra-national system which lacked any cohesive national identity common to all its subject peoples.[4]

Contrary to conventional wisdom, Grillparzer was not a simple reactionary. His poetry, epigrams and diary are full of slashing attacks on Metternich and on Austrian and Russian abolutism and reaction.[5] His poems, of the 1830s especially, often support liberal causes most vehemently: the victory of constitutionalism in France in the revolution of 1830[6] and the heroic struggle of the Poles against Tsarist oppression in 1831,[7] while for Austria itself, Grillparzer has the spirit of the dead Emperor Joseph speak from his statue to lambast the blinkered authoritarianism that was destroying his progressive reforming work.[8]

Equally, Grillparzer was no liberal. He did not share the liberals' naive faith in the progressive route to a perfect democratic society. He was especially scornful of the shallow rationalism with which the liberals approached complex social and political problems; a poem like 'Fortschritt-Männer' ('Men of Progess') (1847) conveys both the belief that rational analysis is inadequate to the complexity of man's existence and also Rudolf's underlying fear that such analysis will act as a solvent eating away the organic bonds of faith and tradition that hold society and civilisation together.[9] Indeed, Grillparzer's late dramas revolve round the quintessentially conservative defence of a traditional order, which has evolved over generations and is thereby legitimated in a religious sense, against the historical forces of change. Consequently, Grillparzer recoiled from the prospect of social anarchy and national disintegration in 1848, composing public celebrations in verse of Radetzky, the imperial Field Marshal who suppressed the revolution in Northern Italy, and of Windisch-grätz and Jelačic, the counter-revolutionary generals who bloodily reduced revolutionary Vienna in October 1848.[10]

Yet Grillparzer had by no means been hostile initially to the revolution that overthrew Metternich on 13 March 1848. On the contrary, his pronouncements on the early, moderate stage of the revolution were unambiguously enthusiastic.[11] It was only the increasing radicalism and violence which caused the imperial family twice to flee Vienna, the mob lynching of the Minister of War, Graf Latour, and the eruption of a full-scale workers' uprising in October 1848, that impelled the cautiously moderate Grillparzer towards the counter-revolutionary camp.

In any case, Grillparzer's attitude to the revolution was decisively influenced by a factor outside the clash between liberalism and conservatism: that factor was nationalism, and in particular the danger that the nationalist forces unleashed by the revolution might cause the Empire to disintegrate entirely. Grillparzer had always set his face resolutely against nationalism, especially that of the two principal national groups challenging the Habsburg state, the Czechs and Hungarians. Grillparzer was bitingly dismissive of Czech claims to national self-determination. In his *Erinnerungen aus dem Revolutionsjahre 1848*, he flatly denies the Czechs the status of a nationality and dismisses their language, the key indicator of their ethnicity, as a mere dialect.[12] He looked even less favourably on Hungarian nationalism, which he again attacked through its language: if Kant had published his *Critique of Pure Reason* in Hungarian, Grillparzer wrote, he would have been lucky to sell three copies.[13] Throughout his reflections on the revolution and its failure runs the argument that it was the intransigent radical Magyar nationalists around Kossuth who were more than anyone else to blame for the revolution's descent into extremism, violence and a chaos of warring national groups.[14] Grillparzer's loathing of nationalism finds its most celebrated expression in his epigram of 1849:

Der Weg der neuern Bildung geht
Von Humanität
Durch Nationalität
Zur Bestialität.

The path of modern thought leads from humanity through nationality to bestiality.[15]

Whereas Grillparzer's cautiously moderate liberalism did not lead him to oppose modest constitutional reform, nationalism, by contrast, was totally incompatible with his political convictions; these he felt could most likely be realised within the framework of the Habsburg *Vielvölkerstaat*. Thus, in the poem 'Des Kaisers Bildsäule' ('The Emperor's Statue'), Grillparzer has the spirit of the Emperor Joseph defend his reforming achievements against its twin foes, the dead hand of reaction and also the strident demands of a fatally divisive nationalism.[16]

Once the threat of the Empire's disintegration had passed in 1849, Grillparzer no longer felt forced to look to the army and to the reactionary government of Schwarzenberg as the only hope of holding the Empire together. He soon reverted from his temporary forced support of the counter-revolutionary Right to his customary stance of cautiously conservative liberalism. Already before the end of 1848, Grillparzer was writing epigrams bitterly critical of the new reactionary politicans and generals, who, he said, had simply exchanged Metternich's courtly stockings for Windischgrätz's military leggings.[17]

The effect of the 1848 Revolution on Grillparzer was therefore clearly not to drive him definitively into the camp of counter-revolutionary reaction, but rather to destroy his already waning hopes of a moderate, sensible solution to the Empire's many problems, through a peaceful process of gradual political evolution. The pattern that emerges here is that of a cautious moderate, leaning in late middle age towards conservatism, who is appalled by the extremes to *both* sides of his position, by the brutally repressive intolerance of the reactionary Right, as much as by the radical excesses of the Left.[18]

Grillparzer's hostility to ideological extremism and fanaticism of all persuasions is the key to an understanding of *Bruderzwist*, where Rudolf similarly stands opposed both to the disintegrating forces of change (personified by his illegitimate son Don Cäsar and by the rebellious Bohemian Estates) and to the Catholic bigotry of the Archduke Ferdinand. This pattern of Grillparzer's rejection of both extremes emerges already in January 1848, when in the prophetic poem 'Vorzeichen' ('Portents'), he accuses the ultra-reactionaries of undermining the whole system by instituting repressive measures so severe that they cause the forces of change that threaten the system to erupt into open rebellion.[19] The parallel with 1618 is clear.

In his study of Metternich, Henry Kissinger analyses the division that a revolutionary situation inevitably creates in the conservative camp, between moderate conservatives and counter-revolutionary extremists. The moderate conservative will seek a conservative compromise that will reconcile the advocates of change to the existing order.[20] This is precisely the position of Rudolf II. For Rudolf, the old order is still sacrosanct, its authority legitimated, its validity unimpaired. But if the conservative once acknowledges his foe to be the advocate of an alternative, revolutionary ideology, he becomes by that token involved in an ideological conflict, in which he fights in the name of an unconditional ideological orthodoxy; he becomes a reactionary. In *Bruderzwist*, this is the position of the Archduke Ferdinand, the later Emperor Ferdinand II, victor of the Battle of the White Mountain and scourge of Bohemian Protestantism.

When Grillparzer wrote that one could best understand the nineteenth century by studying the history of the Crusades in the twelfth,[21] he was expressing his belief that he was living in an age when political ideologies were fighting out a struggle to the death akin to the fanaticism with which religious controversies had been fought out in earlier ages. It is therefore hardly surprising that we should find him distilling the political insights of his mature years into a play about the outbreak of the Thirty Years War, the most famous of European religious conflicts. As the 1840s wore on, Grillparzer became increasingly convinced that the clash of the ideological extremes would doom the moderate conservative position to oblivion. It is for this reason that his Rudolf II can only fight a hopeless rearguard action against the coming explosion. *Bruderzwist* ends in total disaster, with the onset of the greatest modern European catastrophe before 1914; the historical pessimism of the play reflects Grillparzer's despair at the future prospects for central Europe. The principal factor behind this was his recognition of the impossibility of securing the Empire's future against both liberal and national aspirations, against the twin heritage of the French Revolution.

In *Bruderzwist*, Grillparzer uses the period that had begun with the Peace of Augsburg (1555) and ended with the outbreak of the Thirty Years War (1618) as a historical paradigm for the development of Europe after 1815. As the Peace of Augsburg had brought only a temporary cessation of religious hostilities between Protestants and Catholics, so the peace settlement of 1815 represented for Grillparzer only a temporary ceasefire in the ideological conflict between the revolutionary forces unleashed by the French Revolution and the reactionary counter-forces. During the reign of Emperor Rudolf II (1576–1612), the progress of the Counter-Reformation and the Protestant reaction to it led to a growing extremism in confessional politics that eventually caused the Augsburg settlement to break down and plunged Europe into the Thirty Years War. Grillparzer's prophecy for the Europe of the mid-nineteenth century was a repetition of that process of ideological conflict intensifying until it erupted into warfare.

The crucial factor common to both historical situations was that both conflicts were struggles for political power reinforced by an underlying ideological conflict. In *Bruderzwist* the Reformation, the origin of the crisis, corresponds to the French Revolution, and the Counter-Reformation to the reactionary Restoration after 1815. To the Protestant reformed religion correspond the radical democratic ideas deriving from 1789; to the religious fanatics of the early seventeenth century correspond the political extremists of the nineteenth; and to the moderate conservatism of Grillparzer's Rudolf II correspond the dramatist's own ideas for the gradual, organic reform of the Habsburg Empire, which were for him perhaps the most notable casualty of the disaster of 1848. Rudolf II is reduced to political impotence and despair, his efforts to preserve the unity of his realm and to avoid open religious conflict rendered ineffective by fanatics – Catholics like Ferdinand, Protestants like the Bohemian Estates – who are bent on ideological absolutes and reject compromise. In the same way, Grillparzer predicts, the

traditional order of the Habsburg Empire, the guarantor of peace in
central Europe, will be torn apart between extremist proponents of
radical egalitarianism and radical nationalism and their reactionary
opponents.

The entire action of *Ein Bruderzwist in Habsburg* consists of the
remorseless demolition of the fragile compromise of 1555 by
characters representing the various forces ranged against the
existing order. The play begins in 1605, when the process of the
undermining of the imperial order is already well advanced. Act I
shows Rudolf II having retired into seclusion in his Prague palace,
the Hradschin. Rudolf's startling neglect of all affairs of state is to
be understood as the result of his despair at the political situation,
which is now so dangerous that the least political act may spark off
a religious war. Lacking Rudolf's wisdom, the other principal
characters on the historical stage are only too keen to act, each in
his own personal or sectional interest. The last factor holding back
the conflicting parties from open strife is removed in Act II, when a
peace with the Turks is concluded (Treaty of Zsitvatorok, 1606).
Rudolf had understood that it was only the war in Hungary against
the common Turkish foe that had kept Catholics and Protestants
from falling on each other. He therefore opposes the signing of the
peace treaty with the Turks, because it opens the way for a far worse
internecine conflict.

It is here that the crucial first breach of the imperial order is
made, when the four Archdukes, meeting in Hungary without
Rudolf's approval, decide to conclude peace without the Emperor's
authority. The Archdukes further decide to give Rudolf's brother,
the opportunistic and power-hungry Archduke Matthias, ple-
nipotentiary powers to conclude the peace treaty and to execute its
provisions, in defiance of the Emperor's authority. This represents
an irreparable blow to the imperial order, the setting up of Matthias
as an alternative imperial power over against Rudolf. Building on
this position, Matthias gains the support of the Hungarian,
Austrian and Moravian Estates, and does not scruple to attract
Protestant support, though he himself remains a convinced
Catholic.

When he marches on Prague, Rudolf's last stronghold, the folly
of Matthias's cynical exploitation of the religious divide becomes
clear, as it triggers the division of the Empire into two warring
confessional camps. On the one hand, the Protestants in Bohemia
seize the opportunity offered them by Rudolf's weak position to
extract from him a guarantee of religious freedom for Protestants.
Rudolf is forced to sign the Letter of Majesty (1609) (Act III), the
contravention of which by the Counter-Reformation party under
Archduke Ferdinand leads to the Protestant uprising in Bohemia in

1618 and to the Thirty Years War. On the other hand, the Catholic party has also been gathering its forces. Archduke Leopold, Ferdinand's younger brother, leads an army into Bohemia to restore Rudolf's position and suppress the rebellious Bohemian Estates. The failure of this ill-starred venture (1611) (Act IV) marks the end of Rudolf's power. He dies in 1612, and is succeeded by Matthias.

Act V depicts the fatal consequences of the policies of the men of action who have ignored Rudolf's wise policy of maintaining the status quo. The feeble Matthias suffers the fate of Rudolf; as he had elbowed the latter aside, so he is now displaced from effective power by the Catholic fanatic Ferdinand. Convinced of the rightness of his cause, Ferdinand does not hesitate to confront the Bohemian Estates over the religious question; the fruits of this policy are soon evident: news comes of the defenestration of the imperial lieutenants in Prague from their chancery, and the Catholic forces jubilantly prepare for war against the rebels.

Grillparzer's drama ends with a panoramic perspective leading into a downward spiral of fanaticism and bloodshed: Rudolf is dead, displaced by Matthias; Matthias, a dying man, is displaced by Ferdinand (elected Emperor in 1619) – but Ferdinand too will suffer the same fate, for at the end of the play an unknown officer, Colonel Wallenstein, is alredy beginning to hijack Ferdinand's authority. The ending of *Bruderzwist* therefore opens out into the most famous of German historical tragedies, Schiller's *Wallenstein* trilogy, so we know that the future holds only guilt, disillusion, defeat and death in store for all the parties: Matthias dies in 1619, a broken man; the Bohemian Estates suffer catastrophic defeat at the Battle of the White Mountain (1620) and the extirpation of Protestantism and independent Bohemian culture; Ferdinand fails to achieve his goal of re-establishing Catholic hegemony in the Empire, is forced, for all his piety, to stoop to the assassination of Wallenstein to preserve his power and dies a disappointed man; Wallenstein, after a spectacular career of war and conquest, dies by the assassin's sword; and central Europe, having once broken away from the divinely sanctioned order represented by Rudolf, God's anointed, endures thirty years of slaughter and devastation.

The historical and ideological forces behind this inexorable descent into war are represented in *Bruderzwist* by the characters who stand opposed to Rudolf and the traditionalist, dynastic order he personifies. They are the bearers of the process whereby confessional dogmatism hardens into political extremism, which forms an instructive parallel to the ideological conflicts of Grillparzer's own era, lying, as he feared it did, on the verge of a fresh cataclysmic contest between the forces and counter-forces unleashed by the French Revolution.

The most obvious transgressor against the imperial order is Archduke Matthias, who usurps Rudolf's crown and whose power-political ambitions set in train the course of events leading to 1618. He represents very clearly the principle of the individualistic revolt against the existing order and traditional authority, which Rudolf also condemns in the Reformation and in Protestantism. Matthias represents the principle of particularism, and autonomy from the central imperial order.[22] Grillparzer devotes some space to Matthias's failed attempt, back in 1577, to take over the government of the Netherlands. Matthias revels in his memories of this fiasco, which he describes as the attempt to build a throne for himself – 'sein eigner Schöpfer ('his own creator') (350) – owing it to no one but himself ('Niemand darum verpflichtet als sich selbst'). His disregard for tradition, for the dynastic principle of legitimacy and for the preservation of the existing sacrosanct order is obvious here; it informs his erection of an independent power and authority of his own, not legitimated by imperial sanction and therefore ultimately disastrous.

By Act V, Matthias has destroyed Rudolf's authority, but has replaced it only with the particularist values of individual ambition and sectional self-interest; he has cleared the way for open hostilities between opposing factions. At the play's end, he acknowledges his guilt for the disaster that his selfish individualism has let loose on central Europe. Matthias is the representative, in his era, of the centrifugal forces of democratic individualism and separatist nationalism that Grillparzer saw at work in his own day.

The most obvious representatives of insurgency are the Protestant Bohemian Estates, who openly rebelled against the imperial order in 1618. The disruption of order and peace is their most prominent achievement in the play. The Protestants are motivated in this political rebellion by religious convictions, and they behave very much like the ideological extremists of Grillparzer's day, especially over the question of the Letter of Majesty, which guarantees them religious freedom. Rudolf's aversion to the Protestants' demands is conveyed in terms that would sit perfectly in the mouth of a nineteenth-century conservative. He dislikes on principle any written contract between ruler and ruled. It is easy to see here the nineteenth-century conservative's disapproval of the written constitutions so beloved of the liberals, because such constitutions represent the attempt to regulate human society by shallow mechanical and rational devices. The Letter of Majesty also establishes a crucial precedent, in that it gives the Estates certain rights independently of the Emperor. This embodies the most treasured principle of nineteenth-century liberalism, the establishment of a parliament with independent legislative powers and a degree of popular sovereignty.

Rudolf also points out to the Estates the example they are setting: if they refuse unconditional allegiance to their sovereign ruler, then their own subordinates will in turn demand independent rights for themselves. Rudolf sees clearly where this will lead: to rule by the majority, which he calls 'Pöbelherrschaft' ('mob rule') (403). Written constitutions, Rudolf believes, act as a rational solvent of the entire traditional order, which is legitimated only by custom and antiquity; social structures that have evolved organically over time are validated solely by the fact that they exist, and cannot be justified before the court of reason, which will inevitably condemn and destroy them (405). Once the traditional order has been dissolved, constitutional rationalism can replace it only with the rule of the majority, based on the principle of 'one man one vote', the rational concept of the equality of all men. Rudolf shrinks from such democratic radicalism, fearing that majority rule (popular sovereignty) will be a majority against 'Ehrfurcht und Gesetz' (404), the respect for traditional customs and laws that have preserved civilised values. The relevance of this to the debates between liberals and conservatives in the post-revolutionary era after 1815 is obvious.

Yet the Estates are the spokesmen in the play not only of democratic liberalism, but also of the other force unleashed by the French Revolution, populist nationalism. Grillparzer perceived that the religious fanaticism of the seventeenth century provided him with a perfect dramatic vehicle to convey the fanaticised nationalism stirring in the nineteenth. The Bohemian setting of the play is also particularly appropriate in this respect. By 1600 Bohemia had developed a strikingly strong national culture, a national identity: this was very closely related to its national religion, Utraquism, which derived from the great Hussite revolt, described by a leading authority on the period as 'a searing national experience'.[23] As a result, politics and religion developed along more clearly national – in Grillparzer's play, nationalistic – lines in Bohemia than anywhere else in Europe. The growth of confessional extremism after 1600 brought with it a growth of national feeling, an alignment of Bohemia into two camps on religious, political and national lines.

Grillparzer skilfully uses the national feeling associated in Bohemia with religion to insert into his play a warning against the dangers of unchecked nationalism. Early in Act III, Rudolf's confidant, Duke Julius of Brunswick, reminds him that Huss's religion is still very much alive and that the Bohemians are above all loyal to 'stammalte[r] Überzeugung', to the faith traditional in their ethnic group (395). Shortly afterwards, in a key passage ignored by critics, Rudolf asks a Bohemian citizen of what faith he is, receiving the reply: 'Herr, Utraquist, des böhmschen Glaubens' ('My Lord, a Utraquist, of the Bohemian faith'). Rudolf, appalled at yet another manifestation of division and conflict, responds: 'Warum des böhmischen und nicht des deutschen?/Des wälschen, griechisch, spanschen?' ('Why of the Bohemian faith, not the German? Or the Italian, the Greek, the Spanish?'). This quite deliberately looks forward to the nineteenth century, an age where nationalism was to be pitted against nationalism in bloodstained conflict. Rudolf concludes with the melancholy insight that each church must have its churchyard, a warning that each national 'church' must have its national cemeteries for the dead that its fanaticism will exact: 'Vergaß ich fast doch, daß es soviel Kirchen/ Als Kirchenräume gibt und – Kirchhofgräber' (397). But the wisdom of the conservative humanist striving after reconciliation passes unheard, as it did when revolutionary nationalist passions were aroused in 1848. And for this the Bohemian Protestants pay a grievous penalty, but one appropriate to their liberal-democratic and religio-nationalist subversion of the imperial order. As Rudolf foresees, when he curses Prague as the centre of the poisons infecting the body politic (427), Bohemia will be ravaged by war, its leaders executed and its religious faith and national autonomy brutally eradicated, in a conflict largely of its own making.

The figure of Don Cäsar, Rudolf's illegitimate son, embodies the forces of disorder, rebellion and destruction of the age. Based on a real figure, Don Giulio, Rudolf's bastard son by Katharina Strada, Don Cäsar is the incarnation of the radical challenge to the legitimate order, to all traditional authority and morality. Thus the opening scene sees Cäsar, himself the fruit of Rudolf's contravention of the moral order, publicly pitted against the law, as he tries to free his condemned friend Rußworm by force from the officers of the law. Cäsar lives a life of dissolution and disorder: first he obsessively pursues the demure Lukrezia, even attempting to have her kidnapped by hired thugs, then he murders her in a fit of jealous passion, and finally he contrives to bleed himself to death in his prison cell, a fitting climax to a career of unmitigated destructiveness. Cäsar personifies the inevitably destructive consequences of the restless desire for change and political action which threatens the stability of the sacrosanct imperial order. Rudolf refers to him as the son of an age contemptuous of established values, 'der freche Sohn der Zeit' (396). Julius of Brunswick describes Cäsar as 'wildverworren' ('in a state of frenzied confusion') (421), and Rudolf twice applies the same epithet to the political situation of the day with which he is wrestling, a situation where the peace of the existing order is challenged by the revolutionary forces of change and the fateful events they inspire (359f.).

When Cäsar clashes with Rudolf over religious freedom, this dispute also encapsulates the crucial *political* conflict of the nineteenth century:[24] the established authority of a conservative order confronts the democratic demand for men's freedom to work out their political salvation for themselves, through the agency of their reason and as independent agents in the political process. Thus, Cäsar rejects Rudolf's accusation that he is a rebel and Lutheran with the argument that only God can judge men's beliefs. This draws from Rudolf the memorable riposte:

Ja, Gott und Du. Ihr beide, nicht wahr?
Glaub du an das, was deine Lehrer glaubten,
Die Weiseren, die Bessern laß entscheiden,
Dann kommts wohl noch an dich.

Yes, God and you. You two, is it not so?/ Believe what your teachers believed in,/ Leave the decisions to wiser men and better,/ Then one day your turn may come (357f.).

The contrast between traditional autocratic conservatism and free-thinking liberal individualism could not be more clearly expressed. Cäsar voices the democrats' advocacy of each man's right to free political self-determination on the basis of equality, but ignores the consequences of his reckless onslaught on order and stability. In Act I, Rudolf laments that the new age that has brought forth Cäsar is one which despises civilised values and traditional social structures. The reformed faith, which Rudolf respects and tolerates as a religious faith, has encouraged men to set their judgment up as the criterion by which all values and institutions must be judged (360). The fruits of this rational, egalitarian aproach to sacrosanct authority and tradition emerge clearly from Cäsar's appalling deeds. Cäsar is the barbarian to whom civilised society has itself given birth and who will lay waste all the achievements of its culture (394).

Through Cäsar, Grillparzer also explores the philosophical foundations of the radicals' opposition to authority and order. In Act IV, Cäsar casts himself as the champion of the individual's reason, devoted above all to the desire to know, to understand and to subject all phenomena to rational analysis. But his glorification of man's reason, stripped of any controlling moral order, degenerates into a lunatic solipsism: in a parody of post-Kantian philosophy, he declares that all phenomena are merely the products of his mind and that his brain can create and destroy them at will (415). The consequences of this insane over-reliance on individual judgment and reason are chaos and destruction: Cäsar murders Lukrezia and dies like a ravening beast ('wie ein verzehrend, reißend Tier'); the forces he represents plunge the Empire into three decades of slaughter.

That this destructive mentality is not restricted to the Protestant, or liberal, camp emerges from Grillparzer's careful pairing of Cäsar with Archduke Leopold, Ferdinand's younger brother and an ardent legitimist. The activities of the two young men are repeatedly described in identical terms, consisting mainly of mounting horses and pursuing women (365, 378, 417). They are also virtually twinned by Rudolf, who repeatedly calls Leopold his son (408) and loves him as he cannot love Cäsar, his real son. Leopold displays the same reckless enthusiasm for war and bloodshed (381f.), the same reliance on action and violence with no thought for the consequences (389). Though Leopold is Rudolf's most devoted supporter, his invasion of Bohemia at the head of a Catholic army, far from assisting Rudolf, proves fatal to the latter's cause. Leopold's army's attack on Prague, which sets Cäsar free to kill Lukrezia, is portrayed in Act IV not as a restoration of good Catholic order, but as an irruption of violence and disorder into a settled community (419). The counter-revolutionary extremists prove to be as destructive of the traditional, patriarchal order as their reforming opponents.

Of no character is this truer than Archduke Ferdinand, the strong man of the Catholic Counter-Reformation. Ferdinand's religious fanaticism is the ideological driving force behind the brutally repressive measures that are taken in an overtly counter-revolutionary fashion against the Protestant church. In Ferdinand, Grillparzer has personified the counter-revolutionary extremists of a later age, whose determination to extirpate their ideological opponents root and branch leads to fanaticised internecine strife. Ferdinand has the same naive confidence as his political enemies in the efficacy of determined action and resolute measures. When Rudolf asks who would dare to cut the Gordian knot of the complex political situation at a stroke, Ferdinand replies: 'Wers wagte? Ich!' ('Who would dare? I would!') (364).[25] Behind Ferdinand's certainty lies an iron faith in the rightness of his religious cause; thus, he can even justify political kidnapping by claiming that his end, the victory of God's church, morally sanctions such means (438).

To understand the political balance of the play correctly, it is vital to appreciate how Grillparzer has set Rudolf apart both from the revolutionary radicalism of Cäsar or the Bohemian Estates and also from Ferdinand's counter-revolutionary extremism; the moderate conservative looks with horror on the bigotry and intolerance of the reactionary fanatic, whose principal achievement is to drive his opponents into open rebellion. Far from seeing in Ferdinand a conservative ally, Rudolf recoils from him politically, appalled by Ferdinand's 'cleansing' of his Styrian lands of heretics: 60,000 are forced to convert to Catholicism, 20,000 are driven out to freeze and starve (364). On the personal level, Rudolf is horrified by the inhuman bigotry of a man who can reject the woman he loves for doctrinal reasons and can justify wooing one he finds physically repulsive with the unctuous words: 'Ihr Herz ist schön vor Gott' ('Her heart is beautiful in the eyes of the Lord') (364).

In his dying speech, Rudolf urges Ferdinand to be strong not only when fighting for his own convictions, but also in respecting the convictions of others (430). This plea for moderation and tolerance falls on deaf ears; Ferdinand vehemently rejects any policy of compromise and equal treatment for Protestants, and curses any political wisdom not directed towards the realisation of what *he* takes to be God's will (434). As Ferdinand had 'cleansed' his lands of heretics, so in 1618 he looks forward to 'cleansing' the whole Empire. His language as war begins – he uses the image of the 'enemy within' striking at the Catholic armies from the rear – chillingly anticipates the use of the 'stab-in-the-back' legend by later German nationalist fanatics (447). Ferdinand's goal, he makes clear, is the actual *physical extermination* of Protestantism (447); accordingly, he deliberately breaches the provisions of the Letter of Majesty and provokes a religious war: the inevitable end result of the fatal interaction of revolutionary radicalism with counter-revolutionary fanaticism.

But Ferdinand will no more emerge triumphant from the struggle than do the Bohemian Protestants whom he devastates after the Battle of the White Mountain. In a striking *coup de théâtre*, Grillparzer has Wallenstein make his first entry just as Bishop Klesel is prophesying Ferdinand's future: the strong man Ferdinand will one day tremble before an over-mighty subject whose will and ambition exceed Ferdinand's (440). That Wallenstein will be the man who reveals the limitations of Ferdinand's power and strength of character is foreshadowed at the play's end, when he takes it upon himself to issue orders to Ferdinand's troops on his own authority (442). Wallenstein is the personification of violence, war and destruction; he represents the lowest common denominator of all the men of action in the play, for he cannot think beyond military action to destroy his opponents. Ferdinand expresses the hope that the campaign in Bohemia will soon be over, but Wallenstein shouts out his exultation in war for its own sake: 'Der Krieg ist gut, and währt' er dreißig Jahr' ('War is good, even if it lasts thirty years') (445). The extremist ideologues have played their part, and the conflict they have provoked will be fought out by the technicians of destruction, ending only when both parties are forced to desist by sheer exhaustion. The drama ends with a sombre warning of the state to which Europe would be reduced, Grillparzer feared, by the conflict unleashed by the great French Revolution, between the revolutionary forces of liberalism and nationalism and the counter-forces of reaction.

NOTES

1. See the letter to his fiancée of 10 March 1834, where he refers to the 'iron law' behind history, in George Büchner, *Sämtliche Werke und Briefe*, ed. Werner R. Lehmann, 2 volumes, (Darmstadt, 1967–71), II (1971), p. 425 f.

2. See Herbert Lindenberger, *Historical Drama: The Relation of Literature and Reality*, Chicago, London, 1975, p. 5 f., Walter Hinck, 'Einleitung: Zur Poetik des Geschichtsdramas', in *Geschichte als Schauspiel: Deutsche Geschichtsdramen. Interpretationen*, ed. Walter Hinck, Frankfurt, 1981, pp. 7–21 (p. 13 f.), and Konrad Schaum, 'Zum Verhältnis von Drama und Geschichte im 19. Jahrhundert', in *Akten des V. Internationalen Germanisten-Kongresses Cambridge 1975*, ed. Leonard Forster and Hans-Gert Roloff, 4 volumes, Berne, Frankfurt, 1976, III, pp. 262–271.

3. One of the outstanding authorities on the literature of the period, Friedrich Sengle, expresses his astonishment at the failure of critics to relate Grillparzer's late dramas to the years leading up to the fresh revolutionary outbreak of 1848, although the plays are, in Sengle's opinion, clearly a response to the climate of those years. (Friedrich Sengle, *Biedermeierzeit: Deutsche Literatur im Spannungsfeld zwischen Restauration und Revolution 1815–1848*, 3 volumes, Stuttgart, 1971–80, III, (1980), p. 76.)

4. Rudolf memorably compares his unifying function, in Act III, to that of a bond holding a sheaf of corn together, itself unfruitful, but necessary because it preserves the unity of the whole. (Franz Grillparzer, *Sämtliche Werke*, ed. Peter Frank and Karl Pörnbacher, 4 volumes, Munich, 1960–65, II, p. 391. This edition will hereafter be referred to as *GW*. Page numbers after references to *Ein Bruderzwist in Habsburg* in the text of this essay refer to this edition of the play.)

5. Grillparzer's scathing attacks on Metternich are exemplified by the epigram 'Grabschrift' ('Epitaph') of 1839, *GW*, I, p. 437, where Metternich is described as 'the Don Quixote of legitimacy', the poem 'Der kranke Feldherr' ('The Sick General') of 1839, I, p. 263 ff., the essay of 1839 'Fürst Metternich', III, pp. 1022–34, and the diary entries on Metternich, III, pp. 1034–36. Grillparzer's bitter complaints about the blinkered authoritarianism and the stifling censorship in Austria form a central part of his autobiographical writings; a spectacularly vitriolic example is the poem 'Alpenszene' ('Alpine Scene') (1838), where Grillparzer sees Emperor succeeding Emperor with the bovine stupidity of placid cows high up on their Alpine pastures, as Trottel I gives way to Trottel II (*GW*, I, p. 257). ('Trottel' is an insulting term for an imbecile, used here to denote the intellectual poverty of the imperial heritage that passed in 1835 from the narrow-minded reactionary Franz I to his mentally retarded successor Ferdinand I.) Grillparzer's distaste for Russian

autocracy comes across in the poem 'Rußland' ('Russia') (1839), *GW*, I, p. 262f.

6. Grillparzer's favourable reaction to the July Revolution is apparent from his diary entry of 5 August 1830, p. *GW*, IV, 461f., and in the reference to July, the 'beautiful harvest month' which will melt the tyranny of reaction, in the final line of the poem 'Warschau' ('Warsaw') (1831), I, p. 204.

7. Especially in the powerful poem 'Warschau', *GW*, I, p. 200 ff.

8. In the remarkably forthright poem 'Des Kaisers Bildsäule' ('The Emperor's Statue') (1837), *GW*, I, p. 252 ff.

9. *GW*, I, p. 311 ff.

10. Most notoriously in the poem 'Feldmarschall Radetzky' (1848), *GW*, I, p. 318 f. See also the poems 'Jellachich und Windischgratz' (1848), I, p. 322 f., and 'Dem Banus', (1849), I, p. 332 f.

11. This appears most remarkably in the poem 'Mein Vaterland' ('My Fatherland') composed for the first number of the newly-founded *Constitutionelle Donau-Zeitung*, 1 April 1848, *GW*, I, p. 317 f.

12. *GW*, IV, p. 214.

13. *GW*, III, p. 1020.

14. See for example *GW*, III, p. 1043, and IV, p. 219.

15. *GW*, I, p. 500.

16. The attack on separatist nationalism comes in lines 21–32 and 61f., *GW*, I, p. 252 f. and 254.

17. In two epigrams about Windischgrätz, *GW*, I, pp. 497 and 499. See also Grillparzer's blunt statement in 1852 that the Austrian state had reestablished itself, with a few enforced innovations, on its old foundations: armed force and stupidity, *GW*, III, p. 1052 f.

18. Grillparzer's sense of lonely isolation between two warring extremes finds expression in two notable epigrams: 'Als liberal einst der Verfolgung Ziel,/ Schilt mich der Freiheitstaumel nur servil,/ Nicht hier noch dort in den Extremen zünftig,/ Ich glaube bald, ich bin vernünftig' (*GW*, I, p. 490) (1848), and 'Die Knechtschaft hat meine Jugend zerstört,/ Des Geistesdruckes Erhalter,/ Nun kommt die Freiheit sinnbetört/ Und raubt mir auch mein Alter' (I, p. 491) (1848).

19. *GW*, I, p. 314 ff.

20. Henry A. Kissinger, 'The Conservative Dilemma: Reflections on the Political Thought of Metternich', *The American Political Science Review*, 48 (1954), 1017–1030 (p. 1018).

21. *GW*, III, p. 948.

22. Archduke Max accuses Bishop Klesel of trying to create for Matthias a new-fangled office half separate from the Emperor's dynastic authority, *GW*, II, p. 379.

23. R.J.W. Evans, *Rudolf II and His World: A Study in Intellectual History 1576–1612*, Oxford, 1973, p. 29.

24. In a diary entry of March 1839, Grillparzer states expressly that Cäsar's excesses reflect not only the rising spirit of his era, but also that of Grillparzer's own age, *GW*, IV, p. 644.

25. In his exchanges with Rudolf in Act I, Ferdinand repeatedly states his confidence that a strong will leading to action will be politically beneficial and effective, *GW*, II, pp. 360 and 364.

The 'Lessons' of the French Revolution

N. Hampson

It is a sign of the times and not, I think, a healthy one, that a residual concern for my academic respectability should have led me to put the operative word of my title in quotation marks. History nowadays is not supposed to teach lessons. 'The study of history is witnessing innovative explorations of the symbolic constructions of reality.' We are the beneficiaries of 'the emergence of a powerful new interpretive paradigm.' It is, admittedly, the University of California Press that sums up the situation in these opaque and inelegant terms, but plenty of professional historians would agree with them. I suspect that the intelligent layman would not, and if historians cannot reach that audience there is not a great deal of significance in what they say to each other. History only matters when it matters to non-historians. I may be quite hopelessly out of date but I should be surprised if many of them were much concerned about 'symbolic constructions of reality'. What they have always expected from history is a story with a moral. That is what they used to get and historians who decide that they shall no longer have it are in danger of cutting themselves off from contemporary life.

The 'story' changes over the generations as the accumulation of research disproves some of the things that had once been taken for granted and weaves new threads into the old tapestries. Argument about these things is quite properly the preserve of specialists. It is their job to expose the meretricious and to distinguish fact from conjecture by a critical dialogue that may only be comprehensible to the initiated. But one does not have to be an architect to enjoy looking at buildings and if the end product is not something that the non-specialist can understand and appreciate, something has gone wrong.

My present concern is not with the 'story' but with the 'moral'. At first sight it looks as though this should be implicit in the story itself, as in Dick Whittington or Cinderella. In practice, things are not so simple. Any historian lives astride two generations, the one he studies and the one in which he lives. Most of what he reads will have been written in or about republican Rome, Renaissance

Perugia or whatever his subject happens to be, but he himself inhabits the world of Gorbachev and Thatcher. This makes him inevitably somewhat schizophrenic: he looks at the past with eyes that live in the present. Each generation is bound to see history in terms of its present preoccupations. This is not a matter of looking for parallels; exact parallels between different societies are never going to exist. In this crude sense, the 'lessons of history' as they are invoked by non-historians, for their own purposes, deserve the robust treatment they were allegedly given by Henry Ford. It remains true that what matters about the past: why things happened the way they did and what it all meant, are matters of judgement and the answers that seem the most convincing will vary from one generation to another, in accordance with its fears, hopes, assumptions and beliefs. One can write the history of that too. So the 'moral' is for the present to decide, while the 'story' was decided by the people who actually made it happen.

Changing ideas about the 'moral' nevertheless have some effect on the 'story'. In one sense the two are quite distinct: no interpretation of history, however 'innovative' can make Napoleon win the battle of Waterloo. But the same 'story' can be told from many angles. Without departing from Shakespeare's account of the events, one could rewrite *Hamlet* from the viewpoint of Claudius, or Ophelia or Danish-Norwegian relations.

My concern is with the lessons of the French Revolution as they appear today. This relieves me of the need to go into the history of the history of the revolution but a word about the origins of the prevailing intellectual climate may be helpful. During the first half of this century a kind of orthodoxy that saw itself as broadly Marxist determined the way in which most French historians interpreted their revolution. This implied the belief that the course of historical change, at least in its general outlines, is determined by laws that remain constant over time. Any specific event or series of events, such as the French Revolution, is therefore a particular manifestation of a universal process and it is only by understanding the nature of the process that one can explain the event and locate it within a wider context. During the 1960s this prevailing view was challenged and, in its original form at least, it has virtually collapsed. This does not mean, of course, that Marxism has been disproved as a philosophy of history. What became apparent was that it had been invoked in a somewhat mechanical way, with results that could be shown to be at variance with the evidence. The 'story', in other words, had been distorted to fit the 'moral'.

The vacuum left by the deflation of a particular kind of Marxist history has not been filled by any subsequent ideological consensus. We have not been without our 'innovative explorations of the symbolic constructions of reality' but they have not left us with any generally accepted global interpretation of the revolution. This has encouraged some historians to look for the significance of the revolution – its 'lessons' – within the revolution itself, to see it, not as the manifestation of any general law, but as a period of exceptional aspiration and conflict. This does not imply that it was wholly unique, in the sense of being utterly unlike anything that has ever happened anywhere else, before or since. Agnosticism about the existence of universal historical laws does not prevent anyone from seeing recurring patterns in social behaviour. The 'story', in other words, is not merely an exciting yarn. It is an account of the reactions of a particular society to certain extreme stresses, which suggests inferences about the ways in which other societies are likely to respond to similar stresses, about the nature of political authority in times of crisis, the relationship between ideas and social structures and the constraints that modify or distort political action.

What follows is inevitably a personal statement. Others will disagree with both the themes I have selected and the conclusions that I have drawn from them. Since we all share a common historical environment, I hope these differences will be pronounced enough to generate dialogue but not so wide as to rule out mutual understanding.

The first of my 'lessons' is that the French Revolution was caused by the inability of the government to continue functioning, rather than by the strength of any revolutionary opposition or the accumulation of tensions that had become uncontrollable. The revolution, in other words, was not the product of any 'revolutionary situation' but the result of avoidable mistakes made by the king and his ministers.

This is not to deny that a number of factors were combining to make the ship of state less seaworthy. The traditional authority of a divinely-sanctioned Church and an anointed king had been sapped by the corrosive rationalism of the intellectual currents that go under the general title of the Enlightenment. Most of the philosophers were not primarily interested in politics and those who were, disagreed about the ways in which things might best be changed, but all of them combined to discredit the idea that authority of any kind could be conferred by tradition or by divine sanction. Henceforth it had to justify itself in terms of public utility, which made it the scapegoat of every ruined harvest or economic recession. Allegiance was becoming conditional, an attitude that the king himself seemed to legitimize when he appealed for public support in the preambles to his decrees and, as Tocqueville pointed out long ago, drew attention to ills that he proved incapable of curing.

The Enlightenment raised expectations and generated the impression that all France's problems could be solved by constitutional algebra or economic geometry, but it was not an ideology of revolution; it was the ideology of men who were to find themselves propelled by circumstances into becoming revolutionaries.

A 'rising bourgeoisie' was continuing to rise – into the ranks of the nobility – as it had been doing for generations. The evidence for any radical change in the functioning of this social escalator during the second half of the eighteenth century does not look very convincing. Successful bourgeois were men who had succeeded – by adapting themselves to the possibilities of a system that they were unlikely to feel like challenging. If they wanted esteem they could hope to buy it. If they wanted a share in political power, there was none to be had by anybody, except for a handful of Court grandees, and they were no worse off in that respect than the provincial nobility.

What actually set off the revolution was the fact that the government could not raise enough taxation to keep pace with its rising expenditure. Whether this was due more to excessive borrowing or to financial extravagance, it was the product of political mistakes. It was the deficit that drove the government from one concession to another and eventually compelled it to call the Estates-General. There were corporate bodies ready enough to exploit this opportunity to force the monarchy into making the kind of concessions that it had been resisting for a century, but their power was more a consequence than a cause of the deficit.

What was lacking before 1787 was any radical political opposition. This seemed to be excluded by the nature of the monarchy. A relatively centralized bureaucracy under the control of the king and his ministers gave an illusion of strength and stability. It excluded the possibility of political action by men who were subjects rather than citizens, denied that opinions about policy might legitimately diverge and excluded local magnates from the kind of regional authority that they enjoyed in England. So long as it went on functioning it generated an impression of omniscience and omnipotence, at least to those unaware of the horse-trading that went on between the ministers on the one hand and the parlements and provincial Estates on the other. In 1789 this bureaucracy was not captured by revolutionaries; it simply disintegrated. A fiscal crisis and a revolt in Paris in which fewer than a hundred men were killed, was enough to bring the whole edifice down. It crumbled into dust and the country was left to its own devices.

The revolutionaries did not so much seek power as find it thrust upon them. In opposition, they had been united in their claims for the modification of the old order. When that order collapsed its critics discovered, rather late in the day, that there had been something to be said for an old system of government that had provided a symbol of unity and legitimacy. It proved impossible to find any substitute for 'Louis, by the Grace of God, King of France and of Navarre' that could command universal acceptance. Those who, with however many reservations, had more or less obeyed Louis XVI, had no intention of obeying each other.

If we are looking for a lesson in all this it is, I suppose, that revolutions may owe more to the weakness of governments than to the strength of revolutionaries. A revolution, in other words, is more like an avalanche than an explosion. Its immediate causes may be accidental but once under way it gathers momentum and what need never have started may soon be beyond the wit of man to stop.

This brings us to our second 'lesson': the political process itself, especially when played by revolutionary rules, may make it impossible to find a solution to some political problems. The most important thing about the crisis of July 1789 was what did *not* happen. There was no decisive trial of strength that left the victors free to impose their will on those whom they had defeated. The king brought up a small army to the vicinity of Paris . . . and sent it away again without using it. Both sides then affected to assume that the crisis had been due to misunderstanding and there was a sense in which this was true. The king was prepared to become a constitutional ruler, although he had his own conception of what that meant. Virtually all the members of the Constituent Assembly were convinced that France must remain a monarchy. Where politics was concerned – religion was another matter – the three Orders of society, clergy, nobles and commoners were broadly in agreement about how France should be reshaped. The *cahiers*, or lists of grievances and instructions given to them by their constituents, had a good deal in common. Such of the deputies as left accounts of their principles and ideas of what should be done, were rather more in agreement with each other than the members of any of the present-day British political parties. What led them first to distrust and eventually to hate and fear each other was primarily a matter of tactics: how to treat the king.

The great majority of the deputies would have agreed that the essential characteristic of a constitutional monarchy, what preserved it from the abuse of power by king or people, was the division of sovereignty. The king had sole control of the executive; he was the personification of national unity and it was his responsibility to preserve domestic order and to protect the country from foreign attack. The Assembly had the initiative in legislation, subject to a royal veto. By its control of taxation it could prevent the king from pursuing policies of which it disapproved. There was general agreement about such principles. What divided the deputies was the question of how to implement them. The Right insisted that the king must be given the powers he needed in order to play his constitutional part and especially to maintain law and order. He had indicated his willingness to resign his theoretically absolute power and if he was to be won over to a whole-hearted acceptance of his diminished role, he had to be conciliated. His ministers must be treated with respect and left to get on with the business of government. The Left could scarcely credit the decisiveness of its almost bloodless victory. It deputies frightened each other with talk of an 'aristocratic plot'. They had been fighting what everyone had called 'ministerial despotism' for so long that they found it impossible to conceive of ministers who were not aspiring to become despots, even when the ministers were taken from the Assembly itself. As they saw it, their primary task was to defend the revolution against an 'executive power' that was determined to subvert it. That meant treating the ministers as enemies and depriving the king of control over the policing of his kingdom, until a new constitution could be completed and the revolution so securely entrenched that it would at last be safe to entrust the executive with the powers it needed for the regime to function.

Each view could be defended with enough plausibility to convince those who wanted to believe the arguments, but the pursuit of either negated the other. The Left was not disposed to take any chances and the Right objected that if the king and his ministers were not given the credit for their good intentions they would eventually be bullied into bad ones. It was not long before each side inflated its conception of the other into a self-justifying myth. The Right convinced itself that its opponents were republicans in all but name, determined to transfer all power to the Assembly and content to tolerate, if they did not positively encourage, lawlessness in the streets and mutiny in the armed forces, in order to intimidate their opponents. The Left believed that those who opposed them were royalist cavaliers, ready to jettison the victories of 1789 in return for the restoration of old privileges or the hope of office. Neither perception was true to begin with, but each tended to be self-validating and it drove its adherents to reject any compromise that must be the thin end of an anarchist or counter-revolutionary wedge. Eventually the gap did become unbridgeable. The Right, which was usually in a minority, opted for the *politique du pire* and came to welcome the adoption of what it believed to be absurd policies that would lead through anarchy to the restoration of order.

The 'lesson' of this, I think, is that parliamentary politics is a way of doing things that encourages posturing and the dramatization of policies in confrontational terms. It may well be the least dangerous method there is, but it is not without its risks, especially in time of revolution, when there are so many new things to be done and those entrusted with doing them are inexperienced, liable to panic, obsessed with their own self-righteousness and inclined to take the grandiloquence of their opponents at its face value. Men whose real intentions are within the scope of compromise may destroy each other, not because of what they are but because of what each side persuades itself that the other must be.

The French Revolution illustrated this gulf between perception and reality in another way. Virtually all the deputies in the various assemblies were educated people of reasonable means. Steeped in the doctrines of the Enlightenment, they aspired to make all French institutions rational, uniform and safe from the exercise of arbitrary power. If all men in authority, from bishops to justices of the peace, were elected by their constituents, government would at last conform to the popular will. The democratic vote and the examination would put merit in the place that had been usurped by birth. The rule of law would make all men liable to the same penalties for the same offences and give everyone an equal opportunity for the peaceful assertion of his rights. To the educated and self-confident, these seemed to be universal benefits that would transform a kingdom of subjects into a free and self-governing citizenry. France would set a peaceful example that the rest of Europe would have no alternative but to emulate. Anyone who refused to recognize the superiority of the new principles over the old could only be regretting former favours. It was these generous and sincere convictions that gave the revolution its inspirational content and its Messianic fervour.

To the poor and uneducated, especially in the country, things often looked very different. The changes were too sudden and too incomprehensible to be assimilated. This was most obvious where religion was concerned. To the secular-minded, often deist, deputies, religion was a matter of disseminating principles of sociability and the clergy were 'officers of morality'. To the peasant, religion often meant ritual practices and the hope of salvation. It seemed logical enough in Paris that a 'moral officer' who refused to take a loyalty oath should forfeit his public employment. Depriving villages of their parish priests, replacing them by unknown men, often unversed in the local patois, men moreover whom the old priest said were not qualified to hear confession or to give effective absolution, was a very different matter. When the Constituent Assembly inflicted this mortal wound on the religious unity of the country, it had no idea of what it was doing.

In secular matters too the new dispensation was not always welcomed or understood by people mistrustful of the law and lawyers, who were used to regulating their own affairs in time-honoured ways. Life had been violent enough in the country before the revolution but the violence had usually been provoked by the infringement of what were regarded as moral norms. The new ways of doing things, substituting political factions for the hierarchy of clientage and clan, greater state intervention in such matters as the requisitioning of food, and the heavy-handed intrusion of National Guards from neighbouring towns; all these were seen as oppression rather than as liberation. When peasants took up arms against the revolution they saw themselves as defending their rights against foreign interlopers and alien ways. The townsmen were both scandalized and alarmed by what they saw as obscurantism and fanaticism and they suspected the hand of the priest and the seigneur behind every protest.

If there is a lesson here, it is presumably that disinterestedness and good intentions are not enough. Politicians are unaware of what they do not know. What may strike them as demonstrably in the national interest may be resisted as a moral outrage. In a way this reinforces my second 'lesson': politics is more akin to art than to algebra and the 'right' solutions in terms of logic, enlightenment and even benevolence, may be the most resented. Since revolutions tend to be things that transform governments before they alter populations, it is in times of revolution that the incomprehension between rulers and ruled is inclined to become most murderous.

When the monarchy was overthrown by the insurrection of 10 August 1792 all pretence of grafting a new regime on to the rootstock of the old came to an end. In September France was declared a republic. To the educated, this implied a regime of an entirely different kind. Montesquieu had taught them that republics were only viable if the public actions of their citizens were based on *vertu*, or disinterested civic spirit. As Robespierre explained to the readers of his newspaper, the French had put the cart before the horse: *vertu* should have produced the republic and what they had done was to proclaim the end without any guarantee that they disposed of the means. Putting the issue in different terms, having repudiated the old principle of legitimacy, they had got to provide themselves with a new one. The only alternative to justifying the exercise of authority in the name of tradition and religion seemed to be to base it on popular sovereignty. It still does. Even the revolutions of modern times that justify themselves by invoking what are alleged to be laws immanent in history itself, still insist that what is done is for the benefit of the people as a whole, even if they cannot recognise this until they have been 'liberated' from their hoary preconceptions.

Popular sovereignty had emerged in the early days of the revolution, as an alternative to the division of sovereignty between king and parliament. By the autumn of 1792 it was the only principle available to the republicans. When eighteenth-century writers had discussed republics their models had been classical city-states, small enough for the entire citizen body to make its own decisions. Whatever popular sovereignty had implied in such a situation, to apply it to a country with a population of 28 million was to open Pandora's box. In theory, sovereignty was inherent in the population as a whole, which was entitled to overthrow any government that it considered oppressive. In practice, this was not conceding very much since so many people with divergent interests had no collective identity and no means of expressing any collective will that they might be considered to possess. To be legitimate, a popular revolt had to be general: a partial revolt was the ultimate crime against the sovereignty of 'the people'. The only way to discover whether or not an insurrection was partial was to wait and see if it succeeded. Popular sovereignty was thus a euphemism for the rule of the strongest, Hobbes in fancy dress.

The only way of escaping from this horn of the dilemma was by impaling one's self on the other one. It was possible to argue, as the British would have done if they had not preferred the comfortable ambiguities of Burke's rhetoric to the rigours of Cartesian logic, that the process of democratic election transferred the exercise of a people's sovereignty to a parliament or assembly. In practice this could only mean that a parliamentary majority – even if it turned on a single vote – was identified with the sovereign will of an entire people. Argument was permissible, indeed necessary, until a vote had been taken. After that all opposition was illegitimate. A minority ought to recognize that it had been mistaken and instead of working for the repeal of the measure that it had unsuccessfully opposed, should accept it as the expression of what its own point of view ought to have been. Since *vox populi* was very quickly equated with *vox dei*, opposition was not merely illegitimate but, as Alexandre Lameth had claimed as far back as 1790, sacrilegious.

That was not the end of it. If sovereignty resided within a majority in the Assembly, opposition was equally illegitimate, whether it came from a minority of the deputies or from the voters who had transferred their sovereignty to the men whom they elected. As Duport had told the Constituent Assembly, its duty was to *faire vouloir le peuple*. His friend Charles Lameth said there might be times when the Assembly had to 'rectify public opinion when it was mistaken and rule it in order to return to it the benefits that we derive from it.' This was the comforting conviction of whatever group happened to be in power at any time. Brissot argued in the Convention in 1792 that the electorate did not have the right to request the return of the monarchy. The doctrine was taken up by the Montagnards after the sovereign people, as personified for the occasion by the Paris National Guards, had disposed of the Girondins. Couthon explained that the right of election was an essential part of popular sovereignty, which could nevertheless be suspended if 'extraordinary circumstances make it necessary for the welfare of the people themselves.' Saint-Just summed it all up when he said that a revolution had taken place within the government but had not yet penetrated civil society. The government, in other words, was more democratic than the people it claimed to represent. This was the politics of *Alice Through the Looking-Glass*.

On one thing all were agreed: those who differed from them had no right to do so. This was not the only reason why the revolution was also a period of civil war but the civil war began in men's minds before anyone took up arms. By 1794 the country had torn itself apart by ideological and political hatreds so bitter and lasting that they endured for over a century and made France virtually ungovernable. One of the first gestures of the Vichy Government in 1940 was to proclaim its repudiation of the principles of 1789 by substituting its somewhat less inspiring *'Travail, Famille, Patrie'* for *'Liberté, Egalité, Fraternité'*. In 1978 François Furet, believing that these were battles long ago, entitled the first section of his *Interpreting the French Revolution*, 'The French Revolution is over'. This was optimistic. Some of the writing inspired by the bicentenary of 1789 suggests that the old wounds bleed as freely as ever.

One could draw all kinds of 'lessons' from this spectacle of a country enslaved to its history. One of the things it suggests is that political practice should be kept as far away as possible from political theory. As that supreme pragmatist, Catherine II put it, men are ticklish creatures and when one tries to inscribe one's political theories on their skins they are inclined to wriggle. The mysteries of sovereignty are best hidden away under thick layers of precedent. Even in purely logical terms, the consequence of modelling what is on what ought to be is likely to end in either totalitarianism or anarchy. In 1792 there was not much else that the French could do, but the results suggest that this was their misfortune rather than their opportunity.

This search for the 'lessons' of the French Revolution might seem to suggest at first sight that the most important one is the merit of leaving well – or even ill – alone. That was the opinion of a good many of those who survived the revolution but they were not the most impartial judges. Revolutions may not be the worst of all possible options but they do tend to generate more problems that revolutionaries expect or care to acknowledge. They have a tendency to maximize self-righteousness and to intensify divisions within a society and they often lead to regimes more oppressive than those whose faults they were intended to rectify.

That, however, is not the end of the story. Revolutions also liberate generous, if utopian aspirations. They dehumanize some by a peculiarly repulsive compound of cruelty and hypocrisy but the ennoble others by inspiring them with the challenge of heroic goals. At a time in European history when heroism is at something of a discount and prudence is all, it is good to remember that without some sort of ideal goals, politics degenerates into a squalid business of buying electoral support by the selective distribution of calculated favours. The lesson that generations of the oppressed found in the French Revolution was one of hope, even if this did involve looking at its aspirations, its own image of what it intended to be, rather than at what it actually was. Despite what Burke wrote, the French proved that it *was* possible to tear a country up by the roots, to repudiate the past and to make a new start. There was a price to pay that was likely to be far higher than anyone expected. Parts of the past were going to survive and they were unlikely to be those that people were most anxious to preserve, but some things could be achieved by revolution that could not be attained in any other way. For the British or the Americans to deny this is to repudiate their own history. Neither owes its freedom to the politics of the pig-trough.

If my final 'lesson' seems to contradict all the others, I can only plead that consistency in a historian is a dangerous virtue. When he makes all his evidence point in the same direction one can be sure that he is, if not inventing it, then at least manipulating it for his own purposes. History is more complicated than historians and, for each of us, the lessons of the French Revolution can only be the ones that we are prepared to learn.

Index